BURIED
in the SKY

▲ ▲ ▲

The Extraordinary Story of the
Sherpa Climbers on K2's Deadliest Day

PETER ZUCKERMAN

and

AMANDA PADOAN

W. W. NORTON & COMPANY

NEW YORK · LONDON

For information about permission to reproduce selections from this
book, write to Permissions, W. W. Norton & Company, Inc.,
500 Fifth Avenue, New York, NY 10110

For information about special discounts for bulk purchases, please
contact W. W. Norton Special Sales at specialsales@wwnorton.com or
800-233-4830

Manufacturing by Courier Westford
Book design by Ellen Cipriano
Maps by Adrian Kitzinger
Production manager: Anna Oler

Library of Congress Cataloging-in-Publication Data

Zuckerman, Peter.
Buried in the sky : the extraordinary story of the Sherpa climbers on
K2's deadliest day / Peter Zuckerman and Amanda Padoan. — 1st ed.
p. cm.
Includes bibliographical references and index.
ISBN 978-0-393-07988-3 (hardcover)
1. Mountaineering—Pakistan—K2 (Mountain)
2. Mountaineers—Pakistan—K2 (Mountain)
3. Mountaineering accidents—Pakistan—K2 (Mountain)
4. Sherpa (Nepalese people)
5. Sherpa (Nepalese people)—Social life and customs.
I. Padoan, Amanda. II. Title.
GV199.44.P182Z84 2012
796.522095491—dc23

2012008490

W. W. Norton & Company, Inc.
500 Fifth Avenue, New York, N.Y. 10110
www.wwnorton.com

W. W. Norton & Company Ltd.
Castle House, 75/76 Wells Street, London W1T 3QT

1 2 3 4 5 6 7 8 9 0

For Abrar, Almas, Asam, Dawa, Jen Jen,

Nima, Rahmin, Umbreen, and Zehan

Contents

PART III: DESCENT

List of Maps

List of Characters

More than seventy people endeavored to climb K2 in 2008. What follows is a list of the climbers, expedition coordinators, rescuers, staff, and weather consultants who played a significant role during the disaster as described in this book.

NAME	AFFILIATION
AAMIR MASOOD	Pakistani Fearless Five pilot
ALBERTO ZERAIN	Basque independent climber
"BIG" PASANG BHOTE★	South Korean K2 Abruzzi Spur Flying Jump
CAS VAN DE GEVEL	Dutch Norit K2 Expedition
CECILIE SKOG	Norwegian K2 Expedition
CHHIRING DORJE SHERPA	American K2 International Expedition
CHRIS KLINKE	American K2 International Expedition
COURT HAEGENS	Dutch Norit K2 Expedition
DREN MANDIĆ★	Serbian K2 Vojvodina Expedition
ERIC MEYER	American K2 International Expedition
FREDRIK STRÄNG	American K2 International Expedition
GERARD (GER) McDONNELL★	Dutch Norit K2 Expedition

GO MI-SUN (MS. GO)	South Korean K2 Abruzzi Spur Flying Jump
HOSELITO BITE	Serbian independent climber
HUGUES D'AUBARÈDE*	French-led Independent Expedition
HWANG DONG-JIN*	South Korean K2 Abruzzi Spur Flying Jump
ISO PLANIĆ	Serbian K2 Vojvodina Expedition
JELLE STALEMAN	Dutch Norit K2 Expedition
JEHAN BAIG*	French-led Independent Expedition
JUMIK BHOTE*	South Korean K2 Abruzzi Spur Flying Jump
KARIM MEHERBAN*	French-led Independent Expedition
KIM JAE-SOO (MR. KIM)	South Korean K2 Abruzzi Spur Flying Jump
KIM HYO-GYEONG*	South Korean K2 Abruzzi Spur Flying Jump
LARS FLATO NESSA	Norwegian K2 Expedition
MARCO CONFORTOLA	Italian K2 Expedition
MAARTEN VAN ECK	Dutch Norit K2 Expedition
MUHAMMAD HUSSEIN	Serbian K2 Vojvodina Expedition
NADIR ALI SHAH	Serbian K2 Vojvodina Expedition
NICK RICE	French-led Independent Expedition
PARK KYEONG-HYO*	South Korean K2 Abruzzi Spur Flying Jump
PASANG LAMA	South Korean K2 Abruzzi Spur Flying Jump
PEMBA GYALJE SHERPA	Dutch Norit K2 Expedition
PREDRAG (PEDJA) ZAGORAC	Serbian K2 Vojvodina Expedition
ROELAND VAN OSS	Dutch Norit K2 Expedition
ROLF BAE*	Norwegian K2 Expedition
SHAHEEN BAIG	Serbian K2 Vojvodina Expedition

SULEMAN AL FAISAL	Pakistani Fearless Five pilot
TSERING LAMA (CHHIRING BHOTE)	South Korean K2 Abruzzi Spur Flying Jump
WILCO VAN ROOIJEN	Dutch Norit K2 Expedition
YAN GIEZENDANNER	French-led Independent Expedition

★ = Climbers who died on K2 in August 2008

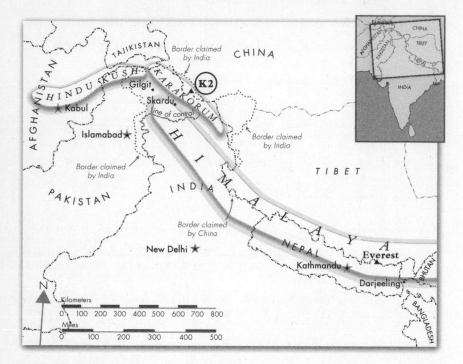

Karakorum, Himalaya, and Hindu Kush: K2 and the surrounding peaks rose from the sea as the Indian continental plate plowed under Eurasia. Still growing, the Karakorum is earth's youngest mountain range. The weather is much harsher than in the Himalaya.

Author's Note

by Peter Zuckerman

Many climbing accounts describe a death-defying struggle up fixed lines. But how did those ropes get there? Who performed the rescues? When your life hangs from a knot, it helps to know who tied it.

But some stories get buried. Western journalists seldom speak Ajak Bhote, Balti, Burushaski, Shar-Khumbu tamgney, Rolwaling Sherpi tamgney, or Wakhi. Reporters can't usually track down indigenous climbers by dialing telephone numbers or sending e-mails, and writers on a deadline rarely have time to trek to remote villages. As a result, testimony from high-altitude workers isn't broadcast far. Survivors of the Death Zone have imperfect recall, and the media maelstrom makes recovery—and accuracy—elusive as families, fans, friends, and publicists all assert claims on a story. Trauma and oxygen deprivation compound the confusion. As in war, eyewitnesses who were standing next to each other sometimes report different versions of the events.

Nonetheless, Amanda and I have tried to get at the truth and to be straightforward about our reporting. We researched for two years. We took seven trips to Nepal, trekking to regions rarely visited by Westerners and off-limits to journalists. We took three trips to Pakistan and obtained unprecedented access to military and government officials, thanks largely to Nazir Sabir, president of the Alpine Club of Pakistan. In total, we interviewed more than two hundred people and spent countless hours at kitchen tables in France, Holland, Ireland, Italy, Norway, Serbia, Spain, Switzerland, and the United States. We relied on more than a thousand photographs and videos. This book re-creates a true story. Please see the background notes for further information on methods and sources.

The death of Amanda's friend Karim Meherban was a catalyst for this book. Nursing a newborn, Amanda couldn't do all the research herself, so I was brought in as coauthor. Amanda and I are cousins, and we've been writing together since I was twelve. Before *Buried in the Sky*, I had a comfortable job as a daily newspaper reporter. I had never strapped on crampons. But when I learned about this story, I had no choice but to quit my job, grab a notebook, and head to the Himalaya. The characters were too inspiring, the goal too important, and the journey too compelling to resist.

Portland, Oregon
November 2011

BURIED
IN THE SKY

▲ ▲ ▲

Prologue

The Death Zone

The Bottleneck of K2, Pakistan
The Death Zone: about 27,000 feet above sea level

Hanging off the face of a cliff, an ice axe the only thing between him and death, a Sherpa climber named Chhiring Dorje swung to the left. A massive ice boulder ripped off above, hurtling toward him.

It was the size of a refrigerator.

The underbelly caught, and the mass flipped, cartwheeling down. It tore past, skimming Chhiring's shoulder, then vanished.

Brooof. It slammed into something below, shattering.

The mountain shook with the impact. Powder shot up in a column.

It was about midnight on August 1, 2008, and Chhiring had only a hazy idea of where he was: on or near the Bottleneck of K2, the deadliest stretch of the most dangerous mountain. At roughly the cruising altitude of a Boeing 737, the Bottleneck stretched away from him into the darkness below. In the starlight, the channel seemed bottomless as wisps of fog slithered into the abyss. Above, a lip of ice curled like the barrel of a crashing wave.

Oxygen depletion had turned Chhiring's mind to mush. Hunger

and exhaustion had broken his body. When he opened his mouth, his tongue froze; when he gasped for breath, the moistureless air scoured his throat and lashed his eyes.

Chhiring felt robotic, cold, too tired to think of what he'd sacrificed to get to K2. The Sherpa mountaineer, who had summited Everest ten times, had been consumed by the mountain for decades. A far more difficult peak than Everest, K2's summit is one of the most prestigious prizes in high-altitude mountaineering. Chhiring had gone despite his wife's tears. Despite the climb costing more money than his father had made in forty years. Despite his Buddhist *lama* warning him that K2's goddess would never tolerate the climb.

Chhiring had made it to the summit of K2 that evening without using bottled oxygen, vaulting him into an elite group of the most successful mountaineers, but the descent wasn't turning out as planned. He had dreamed of the achievement, a heroic reception, even fame. None of that mattered now. Chhiring had a wife, two daughters, a thriving business, and a dozen relatives who depended on him. All he wanted was to get home. Alive.

Normally, descent would be safer. Climbers usually go down during the early afternoon when it's warmer and daylight shows the way. They rappel, leapfrogging off the ice while attached to a fixed line to control their speed. In avalanche-prone areas around the Bottleneck, climbers descend as quickly as possible. This cuts exposure time, minimizing the chance of getting buried. Getting down fast was what Chhiring had planned on, depended on.

Now it was black and moonless. The fixed lines had vanished, severed by falling ice. Turning back wasn't an option. Without rope to catch him, Chhiring had only his axe to arrest a fall. And more than one life was in play: another climber was hanging from his harness.

The man suspended below him was Pasang Lama. Three hours earlier, Pasang had given up his ice axe to help more vulnerable climbers.

He had thought he could survive without it. Like Chhiring, Pasang had planned to rappel down the mountain using the fixed lines.

When the ropes through the Bottleneck disappeared, Pasang had figured it was his time to die. Stranded, he was unable to climb up or down without help. Why would anyone try to save him? A climber who attached himself to Pasang would surely fall, too. Using an ice axe to check the weight of one mountaineer skidding down the Bottleneck is nearly impossible. Stopping two bodies presents twice the difficulty, twice the risk. A rescue would be suicidal, Pasang thought. Mountaineers are supposed to be self-sufficient. Any pragmatic person would leave him to die.

As expected, one Sherpa already had. Pasang assumed Chhiring would do the same. Chhiring and Pasang were on separate teams. Chhiring had no obligation to help. But now Pasang hung three yards below him, attached to Chhiring's harness by a tether.

After dodging the block of ice, the two men bowed their heads and silently negotiated with the mountain goddess. She responded a few seconds later. The sound was electronic, the amplified pluck of a rubber band run through distortion pedals. *Zoing.* It continued, echoing louder, longer, faster, lower-pitched, from the left, from the right. The climbers knew what it meant. The ice around them was calving. With each *zoing*, fractures zigzagged across the glacier, ready to drop cinder blocks of ice.

If the men sensed one coming, they could shuffle to the side and contort themselves away. Failing that, they could sustain a hit. But eventually a mass the size of a bus would break off. Not much to do when that happens, except pray. Chhiring and Pasang had to get down before the falling ice crushed them.

Chuck. Chhiring hacked his axe into the ice. *Shink.* He kicked, stabbing the ice with his crampons. He descended like this for a few feet—*chuck, shink, shink, chuck, shink, shink*—and jammed himself against the slope so that the man attached to him could move to the same rhythm.

Pasang punched the hard ice with his fist, trying to compact it into a dent he could grip. Shallow and slick, the hold couldn't bear his weight. As Pasang extended his leg downward, he leaned on the safety tether that tied him to Chhiring. *Shink.* Pasang kicked in his crampons, relieving the pressure on the tether.

The weight on the rope threatened to pry Chhiring off the mountain's face, but he managed to cling on as they maneuvered around the bulges, cracks, dips, and lumps. Sometimes he and Pasang went side by side, holding hands, coordinating their movements. At other times Pasang went first, while Chhiring braced in a holding position with the axe and controlled the safety tether between them.

Rocks and chunks of ice spun at them, dinging their helmets, but they were halfway down and thought they'd survive. The night was windless—minus four degrees Fahrenheit—almost warm for K2. The lights of high camp were smoldering below. Chhiring and Pasang didn't expect it to happen.

A chunk of ice or rock knocked Pasang on the head. Batted off the ice, he swung like a piñata.

The force of Pasang's body on the rope peeled Chhiring from the slope.

The men tore downward.

Chhiring gripped his axe with both hands and slammed it into the mountain. The blade wouldn't catch. It cut surgically through the snow.

Sliding faster, Chhiring heaved his chest against the adze of his axe, digging into the slope. No good. Chhiring fell faster, another seven yards, another ten.

Pasang punched the slope with his fists and tried to grip, but his fingers skated along the ice.

The men dropped farther into the darkness.

Their shrieks, muffled by snow, must have funneled up the Bottleneck to the southeast face, but the survivors there heard nothing. They were deaf to the thud of falling bodies. All of them were lost. Dazed and hallucinating, some wandered off-route. Others calmed themselves enough to make a measured decision between two grim options: free-climb down the Bottleneck in the darkness or bivouac in the Death Zone.

Gerard McDonnell, who hours before had become the first Irishman to summit K2, cut a shallow ledge to sit on and another to brace his feet. Patience wouldn't stop an avalanche, but at least he had a perch to wait out the night.

Another climber, an Italian named Marco Confortola, squished in beside him. To stay awake, they forced themselves to sing. With hoarse voices, the men crooned the songs they could remember, anything to avoid dying in their sleep.

Earlier, a French summiter had made a promise to his girlfriend. "I'll never leave you again," Hugues d'Aubarède had told her via satellite phone. "I'm finished now. This time next year, we'll all be at the beach." That night, he slid down the Bottleneck to his death. His Pakistani high-altitude porter, Karim Meherban, strayed off-route, reaching the crown of the glacier that hulks over the Bottleneck. He slumped down and waited to freeze.

Farther down, a Norwegian newlywed had just lost her husband to several tons of ice. This climb had been their honeymoon. Now she was clawing down the mountain without him.

Many of the alpinists considered themselves to be among the best in the world. They hailed from France, Holland, Italy, Ireland, Nepal, Norway, Pakistan, Serbia, South Korea, Spain, Sweden, and the United States. Some had risked everything to scale K2. Their climb had devolved into a catastrophe. The final toll was bleak: within twenty-seven hours, eleven climbers had died in the deadliest single disaster in K2's history.

What had gone wrong? Why had the climbers continued up when they knew they'd never make it down before nightfall? How had they made so many simple mistakes, such as failing to bring enough rope?

The story became an international media sensation, landing on the covers of the *New York Times*, *National Geographic Adventure*, *Outside*, and in more than a thousand other publications. It ricocheted around the blogosphere and inspired speculation, documentaries, a stage-play revival, memoirs, and talk shows.

Some considered the climb an example of hubris, a waste of life fueled by machismo or madness: thrill-seekers trying too hard to get noticed by corporate sponsorship; lunatics climbing in a final act of escape; oblivious Westerners exploiting the lives of impoverished Nepalis and Pakistanis in a bid for glory; the media feeding off deaths to sell papers and products; gawkers observing the spectacle for entertainment.

"You want to risk your life?" a response to one of the *New York Times* stories said. "Then do it in service of your country, or family, or neighborhood. Climbing K2 or Everest is a selfish stunt that benefits nothing."

"Heroes my ass," sniffed another; ". . . these egomaniacs should stay off mountains."

Other people saw courage: explorers pitted against the adversity of nature; lost souls embracing risk to find meaning in an empty world.

"Climbing can expand the view of human potential for all of us," read a letter to the media from Phil Powers, executive director of the American Alpine Club.

Paraphrasing Teddy Roosevelt, another letter read, "Far better to dare mighty things, to win glorious triumphs, even though checkered by failure, than to rank with those poor spirits who neither enjoy nor suffer because they live in a gray twilight that knows not victory nor defeat."

Others raised basic questions: What do men and women do when they are on top of a mountain, dying? And why are some people driven to take such risks?

Before they were trapped on the mountaintop; before the deaths and funerals; before the rescues and reunions; before the fistfights and friendships; before the recriminations and reconciliations—everything had seemed perfect. The equipment was checked and rechecked; the routes, established; the weather, cooperative; the teams, intact. The moment they had spent so much time and training and money to reach—summit day—had finally come. They were going to conquer K2, stand on top of the most vicious mountain on earth, howl in triumph, unfurl their flags, and call their sweethearts.

Chhiring and Pasang, as they fell into the blackness, must have wondered: How did this happen?

PART I

AMBITION

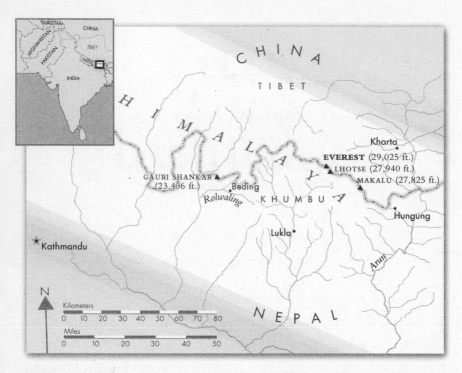

Rolwaling, Khumbu, and Arun regions of Nepal: The Sherpas in Chhiring's village of Beding (center) believe they are protected by a goddess who inhabits the mountain of Gauri Sankar. Pasang grew up in Hungung (far right), which became a war zone as the Maoists wrested control from Nepal's monarchy.

1

Summit Fever

Rolwaling Valley, Nepal
12,000 feet above sea level

His walk was more of a jog. He didn't drive a car; he rocketed through traffic on a black Honda Hero motorcycle. In the seven languages he spoke conversationally, Chhiring Dorje Sherpa talked so quickly it seemed as though each sentence were one long word punctuated by exclamation points. Everything about him was accelerated: his eating, his thinking, his climbing, his praying. He couldn't control the pace. Speed was hardwired into his DNA.

His first name meant "long life," but its pronunciation to English speakers—CHEER-ing—personified him. Cheerful determination radiated from Chhiring. It got him noticed. Clients praised his you-can-do-it, let's-rock-'n'-roll, give-me-your-pack attitude. It was contagious. How could you sit still in camp when every few minutes he would lurch up, stride forward, chop his arms through the air, make a pronouncement, plop down, and spring up again? There was a reason this thirty-four-year-old dynamo rarely drank coffee. He was caffeinated enough.

"Chhiring was always crazy," said his father, Ngawang Thundu

Sherpa. "He was a naughty child, and I knew he'd be a naughty adult."

"We have relied on his climbing for income," explained Chhiring's younger brother, also named Ngawang Sherpa. "Without his money, we wouldn't be where we are. But Chhiring became too ambitious. I was always telling him: 'Slow down.'" The family complained that Chhiring's line of work offended the gods and disrupted village life. His relatives wouldn't state the obvious: Chhiring's job could get him killed.

The summit of K2 was a long way from where Chhiring started. Before he climbed mountains, Chhiring lived in Beding, a remote village in Nepal. Wedged between India and Tibet, "like a yam between two boulders," Nepal is on the collision zone between two continental plates. This region of Southeast Asia used to be flat, submerged beneath the Tethys Sea, but for sixty-five million years, the Indian plate, moving north at twice the speed of a growing fingernail, has been jacking up the Tibetan crust, lifting the ancient seabed. It's now earth's highest mountain range. Nepal hosts a third of the Himalaya, including the south side of Everest.

Chhiring describes his birthplace as "mostly rock and ice." About 12,100 feet above sea level, the village of Beding seldom appears on maps, and when it does, it is plotted at different locations and, like many remote villages, goes by different names. Beding is about thirty miles west of Everest in a valley known as Rolwaling. Getting there takes a trek. First, travelers must jostle over a jeep track that ends near a cliff. Afterward, they zigzag up switchbacks, ford rivers, and wobble over chain-link bridges. After six days of lugging their own food and shelter, travelers see the village *chorten*, a shrine painted with unblinking blue eyes, rimmed in red. Symbolizing Buddha's gaze, the eyes stare down on Beding, inspiring the devout and spooking evil spirits.

Glaciated peaks surround the village, which is constructed of rocks, wood, mud, and dung mortar. A film of gray dust off the moraine coats the children. The air smells of threshed grass, blue smoke billows from fire pits, and the clouds seem so close you could jump up and punch them. Goats, sheep, cows, and yak-hybrids called *dzos* graze on steep terraces that resemble giant staircases. Below, the Rolwaling River shoots iridescent spray into the air.

Sherpas inhabit Beding and the other villages of the Rolwaling Valley. Although *sherpa*, with a lowercase *S*, is used colloquially as a job description, *Sherpa* is also an ethnicity, just as Greek, Hawaiian, and Basque are. And the Sherpas are a tiny ethnicity at that: The 150,000 Sherpas in Nepal make up less than one percent of the country's population.

Chhiring's village is often described by a list of what's missing: antibiotics, electricity, machinery, public sanitation, roads, running water, telephones. Residents lack formal education. Some don't know how to spell their names or read a clock, and many are told when they were born not by day but by season. A calendar's main function is to track dates commemorating the life of Buddha.

The Sherpas of Rolwaling seldom characterize themselves this way. They prefer to recognize what they have: faith and a self-reliant community. The gods are near, and neighbors are family. In Beding, locals take time to chat, drink tea, and play *Carrom*, a hybrid of billiards and shuffleboard in which players flick pucks at targets. They have a sophisticated knowledge of folklore, farming, and the region's topography, and they speak an unwritten language that combines eastern and central dialects of Tibetan, reflecting their long journey into Nepal. Rolwaling Sherpi tamgney is spoken nowhere else.

As with many Sherpa communities, the residents of Rolwaling rotate among three villages according to the season. The winter village heats up too much in the summer, the summer village cools down too much in the winter, and the central village, Beding, is more hospitable for crops and livestock in the fall. Residents live off the land, growing and eating astonishing amounts of potatoes. As Buddhists, they follow a tradition variously described as Tantrayana, Vajrayana, Nyingma, or, by detractors, Lamaism.

Written history on Rolwaling is hard to come by, and the legends vary, depending on the imagination of the storyteller. Anthropologist Janice Sacherer has studied the Sherpas of Rolwaling since the 1970s. "Piety they have," she said while discussing the challenges of studying their folklore. "Consistency they do not."

According to Tibetan scripture, Rolwaling is a *beyul*, a sacred valley formed as a refuge for Buddhists during times of turmoil and hidden until divinely revealed. Guru Rinpoche, who converted Tibetans to Buddhism in the seventh century, is credited with finding the *beyul* of Rolwaling, or even creating it with a giant horse and plow. Five centuries later, when Mongols were invading Tibet, the ancestors of the Sherpas moved to Nepal, and Buddhist visionaries told followers about the *beyuls* on the southern flanks of the Himalaya. Full of caves and rock monuments with spiritual properties, the *beyuls* are tributes to Guru Rinpoche and his consort, Yeshi Tsogyel, who aimed to peacefully enlighten all sentient beings.

At the hands of Chhiring's father and his elderly friends, however, these legends take on a less Buddhist tone. According to them, the Rolwaling Valley is the center of the universe and the cradle of life. The world began eight hundred years ago, before time was linear. Guru Rinpoche and his wife were meditating in a cave near Beding. After two days, the couple made a pact to rid the valley of evil. They stormed out and waged war against the demons.

Wings and scales were stripped like husks. Limbs were twisted; fangs, extracted. The demons rallied and tried to blot out the sun, stirring up dust to choke the gods. Guru Rinpoche summoned support, instructing his troops to gouge out their enemies' eyes. Crippled demons, swooping blindly, plunged into the Rolwaling River. Some of them sank. Guru Rinpoche waded in after the others, forcing their heads beneath the surface. Those who wiggled free of his grasp retreated to clefts in the rocks.

In the end, almost all of the demons were killed or tamed, but the war had taken a toll on the land. Features of Rolwaling's landscape—a massive rock on a level plain, a deep pit in the hills, a crack cleaving a boulder in two—attest to the battle. Afterward, the gods retired to the mountains, and Guru Rinpoche and his wife conceived five children, who became the genesis of all others. A few stayed. Most left the valley and became corrupt. That's the rest of us.

These days, the gods are impatient with the world outside Rolwaling. The elders predict that these gods will wipe out civilization fairly soon, maybe tomorrow, sparing only those who live in the valley. They frown upon anyone leaving. Deserters will be butchered along with everyone else.

The younger generation is less concerned. They say the apocalyptic legend is a scare tactic their grandparents use to get them to visit more often. In the standard Buddhist version of the founding myth, Guru Rinpoche traveled across the Himalaya like a sacred bounty hunter, tracking down demons and proselytizing them without the use of force. At that time, five sisters inhabited the crags in Rolwaling. Predating Buddhism by centuries, they were goddesses of an ancient Tibetan sect that demanded blood sacrifice.

As Guru Rinpoche entered the valley, chalk-faced Tseringma, the eldest, sent a snow leopard in pursuit. The guru charmed the cat until it purred and spoke of Buddhism, without pausing to eat or sleep, until Tseringma reformed.

Tseringma ascended a nearby mountain that now bears her name—but known to Hindus as Gauri Shankar—and renounced her diet of human flesh. Tseringma, the goddess of longevity, still lives on the 23,405-foot peak above Beding. Snowmelt from her glacier surges into the Rolwaling River, and its properties are miraculous. Some elders claim to be 120 years old, thanks to the water's effects.

After Guru Rinpoche subdued Tseringma, he pursued her four younger sisters. One by one, they repented and became Buddhist deities, moving to mountains of their own. Miyolangsangma patrols the summit of Everest on the back of a tigress. Now the goddess of prosperity, her face shines like 24-carat gold. Thingi Shalsangma, her body a pale shade of blue, became the goddess of healing after galloping on a zebra to the top of Shishapangma, a 26,289-foot peak in Tibet. Chopi Drinsangma, with a face in perpetual blush, became the goddess of attraction. She chose a deer instead of a zebra and settled on Kanchenjunga, a 28,169-foot peak in Nepal.

The final sister—Takar Dolsangma, the youngest, with a green face—was a hard case. She mounted a turquoise dragon and fled northward to the land of three borders. In the modern Rolwaling folklore, this is Pakistan. Guru Rinpoche chased after her and eventually cornered her on a glacier called the Chogo Lungma. Takar Dolsangma appeared remorseful and, spurring her dragon, ascended K2, accepting a new position as the goddess of security. Although Guru Rinpoche never doubted her sincerity, maybe he should have: Takar Dolsangma, it seems, still enjoys the taste of human flesh.

▲ ▲ ▲

Rolwaling is a *beyul*, a frontier community that granted amnesty to refugees. It was thought to be guarded by a powerful mountain goddess. By the mid-nineteenth century, the valley was a popular destination for debtors and thugs to settle down and become pious. At first, famine limited population growth. In the 1880s, the introduction of the potato provided a measure of food security, and the population quadrupled to about two hundred.

The next significant incursion, after the potato, was Edmund Hillary. Two years before he achieved the first ascent of Everest in 1953, Hillary trekked through Rolwaling with a British reconnaissance team, searching for the best route to Everest. The British ultimately chose a different approach, through the Khumbu Valley to the east, but some Rolwaling Sherpas were offered jobs, including Hrita Sherpa, who broke trail for Tenzing Norgay and Hillary days before their first ascent.

Rolwaling never underwent development like the Khumbu, where Everest-bound tourists injected money and jobs and Hillary built schools, a hospital, and an airstrip. During Chhiring's childhood in the 1970s, Rolwaling was the "most isolated, traditional and economically backward of all the Sherpa communities in Nepal."

Traders seldom passed through, and beasts of burden could barely scramble up the banks of scree. The Sherpas relied on local materials and their own labor to feed and clothe themselves. No one owned a cotton T-shirt; yak wool was woven into cloth. Chhiring's father dressed in a *chuba*, a wool robe secured by a sash over his trousers. In the winter, he wore buffalo leather boots that were padded with dried moss. His mother wore an *ungi*, a sleeveless tunic draped with a blue-striped apron that covered her front and back. To signify her unmarried status, Chhiring's younger sister wore an apron only on her back.

Chhiring was born in 1974 on the floor of a room that served as his family's kitchen, barn, and bedroom. The boy—said Chhiring's father, aunt, and uncle—was a slacker who loved to sneak away and explore the mountains. His relatives still tell the story of his gravest transgression: the time when, as an eight-year-old playing with fire, Chhiring set the hills ablaze. The flames burned the winter reserves of feed, and the animals went hungry. Chhiring's father beat him with a stick, and, twenty-six years later, still hadn't forgiven him.

It was a childhood disrupted by death. Chhiring's younger sister returned from the fields one afternoon with red blisters crawling up her skin. As the pustules clustered on her tongue, she suffocated. Another sister was carrying water from the river when a rock dropped off a cliff and crushed her internal organs. No one could figure out what happened to Chhiring's two-year-old brother. Perhaps he ate something toxic. One day, his gut inflated. With his stomach painfully distended, the child soon died. A third sister's birth left Chhiring's mother, Lakpa Futi, hemorrhaging. Mother and infant died.

Chhiring watched the *lama* perform the death rites on his mother, yanking her hair to let her spirit leave through the head, whispering into her ear advice about the afterlife. Chhiring tried not to cry, believing it could cause a veil of blood to cover her eyes and obscure her way into the next life. He was too young to go up the hill for the cremation, so he sat in the room where he was born and watched his mother's smoke lift into the sky. His father, Ngawang Thundu Sherpa, returned home and collapsed.

From then on, Ngawang passed out several times a day. Villagers suspected that a demon possessed him. As the fainting became more frequent, Chhiring's father stopped caring for the four remaining children. He fell mute and forgot to eat and bathe. When he slept, he woke crying, and sobbed until he fainted again.

The fields withered, the animals strayed, and the house fell into disrepair. The family ran low on food. The children's shoes and clothing wore out. No matter how hard he tried, Ngawang could not motivate himself to work. When able to rouse himself, he spent all his effort praying, trying to appease the gods. "I didn't understand what I had done to make them punish me," he recalled.

Chhiring, then twelve years old, became head of the household. He sold off livestock and bartered for food to feed his siblings but soon ran out of things to trade. In exchange for potatoes, he worked for other families, fetching water, gathering firewood, and sweeping. His sister, Nima, cared for their father and the two youngest children.

Chhiring didn't make enough to afford shoes, but he and his family didn't starve, and relatives helped when they became desperate.

Around the time he turned fourteen, Chhiring's aunts and uncles told him he had no choice: He was a man now, old enough to marry, and he had to find a faster way to pay off his father's debts. Some suggested he leave the village to carry fuel and equipment for European climbers and trekkers. Chhiring was reluctant. He had never wandered far from the sacred valley. At that time, few Sherpas had left Rolwaling, and those who had entered the climbing industry described it as miserable and speculative. "Chhiring seemed too young to be a porter, too small to carry loads for foreigners," recalled his uncle, Ang Tenzing Sherpa. "I told him it was a bad idea."

Furthermore, Chhiring worried about the deities who lived on the mountains; the glaciers were their embodiment. Climbing the spine of a goddess or trespassing into her home amounted to insolence, even blasphemy. Chhiring's grandfather, Pem Phutar, had carried loads for a 1955 British expedition to Gauri Shankar, the sacred peak where Tseringma resides, but the family rarely spoke of it. Many villagers looked down on mountaineers and told disparaging stories about them.

These tales had the same theme and usually ended with a broken man from Germany. Fifteen sherpas were infamously killed on German expeditions to Nanga Parbat in 1934 and 1937. Even Hitler's *Reichssportführer* had condemned two members of the 1934 expedition who abandoned their team in a storm, and a strange stereotype evidently developed among the Sherpas. For example, villagers in Beding spoke of a once-successful German businessman who tried to climb Gauri Shankar. He failed, of course, and the mountain goddess punished him. Within a year, the German lost his teeth, contracted leprosy, and was robbed of everything but his wife. When she left him, he died of despair.

Although that story must be apocryphal, another one isn't. In 1979, American mountaineer John Roskelley decided to conquer Gauri Shankar. Pitch after pitch, conditions on the peak were so frustrating that Roskelley found the experience vaguely erotic. The "goddess of love," he surmised, wanted to "remain a virgin." Approaching the summit, he had nearly seduced her when his climbing partner—"a young and upcoming Sherpa 'tiger' " named Dorje—begged him to stop. Roskelley, nonetheless, "hugged [the peak] like a fat lady's bottom and shimmied up," Dorje in tow. "Gauri Shankar was ours," he gloated. "We were the first non–deities to reach its 23,405-foot summit."

Although Roskelley didn't suffer any ill effects from the climb, residents of Rolwaling believe they did. Soon after Roskelley's summit, a glacial lake on the flanks of Gauri Shankar burst through a natural dam, triggering a flash flood. Icemelt and debris submerged three women working at a water-powered gristmill. Two were fished out alive. The third died.

Chhiring didn't want to end up like the German or cause a flash flood as John Roskelley had. He considered it risky even to speak to mountaineers and figured they all were crackpots. Why would anyone spend so much money to climb without any practical purpose? And why weren't they strong enough to carry their own food and gear, as the rest of the world did?

But necessity and curiosity got the best of him. His family needed money, and Chhiring couldn't make enough gathering firewood. His uncle Sonam Tsering, a mountaineer, told him that portering was the solution. The gods would overlook the offense, given his circumstances, and Chhiring could return home rich. So at the age of fourteen, Chhiring left for the city, walking most of the way.

When he arrived in Kathmandu, Chhiring discovered that the elders weren't exaggerating. The apocalypse, predicted to occur outside Rolwaling, was known to the general public. Even the U.S. Embassy was issuing survival kits. The capital was doomed.

▲ ▲ ▲

Kathmandu is still waiting for the Big One, an earthquake that could flatten the city. The tremors of 1253, 1259, 1407, 1680, 1810, 1833, 1860, and 1934 knocked down temples and killed tens of thousands. The next quake will be worse. Kathmandu has swelled to a million residents, and most of them live in brick warrens tottering atop shallow foundations. Assessing the risk, the United Nations has waged a campaign to promote earthquake preparedness, but nobody seems flustered. Fatalism is part of Kathmandu's character.

If driving rules exist in the city, they're Darwinian. A green light means full speed ahead; a yellow light means full speed ahead; a red light means full speed ahead and honk. Traffic spills into a medieval grid too narrow for the modern world, and no meaningful lines are painted on the road. Seat belts are a novelty, and drivers and pedestrians go wherever they dare, braving a crush of buses, bicycles, cows, chickens, children, dogs, food carts, lepers, motorbikes, peddlers, pilgrims, protesters, rats, rickshaws, sewage, strollers, taxis, trucks, and trash.

A moonscape of brick factories rings the city, and soot thickens the air and congeals in the slits between the tenements. The smog, cupped inside an amphitheater of mountains, rarely disperses from Kathmandu, even at night. The particulate matter in the air almost always exceeds World Health Organization standards, and pedestrians wear surgical masks so they can breathe through the grit that settles in the lungs.

Paradoxically, this polluted city started with a shade tree. According to legend, the Hindu god Gorakhnath, like many modern commuters, didn't respect the right of way. Racing to a festival, he plowed into a chariot processional, and, to avoid embarrassment, tried to impersonate a human. Fortunately, a responsible bystander made a citizen's arrest. To post bail, Gorakhnath planted a seed in the mud. It sprouted into a sal tree that grew tall enough to scrape the firmament. A monk felled the tree and used the wood to build Kasthamandap, a three-tiered pavilion. Still standing, it's one of the world's oldest wooden structures. Kasthamandap is Kathmandu's namesake.

In the 1950s, Kathmandu became a launching pad for mountaineering expeditions. Hippies followed in the 1960s, and Freak Street, acrid with incense, remains an asylum for the New Age movement. Tourism makes up a large percentage of Nepal's economy, and Kathmandu depends on it. Tour guides, prostitutes, drug dealers, and self-appointed messiahs hustle near the city's Durbar Square seven days a week.

When Chhiring arrived in Kathmandu for the first time, he had never switched on a lightbulb. The teenager settled in Little Tibet, a community of Buddhist refugees who had fled the Chinese invasion in the 1950s. Chhiring's neighbors helped him adapt to city life, and the nearby Boudhanath *stupa* gave him a sense of permanence. Considered one of the holiest Buddhist sites in Nepal, Boudhanath is a reliquary buried beneath an enormous mound of soil. The *stupa*'s shape symbolizes Mount Meru, the center of the Buddhist cosmos, with its summit in the heavens and its bedrock in hell. As soon as he arrived in Little Tibet, Chhiring joined the crowd of worshippers, pacing clockwise around the *stupa* in prayer. He repeated the ritual each morning until his uncle found him a portering job that paid $3 a day.

For that job, Chhiring spent a month hauling seventy pounds of kerosene, stoves, and climbing gear to Island Peak, near the base of Everest. The Japanese clients were surprised that a teenager could lug so much up steep trails without complaining, and they praised his upbeat attitude. To Chhiring, these trekkers seemed normal enough—and by the end of the month he had earned $90. Never had he seen so much money.

He spent half his wages on food, shoes, and clothes, which he took to his family in Beding. He returned to Kathmandu a few weeks later to find another job. It wasn't long before Chhiring was spending six months of the year outside Rolwaling, accepting one portering job after another. The work fit his talents. He befriended clients and picked up their languages, becoming a leader among the porters because he could serve as an interpreter. Around the time he turned sixteen, a women's team, impressed with Chhiring's endurance and command of English, invited him to carry loads on Everest. Chhiring had never climbed on a glacier but agreed to do it.

Western climbers spend years preparing for Everest; for many Sherpas, it's their training ground. During their first week on the job, some Sherpas who have never climbed will be breaking trail, hauling gear, and establishing camps for professional guides and their clients. It makes a certain kind of sense on Everest. Thousands of people have summited it. The routes are well established, the climbing is nontechnical, and the wage for each support climber is substantial—about $3,000 plus a bonus for each client who tops out. Sherpas from mountain villages are better acclimatized than their clients and often have superior strength and balance at high altitude. On Everest, these abilities can compensate for inexperience.

Sherpas begin with Everest for another reason too. Most believe the mountain can be climbed without retribution. Miyolangsangma, the goddess who resides on Everest, only occasionally punishes trespassers. If she dislikes being climbed, pragmatism offsets her displeasure. The goddess of prosperity loves to see Sherpas make money. "As long as you treat Miyolangsangma with respect, ask forgiveness and get paid well, she'll tolerate the climb," said Ngawang Oser Sherpa, the head *lama* of Rolwaling. "You shouldn't do it, but she is the most forgiving of the five sisters."

Chhiring went up Everest for the first time in 1991. In the beginning, the climb was straightforward. He didn't have much gear or formal training, but other Sherpas showed him how to strap on crampons and grip an ice axe, and he carried seventy pounds of bottled oxygen to the South Col at 26,200 feet. On his way down, however, a storm rolled in. The temperature dropped and Chhiring's fingers turned gray. As everyone rushed to camp, Chhiring tried to catch up, but he stepped on a smooth plate of ice. It gave way under him like a trapdoor. Chhiring sank down to his shoulders. He clawed at snow, but his fingers were too stiff to grab hold, and he slid deeper. Waiting, he hung, his feet dangling in space.

It seemed as though hours had passed, and he was nearly unconscious when another climber, also named Chhiring Sherpa, pulled him out by the collar. The older Chhiring was furious. He scolded the teenager. You're too young to be on Everest, he said. Nobody your age should be up this high.

The warning had an unintended effect. It humiliated Chhiring and made him want to climb even more. Something about failing, knowing he might have reached the top of the world if he'd worn thicker gloves and boots, made him want the summit. He decided he would learn to climb better than the Sherpa who had saved him—or anyone else. Money was another incentive. He made 35,000 rupees, or about $450, from his first Everest climb. Although it wasn't a fifth of what experienced climbers were receiving, it was more than the average Nepali made in a year, and he had earned it in a month.

For the next two years, Chhiring continued to work on high mountains, to seek advice and help from his uncle Sonam. Then, in 1993, Sonam left on an expedition that would be his last. Sonam, with four Everest summits to his credit, was joining Pasang Lahmu, a friend aiming to become the first Nepali woman on the summit of Everest. The duo topped out on April 22.

Sonam may have prayed to Miyolangsangma, the goddess of Everest, and apologized for violating her sacred space. Nevertheless, as he and Pasang Lahmu descended toward the South Col, an upturned bowl of swirling clouds coalesced around the summit. The lenticular formation meant brutal weather blowing in. With no time to strategize, Pasang and Sonam joined three teammates in a forced bivouac. Huddling together in the open, they braced against raging winds.

Miyolangsangma refused to intercede. The gale pounded them, and, after two days, they were presumed dead. Sonam may have forced himself to stagger several hundred meters before he fell. Climbers discovered his pack below Pasang Lahmu's body.

As confirmation of Sonam's death spread to Kathmandu, Chhiring couldn't accept it. He remembered how Sonam had assured him that Everest could be climbed without consequence. "I saw he was mistaken about that," Chhiring said. "My head was telling me to quit and go home." Yet when he returned to Beding, Chhiring saw the power of money. His six-year-old brother Ngawang was plump and wore new shoes. His father had installed a corrugated tin roof. His sister was learning to read. Although the family mourned Sonam, none of Chhiring's siblings were asking him to quit. "And I couldn't," he said. "I didn't want to."

The following year, Chhiring was back on Everest with a Norwegian team. Climbers recognized his endurance at altitude and recruited him to work for them on subsequent expeditions. Soon Chhiring had joined teams from Belgium, England, France, Germany, India, Japan, Norway, Russia, Switzerland, and the United States.

As Chhiring landed more jobs, he became more ambitious. When clients asked him to carry a forty-five-pound load, he hauled ninety. Instead of simply carrying, he volunteered to fix ropes, break trails, lead pitches, organize expeditions. He stopped using bottled oxygen, which purists regard as doping. He worked Everest as a yearly routine, reaching the summit ten times, and broke an endurance record for topping out three times in two weeks.

Family members saw him change. He became wealthy by Nepali standards and seemed indifferent to the elders' prophecy. Sometimes he climbed not for the money but for the exhilaration. His *lama* warned that it was only a matter of time before he'd be cursed. Chhiring's father, now healthy, decided that his son had gone mad. Villagers were afraid Chhiring's riches would tempt the younger generation to leave.

They were right. When Chhiring returned to Rolwaling during the off-season, he wore La Sportiva boots and a North Face jacket. He brought provisions for the village—fuel, rice, socks, wool sweaters— and described urban novelties, such as motorcycles and televisions. The teenagers were awed. Mountaineering may be a sin, but it sure made you rich. Villagers flocked to Kathmandu.

Chhiring gave them a place to stay, found them jobs, and started an expedition company, Rolwaling Excursion. The elders appreciated the clothing he brought back, and their opposition softened, even as Beding's population crashed to twenty-three permanent residents.

Chhiring's accomplishments impressed his peers, but critics dismissed his achievements because they were on Everest. Anyone can climb Everest over and over, they argued, even a *Playboy* centerfold. The mountain has fixed lines strung from nearly start to finish. Everest is commercial, more a jungle gym for tourists than one of the great climbing challenges. Although this guy may hold an endurance record, it's from high camp, not Base Camp. Real climbers take on real mountains, like K2. Chhiring craved the chance to prove himself, but getting to K2 cost money, and he was about to settle down.

At sixteen, Chhiring had fallen for Dawa Sherpani, a girl he'd seen herding yaks. Dawa hadn't taken him seriously then. Now she owned a teashop near Boudhanath, and Chhiring was a regular. He'd sit at a corner table, swilling black tea, and jump up, making his presence felt, if a male patron paid Dawa too much attention. Dawa wasn't impressed, but Chhiring had learned to move fast. He persuaded Dawa to consult his *lama* to see whether their horoscopes were compatible. It was a perfect match.

They skipped the traditional three-day ceremony, exchanged vows in an hour, and went to his place. Their daughter, Tshering Namdu Sherpa, arrived in the spring. Four years later, Dawa gave birth to a second daughter, Tensing Futi Sherpa. The family, along with Chhiring's brothers and sisters and Dolkar, a white spaniel, moved into a cream-colored townhouse that resembled a four-tier wedding cake. It had more than just running water and electricity; Chhiring's home had a television, a microwave oven, an office, a prayer room, two computers, and four bathtubs—luxuries he'd never dreamed of as a child.

Compared to Beding, this was easy living. Chhiring's expedition company boomed, nearly doubling in size every year. Chhiring began organizing climbs with dozens of employees, many from his village. By now a major patron of Rolwaling's monastery, Chhiring finally had won approval from the elders. He held platinum elite status at the Mount Everest Summiters Club. His daughters were becoming fluent in English and attended a private prep school. Only his wife seemed worried.

"So many people relied on him," Dawa said. "If he got killed in the mountains, Chhiring wouldn't just be hurting himself. He'd be hurting me and the children. I didn't know what we'd do if he died."

Doorway to Heaven

K2 was born during a period of mass extinction. Sixty-five million years ago, as dinosaurs were dying off, the Indian continental plate sped north at six inches a year, a reckless pace in geological time. It plowed into Eurasia, wedging itself under the larger continent, and K2, like Everest, rose from the sea. Still rising, the Karakorum is earth's youngest mountain range, with jagged edges unfiled by the elements.

The word *Karakorum* stems from several languages in the Altaic linguistic family of Central Asia: *kara* means "black" and *kor'um* means "gravel" or "rock." The city of Karakorum was Genghis Khan's opulent capital in thirteenth-century Mongolia, and traders used *karakorum* to describe the highest pass along the way. The British explorer William Moorcroft climbed the Karakorum Pass in the 1820s and applied the name to the mountains around it. In the 1930s, the Royal Geographical Society affirmed the title.

The range extends southeast through Kashmir, along the borders

of Pakistan and China, and latches into the Himalaya. The Karakorum has the world's largest concentration of peaks more than five
miles high. Harsher than the Himalaya, it is the most glaciated place
outside the polar regions—so remote that Western explorers hadn't
mapped it until the mid-nineteenth century.

The mountain now called K2 entered surveyors' books in 1856.
The Great Trigonometric Survey of India had ordered British lieutenant Thomas Montgomerie to map Kashmir as part of an empire-
wide effort to determine the exact shape of the earth. With help from
Kashmiri porters, Montgomerie spent four days towing a plane table,
heliostat, and brass theodolite up Mount Haramukh in the Himalayan foothills. The climb rewarded him with a panorama of spires.
Two peaks 130 miles northeast jutted from the range's spine, towering
above the rest. Montgomerie peered through the theodolite, took the
mountains' bearings, and inked their outlines in his field book.

The closest peak, a hexagon with two summits, appeared taller to
him. He labeled it K1. *K* stood for "Karakorum"; the numeral signi-
fied that it was the first peak in his survey. He marked the glistening
pyramid farther away as K2 and later logged more mountains, all
the way to K32. Along with the other peaks, K1 reverted to its local
name, *Masherbrum*, or "mountain of fire" in Balti, the local language.
K2's designation stuck. Mapmakers thought its local name, *Chogori*,
was a cursory description the Baltis used to signify a big peak. *Chogori*
is actually a Tibetan word that means "doorway to heaven." The Buddhist ancestors of the Baltis probably named the mountain soon after
they migrated from Tibet.

Montgomerie's visual estimate was off by 2,592 feet. K2 towers
over Masherbrum. Straddling the borders of China and Pakistan, the
peak looms above the Karakorum, soaring 28,251 feet, making it the
second-tallest mountain on earth. Everest stands just 778 feet higher.
From a distance, K2 resembles a prehistoric shark tooth. Closer in,

Thomas Montgomerie's Sketch of K2: A British lieutenant sketched the mountain's profile in his field book and labeled it K, for the Karakorum mountain range, and 2, for the second mountain in the survey. To locals, K2 is *Chogori*, or "doorway to heaven" in Tibetan. Mountaineers often refer to it as the Savage Mountain.

you can see its striated gneissic rock, encased in ice. On clear mornings, the summit floats imperiously above the clouds and the sun bathes its glaciers with golden light.

K2 lacks the mass of Everest, but it's sleeker—and meaner. Climbers call it "The Savage Mountain." The peak has all the obstacles of Everest, and more. K2's glaciers are riddled with fissures concealed by layers of snow; climbers step on these crevasses, punch through, and, if unroped, disappear. Blocks of ice cleave off overhanging glaciers; avalanches roar down icy flanks. And then there's the altitude. No human, plant, or animal can tolerate such harsh conditions for more than a few days. With each lungful of air, climbers on the summit suck in only a third of the oxygen they breathe at sea level. Oxygen deprivation saps their strength and compromises their judgment. Altitude illness breaks them, giving some the coordination of toddlers.

As if these difficulties weren't enough, storms are harsher on K2. It stands 882 miles northwest of Everest, and, being farther from the equator, is more vulnerable to extratropical cyclones and their accompanying jet streams. Everest at least follows a reliable weather pattern: Water evaporates from the Bay of Bengal east of India, forming cloud banks; they float northward over the Himalaya, nudging the jet stream off the summit, in advance of the monsoon. In May, relatively windless weather graces Everest for as long as two weeks. In contrast, K2's weather window is a crapshoot. Climbers don't know when the window will open—or whether it will open at all.

All this makes for dismal statistics. Before 2008, only 278 people had stood on K2's summit. Everest's summit roll was 4,115, and its fatality rate—the percentage of climbers who went above Base Camp and died—had averaged 0.7 for the previous decade. Although the Himalayan Database crunches the numbers for Everest, no accurate statistics exist for K2. Climbers of the Savage Mountain can't reliably approximate their chances of survival and don't want to. In 2008, the fatality rate of those leaving Base Camp for a summit bid was 30.5 percent, higher than the casualty rate at Omaha Beach on D-day. Among high-altitude climbers if not statisticians, there's no comparison: K2 is more lethal than Everest.

It took a century of alpinism before a mortal stood on K2's summit. One early attempt involved "The Wickedest Man on Earth." Mountaineer, author, pornographer, and occultist, Aleister Crowley had eclectic passions, attracting admirers long after his death. The Beatles featured him on the album jacket of *Sgt. Pepper's Lonely Hearts Club Band* just as prominently as Karl Marx and Marilyn Monroe. In 1902, Crowley and his friend Oscar Eckenstein decided to climb K2.

On the way to the mountain, Eckenstein was arrested for espionage. Crowley, meanwhile, loaded the packs with tomes by Milton and whipped the porters. Some of these porters deserted, stealing Crowley's clothes.

As Crowley and his teammates negotiated K2's Northeast Ridge, weather pushed him back five times. One man's lungs filled with fluid, and Crowley was hallucinating from a combination of altitude and opium. At high camp, Crowley pulled out a revolver and tried to discipline a teammate, who knocked the gun away and socked him in the gut. Crowley accused another climber of hoarding food and going mad. He booted the hungry man off the team.

After nine weeks and five summit bids, they failed to reach the top, but Crowley's expedition achieved a measure of success. They spent a record amount of time at high altitude—more than two months—and climbed to a respectable 21,400 feet, a record on K2 that stood for decades.

If Crowley embodies the climbing nut, the leader of the next major expedition epitomizes the climbing aristocrat. Luigi Amedeo Giuseppe Maria Ferdinando Francesco di Savoia-Aosta, more concisely known as the Duke of the Abruzzi, was a veteran explorer who had lost four fingertips trying to reach the North Pole. Fleeing a scandalous romance in 1909, he decided to head for the hills. The duke failed to get permission to scale Everest, so he christened K2 as the Third Pole and left his *palazzo* to climb it.

Abruzzi departed Europe on the steamer *Oceana*, laden with 10,454 pounds of luggage, including a brass bedstead, feather pillows, and sleeping bags layered with four types of animal hides. Trekking through the princely states of Kashmir, he was slowed by banquets, polo matches, and gift-giving ceremonies. Runners brought in daily mail and newspapers, and one of the duke's early concerns was, to quote the expedition diary, "the smell of the natives," who were "unbearable, even in open air."

But even as Abruzzi pressed a scented handkerchief to his nostrils, he took in a majestic vista. K2 was "the indisputable sovereign of the region, gigantic and solitary, hidden from human sight in innumerable ranges, jealously defended by a vast throng of vassal peaks, protected from invasion by miles and miles of glaciers." The landscape impressed him enough to bestow his own name on its features. Some of these names, such as K2's Abruzzi Spur and the nearby Savoia Glacier, are still used today.

The duke spent six weeks trying one route after another, surveying and posing for photographs. He never made it above 20,500 feet. "If anyone does get to the top," he later informed the Italian Alpine Club, "it will be a pilot, not a mountaineer."

▲ ▲ ▲

The duke's prediction held for nearly half a century, but two men almost disproved it in 1939 during what became "the most bizarre tragedy in the history of Himalayan mountaineering."

Fritz Wiessner—"Baby Face" to his friends—had the dimples of a cherub and the charm of a hornet. Famous for first ascents on monoliths such as Devils Tower in Wyoming, he had hired eight Sherpas to help him bag K2. On the evening of July 19, one of them, Pasang Dawa Lama, had him on belay 750 feet below the summit. As the sun dipped, trailed by a sliver of moon, Pasang heard a rustle. Blue scales flared in the dusk.

According to *lamas* who mythologize the climb, Pasang was familiar with the goddess of K2 and her appetite for human flesh. He watched in horror as Takar Dolsangma dismounted her dragon, hitched the beast to the slope by its tongue, and sniffed the air. It had been 1,122 years since her last meal.

Pasang "was so afraid," recounted Wiessner. Oblivious of the danger, he shouted for more slack.

"No, sahib," Pasang responded, gripping the rope. "Tomorrow."

Incredulous, Wiessner turned back. The retreat, however, did not appease the goddess. As Pasang rappelled down the ice, she gripped the dragon's withers and soared into the sky. Spiraling toward Pasang, the dragon grazed his pack, knocking two pairs of crampons down the slope. Attempting the summit was now hopeless, and Pasang began strategizing about how to get down.

His first challenge was Wiessner, who was bent on topping out. The next day, as the men recuperated at high camp, Pasang watched for dragons, and Wiessner sunbathed nude. "Since the day before, [Pasang Lama] had no longer been his old self," Wiessner recounted. "[H]e had been living in great fear of the evil spirits, constantly murmuring prayers, and had lost his appetite."

At dawn, the men climbed to the Bottleneck and examined the ice. "With crampons, we could have practically run up," Wiessner puffed, but without crampons there was no choice. They turned around for the last time.

On descent, Pasang relaxed. The camps below would be stocked with supplies and armed with Sherpa support. He had provoked Takar Dolsangma yet somehow survived.

But she hadn't forgiven him. On an icy slope above Camp 8, Pasang's body lurched forward, as if jabbed by an invisible elbow. His throat let loose "a funny little noise" as he began to slide. Wiessner knew what to do. "I put myself in position, dug in as much as possible, and held him on the rope." Pasang regained balance, but what he encountered in the next camp shook him more than the fall. There was nothing: no additional supplies and no one except a dehydrated straggler, American millionaire Dudley Wolfe, who was slurping snowmelt from the folds of a tent.

Wolfe joined the rope team, and the trio descended through the fog until the goddess evidently tripped Wolfe. The line pulled taut and jerked all the men off their feet. They barreled toward a 600-story drop, gear spilling from their packs. "All I was thinking was, how stupid this has to happen like this," Wiessner recounted. About 20 yards before the cliff, he flipped onto his stomach, swung his axe, and broke the fall. All skulls were intact, but only one sleeping bag had survived. The men would have to share it.

In the next camp, it appeared as though a dragon-size raccoon had rummaged through the tents—shredding the fabric, sampling the food, and scattering trash. The air mattresses and sleeping bags had vanished. "I could hardly speak," Wiessner recalled. "We almost knew that we had been sabotaged." The men dug out a tent, pulled the remaining sleeping bag across their chests, and shivered through the night.

In the morning, Wolfe could barely stand. Pasang and Wiessner left to look for help but found camp after camp had been emptied. The reason for this became clear when they finally stumbled into Base Camp: Pasang, Wiessner, and Wolfe had been presumed dead.

The Sherpas mobilized to rescue Wolfe, but by the time they reached him, critical days had been lost. Wolfe, too debilitated to crawl outside, was using his tent as a latrine. The Sherpas pulled him out of the sewage, poured tea down his gullet, and descended to thicker air, aiming to haul him down the next morning.

A storm grounded the rescue for another day. Then, as the skies cleared on July 31, three rescuers—Kikuli, Kitar, and Phinsoo—went up to fetch Wolfe. They never returned. The slope, packed with fresh snow, avalanched, likely burying them alive. Wolfe presumably died in his tent. The Savage Mountain had claimed its first four victims.

Wiessner trudged home defensive: "On big mountains, as in war," he told the media, "one must expect casualties." He, like the Sherpas, developed a mythological version of the events. As the years passed, he began to claim that a nearly full moon had illuminated the sky on the night of his summit bid. This fostered a myth that Wiessner might have pioneered the first ascent of K2 if a superstitious Sherpa hadn't held him back. But lunar charts show that July 19 was three days past a new moon, and, as seen from K2, that moon was a useless sliver that stayed visible only three hours after dark. Pasang and Wiessner had confronted a bigger problem than a turquoise dragon: Headlamps wouldn't be invented for another thirty-three years, and they faced pitch-blackness. In the gathering dusk, Pasang's insistence on turning around probably saved Wiessner's life.

▲ ▲ ▲

Nobody attempted K2 during World War II. In the aftermath, the British relinquished their Indian empire, which split into two independent nations: Pakistan and India. Suddenly K2 had changed hands, ending up in Pakistan-administered Kashmir, a territory claimed by both countries.

The 1947 Partition of British India led to one of the largest and bloodiest exoduses in modern history. Religious persecution took the form of mob violence as fourteen million people dispersed to their respective nations: Hindus fleeing from Pakistan to India and many Muslims flowing in reverse. Their desperate caravans were ambushed by fanatics of the opposing faith. Refugees were butchered on the railway, and train cars stuffed with mutilated corpses had to be hosed out when they reached their destinations. One million were killed, and the new governments of India and Pakistan blamed each other. There has been constant hostility around K2 ever since.

Nevertheless, mountaineering revived, and the Karakorum reopened for business. A group of Americans cinched a permit for K2 in 1953, and their expedition came to define decency on a mountain.

As the team left for the Karakorum, Art Gilkey, a twenty-seven-year-old geologist, learned that Everest had just been conquered. Gilkey had hoped this would be his lucky summer, too, but eight weeks later he found himself dying at 25,500 feet. He was suffering from what felt like a charley horse in his left calf. He couldn't walk it off, and the leg kept swelling. A storm blew in, stranding Gilkey and several teammates. The gale pounded their tent for five days. When the wind slowed, Gilkey crawled outside and tried to stand. He collapsed.

A doctor named Charlie Houston examined Gilkey and diagnosed thrombophlebitis, or potentially lethal blood clots that can form when a climber is dehydrated, oxygen-deprived, and immobile for too long. Unwilling to let him die, the team tried to bring Gilkey down. Winds blasted them back, foiling their first evacuation attempt and trapping them inside the tents for another three days. Gilkey's cough became an incessant hack. As is often the case with thrombophlebitis, the clots had probably broken off and barged through Gilkey's main pulmonary artery, clogging his lungs. The resulting embolism would have impaired Gilkey's breathing and circulation.

After a break in the weather, the men decided to try again. They zipped Gilkey into a sleeping bag, wrapped a tent around his torso, stuffed his feet into a pack, and bound him with ropes. They dragged the improvised gurney through the snow with towlines, lowering him through the steepest sections.

When rescuers fanned out to scout the route ahead, one man, roped to a second, lost his balance and slid, yanking his partner and trolling him down the slope. Gaining speed, the pair clotheslined another two. This tangle of four snagged the rope connected to a fifth and to Gilkey. All six men flailed down the mountain, about to launch off a 7,000-foot drop. "This is it!" thought Bob Bates, one of the climbers. "There was nothing I could do now."

Above them was Pete Schoening, a twenty-six-year-old from Seattle. He leaped up and grabbed a rope attached to Gilkey, who—through a series of towlines, tangles, and tie-offs—was also connected to the five tumbling climbers. Schoening wound the line around his shoulders and anchored the wooden shaft of his axe behind a rock.

The line yanked Schoening, but he held the axe and simultaneously clenched the rope. Somehow, it didn't snap, and Schoening checked the momentum of five falling men while also bearing the weight of Gilkey's gurney. Mountaineers call this feat the Miracle Belay.

Almost as miraculously, the injuries were manageable. One man lost his mittens, pack, and glasses; another lost his short-term memory. Two were ensnared around a third, who was partially sliced by the rope. But one by one, they untangled themselves and got to their feet. The rescuers re-anchored Gilkey's gurney and went ahead to scout a route and pitch camp.

Some of them heard the muffled shout. The climbers returned to where Gilkey had been tied and saw freshly plowed snow. Charlie Houston later speculated that Gilkey "wiggled himself loose from the line" so his teammates wouldn't have to risk their lives to save him. It's more likely that an avalanche swept him off the slope. Whatever the truth, Gilkey was gone. His friends limped down the mountain, devastated but alive. Near Base Camp, their porters piled up stones, creating a memorial cairn that remains today. Although the team had lost Gilkey and the summit, their expedition was hailed as a high point in alpinism. The team had banded together, and no one had sacrificed his humanity for self-preservation.

▲ ▲ ▲

After Gilkey's death, the Savage Mountain became an object of desire for Italians. Frederick Cook and Robert Peary had touched the North Pole; Roald Amundsen had tagged the South; Tenzing Norgay and Edmund Hillary had summited Everest—but no one could conquer K2. Now the highest untouched summit, it was the hardest place to reach above sea level.

Still demoralized by World War II, the Italians pursued the mountain to restore national pride. Expedition leader Ardito Desio secured a permit for 1954 and made sure his climbers understood the stakes: "If you succeed in scaling the peak, as I am confident you will, the entire world will hail you as champions of your race long after you are dead." The Italian expedition was to become K2's most controversial, triggering fifty years of polemic—all over the disappearance of a tent.

The climb began with six hundred Pakistani porters carrying thirteen tons of gear to Base Camp, including 230 vermilion oxygen cylinders, but by late July, only four men were in serious contention for the summit. The strongest of them, twenty-four-year-old Walter Bonatti, had been relegated to the B-Team.

Two days before the summit bid, Bonatti was ordered to lug eighty pounds of oxygen cylinders to the two members of the A-Team. To manage it, Bonatti wanted to enlist help from Amir Mehdi, a Pakistani high-altitude porter who had carried Austrian mountaineer Hermann Buhl down Nanga Parbat the year before. Mehdi wanted the summit for himself, so Bonatti cut him a deal: If Mehdi delivered the oxygen to high camp, he could sleep in the A-Team's tent and join their summit bid. Mehdi agreed, and the next day he and Bonatti left for the drop-off point at 26,600 feet.

But when they arrived that evening, the A-Team had disappeared, along with their tent. Bonatti scoured the slopes for shelter, shouting for the missing climbers. At one point, Bonatti heard someone hollering instructions—"Leave the oxygen and descend." Mehdi, meanwhile, was pacing and kicking the snow "like an unchained force of nature . . . yelling crazily," as Bonatti recounted. Mehdi's toes were cramped inside Italian army boots two sizes too small.

Bonatti decided it was insane to descend in the dark with a screaming man who couldn't feel his feet, so he gave up looking for the tent and stomped out a platform in the ice. He and Mehdi huddled together chewing caramels, expecting to die. Frostbite consumed all of Mehdi's toes and about a third of one foot. In 1954, it was the highest open bivouac in history.

Meanwhile, Achille Compagnoni, the captain of the A-Team, was resting in his tent, quietly sipping chamomile and clutching a typed memorandum stating that he was in charge. But a soggy paper has no authority in the Death Zone, so Compagnoni had taken another precaution: He'd moved his tent to an unstable traverse so Bonatti couldn't supplant him on summit day.

At first light, Bonatti and Mehdi left the oxygen cylinders and descended. Only then did Compagnoni and his climbing partner, Lino' Lacedelli, crawl out of their tent to retrieve the oxygen. They avoided the Bottleneck, but the rocks below the southeast face were no easier. The oxygen allegedly ran out, and the men staggered and slipped. Hallucinating, Lacedelli saw his fiancée tailing him. Compagnoni met the ghost of a teammate who had died in June. Their Due Lupe gloves became soaked and froze over their thumbs. Finally, at dusk on July 31, 1954, the A-Team planted the Italian flag on the summit. They descended in darkness, resting to take a swig of brandy, and reached their tent late that night.

Once at Base Camp, Compagnoni was unapologetic about hiding the tent and demanded to know why his oxygen cylinders had run dry, but euphoria soon smothered all argument. Steaming home on the *Asia*, a luxury cruise ship, the climbers presented a united front. No one disclosed the details of the forced bivouac. Radio and TV stations broadcast Italy's triumph worldwide; the Italian and Pakistani governments decorated the climbers; Pope Pius XII offered blessings. Compagnoni and Lacedelli were emblazoned on postage stamps. As mountaineer Reinhold Messner later put it, the victory on K2 helped bring a "psychological reconstruction of Italians" after the trauma of fascism and war.

But a decade later, bizarre allegations emerged. Through a journalist, Compagnoni accused Bonatti of siphoning oxygen from his bottles, even though the mask and tubing had been inside Compagnoni's own tent. Furious, Bonatti successfully sued for libel. "Like an elephant," he never forgot the sins of the A-Team, and neither did anyone else. When Compagnoni died fifty-four years after the climb, his obituary in the *New York Times* focused on his choice to move the tent. A snap decision on K2 had cemented his reputation as the Judas of mountaineering.

Mehdi, after the amputation of his toes, returned home to Hunza and left his ice axe in the garden shed. Gradually, he learned to walk on his stumps. He was informed by mail that the Italian government had awarded him Cavaliere status, the equivalent of knighthood. Compagnoni sent him dozens of letters over the years, but Mehdi never had them translated.

▲ ▲ ▲

After the operatics of 1954, the Savage Mountain permitted no summits for twenty-two years. A Japanese team finally succeeded in 1977, with help from an army of 1,500 porters. In the late 1970s, Pakistan, which had limited the number of K2 expeditions to one a year, began allowing many more. Overcrowding contributed to the death toll, which spiked in 1986 when thirteen climbers perished in a single summer.

At the same time, the spirit of the sport was changing. The first generation of high-altitude mountaineers were the proud "Conquistadors of the Useless," pioneering first ascents. But what was left once all the major peaks had been conquered? Mountaineers scrambled for ways to distinguish themselves. Competing for media attention and corporate sponsorship, they took on more daring routes under ever-more-harrowing conditions. Reaching the top wasn't enough. Climbers had to ascend without bottled oxygen; claw up hypertechnical routes; race up two mountains, one right after the other; climb during the Himalayan winter; bag every summit higher than 8,000 meters. And all of this had to be documented, on camera, for the Discovery Channel.

Technology improved. GPS guided climbers through whiteouts;

satellite phones buzzed; supercomputers predicted storms; crampons grew front points; DryLoft replaced reindeer skin. As new tools and equipment allowed the sport to become more extreme, they simultaneously made it more accessible. Western guide companies such as Peak Freaks and Mountain Madness appeared in the 1990s. For popular destinations like Everest, these companies organized all the logistics, obtained permits, hired staff, fixed routes, and charged $30,000 to $120,000 a head.

Crowds packed the mountain. Amateurs who had trained on sea-level StepMills arrived at Everest, clipped their ascenders onto a fixed line, and winched their way through the clouds. Most Sherpas, grateful for the work, recognized that clients sometimes lacked technical expertise, but their dependence could be managed. They instructed weak climbers to avoid overexerting themselves and focus on their health. "We climb Everest twice," Chhiring explained. "First, Sherpas go up to set the ropes and camps, then we go down to collect our clients and take them to the top." A headline in *The Guardian* summarized the phenomenon: "Mount Everest: a not so novel feat." The subhead observed: "So many people, and celebrities, are conquering Everest that it's more resort than wilderness." Sherpas did the heavy lifting, and thousands of happy amateurs joined the Mount Everest summit roll.

The inadequacies of commercial climbing hit the spotlight in 1996 when fifteen climbers lost their lives on Everest, eight in a single day. Jon Krakauer's memoir about the tragedy, *Into Thin Air*, sold four million copies and became a finalist for the Pulitzer Prize. The book should have scared rational creatures away from the sport; instead, the "Krakauer effect" galvanized commercial mountaineering. Most newcomers arrived at Base Camp with the requisite experience, but a few imagined that their $65,000 expedition fee was a chairlift to the top, weather and ability be damned. Forced to turn back for their own safety, they sued for breach of contract. Even Sir Edmund Hillary worried that dilettantes were "engendering disrespect for the mountain."

The death of David Sharp in 2006 epitomized this decline. A thirty-four-year-old math teacher, Sharp was descending from the summit of Everest when he collapsed, still clipped to the fixed line, fewer than 800 feet above the highest camp. Over the next twelve hours, as many as forty summit-hungry climbers reportedly passed him as he lay dying. Some witnesses said they thought Sharp was merely resting. Others said he was in obvious distress and could have been rescued if anyone else had agreed to help. Nobody made an effort until they were descending from the summit, but by then it was too late. Sharp had been left to die; summit fever had trumped common humanity.

As an Everest conquest lost its purity and prestige, professional climbers and avid amateurs defected to K2. Its difficulty resisted commercialization. A successful ascent without bottled oxygen was a shortcut to media attention, fame, and sponsorship. The Savage Mountain got a second moniker—The Mountaineer's Mountain—and Sherpas wanted to bag it, too. Sherpas were the strongest on Everest. They held the records for the first, fastest, and greatest number of summits, and it was getting hard for them to distinguish themselves there. Hundreds of Sherpas had climbed Everest, but only two had succeeded on K2 without using bottled oxygen.

Chhiring intended to be the third, but his wife, Dawa, thought his ambitions were perverse. Now in his midthirties, Chhiring had a family, a house, a business, and a potbelly. By 2007, Dawa thought she'd persuaded him to give up on K2. "He had become more sensible," Dawa said. "K2 was a fantasy. And even if he got the chance, I knew I could stop him." But in his mind, Chhiring never relinquished the mountain. He kept looking for a way. After a decade of dreaming, he found a solution: a man named Eric Meyer.

▲ ▲ ▲

An anesthesiologist from Colorado, Eric Meyer had lived in a decompression chamber for six weeks in the mid-1980s. Researchers for Operation Everest II, a study on oxygen deprivation, barraged him with fitness tests to analyze how hypoxia had withered his body. They drilled cores out of his legs to determine how his muscles atrophied under high-altitude conditions. They forced tubes up his arteries to examine how his heart deteriorated. In exchange, Eric earned $4,000. He spent it on a climbing trip.

The ultra runner and triathlete tested his limits, cultivating his mind and body in tandem. He practiced yoga every morning for an hour, studied martial arts in Asia, and stocked his Sub-Zero refrigerator with green smoothies made of puréed algae, broccoli juice, and barley grass. These efforts cast an enchantment over his appearance. His skin was so smooth it seemed varnished. His hair was so radiant it practically glowed in the dark. He had virtually no body fat. Graceful and relaxed, he spoke with the mellow authority of a meditation guru.

In 2004, recovering from a divorce, Eric spotted Chhiring when climbing Everest. While everyone else at Advanced Base Camp seemed wasted, Chhiring bristled with energy. The Sherpa had arms thicker than most climbers' thighs. He pitched tents and set ropes faster than anyone. His five-foot-nine frame supported outrageous, unbelievable loads. "I'd never seen anyone so strong," Eric recalled. "I had to get to know him. We started talking, and we bonded instantly. I knew I'd made a friend for life."

Chhiring told Eric about his dream of climbing K2, his daughters, his village, and his mother dying in childbirth; Eric told Chhiring about his volunteer work to improve health care and reduce infant mortality in the developing world. Chhiring and Eric shared meals of rice and dal. They swapped stories and traded tips on climbing technique. They meditated. "He didn't treat me like a sherpa," Chhiring said. "To Eric, I was an equal. We became brothers." After climbing to the top of Everest, Eric asked Chhiring to visit him in Colorado.

In the summer of 2007, Chhiring and Dawa arrived in Steamboat Springs, a ski town known for its powder. In Steamboat, delis name their sandwiches after explorers, and toddlers learn to slalom almost as soon as they can walk. Chhiring fit right in. He and Eric pedaled up mountain trails and scaled crags. They carbo-loaded on noodles Dawa cooked in Eric's kitchen and ran marathons. Chhiring learned to drive a pickup along the back roads and laid cement foundations to stay in shape. "He never seemed to get tired of carrying bags of concrete," observed Eric's friend Dana Tredway. It was the perfect vacation until K2 got in the way.

Eric told Chhiring he planned to quit his job, secure a permit from Pakistan, and climb the Savage Mountain. Maybe Chhiring could join him—not as a support climber but as a full-fledged team member? Five friends were already planning to join up: three Americans, a Swede, and an Australian. Sponsors such as Warid Telecom would defray the cost, so Chhiring would only need to cover $3,000. As a team member rather than staff, Chhiring wouldn't have to babysit anyone. He could focus on reaching the summit. The team would follow the Abruzzi Spur, K2's southeast flank, the sanest way up. They wouldn't dope on bottled oxygen. Chhiring would join the ranks of the most elite climbers.

Chhiring didn't need convincing. Dawa did. "And I didn't want to step in the middle of it," Eric recalled. "There are plenty of reasons not to climb K2. I couldn't promise her he'd come back."

Dawa couldn't speak English as well as her husband, and she was oblivious to the plans that he and Eric were hatching. Chhiring tried to ease her into them before the end of summer. During the final week of their vacation, he sat her down on Eric's couch, slid a disk into the DVD player, and punched some buttons on the remote. A six-inch gorilla in a red Hawaiian shirt appeared on the flat screen. The puppet assumed a Kermit-the-Frog twang: "I'm Murph. I may not look like much, but I get around."

Murph Goes to K2, a hokey documentary for children, explained to Dawa how a puppet safely ascended the world's deadliest peak. When the screen went black, Dawa turned to her husband in disbelief. Now she understood what Eric and Chhiring had been talking about in English. Did Chhiring actually think he was going to climb K2 like a stupid puppet?

She wanted to leave Eric's home and walk the three miles to the airport. Instead, Dawa forced a smile and sat quietly for two hours as her husband and Eric joked in a language she couldn't understand.

When Chhiring and Dawa returned to their A-frame guesthouse for the night, Chhiring acted as though everything had gone well. He took off his shoes, sat cross-legged on the floor, and began the evening prayer. Facing the Rockies, he gripped his *mala* rosary and repeated a mantra: *Om mani padme um*. The rite, which Chhiring performed twice a day, is meant to invoke compassion. Dawa usually joined him in prayer, but she'd been compassionate enough that evening. Now it was her turn to talk. "You offend the gods," she said.

Chhiring kept repeating the mantra.

"Did you hear me, Chhiring? Climbing K2 is a sin."

Chhiring recited *Om mani padme um* for ten more minutes. Once he stopped, he got up and slinked into the bedroom, avoiding eye contact with Dawa.

Dawa watched him leave and took a moment to collect herself. She wouldn't call him a bad father, a bad husband, a bad brother, a bad son. Chhiring was none of those things, but she would tell him what he was. Dawa opened the bedroom door. "You're an addict," she said.

Chhiring, sprawled on the mattress, turned his head to the wall.

Later that night, Dawa lay beside him and waited for sleep to come. An hour passed. She listened to her husband's breathing. She knew he was still awake, so she decided to speak her mind. "If you go to that mountain," Dawa told him, "I will leave."

She'd never said that to him before, and even this was a bluff. A woman with two young children seldom divorces her husband in Nepal. Social mores are against it. So is the legal system. "But what else could I do?" Dawa recalled. "I could beg, I could cry, I could tell him why he shouldn't go, but he's a man. And in Nepal, men decide everything."

Dawa cried anyway. After a moment, Chhiring told her what she wanted to hear. Nobody should climb K2. Not a Buddhist. Not a parent. Not when it costs as much as a house. Chhiring couldn't justify gambling his life to stand on top of a mountain. K2 had worse odds of survival than Russian roulette. It didn't make sense.

But people don't climb because it makes sense. You can come up with reasons—it gives direction to the lost, friends to the loner, honor to the reprobate, thrills to the bored—but, ultimately, the quest for a summit defies logic. So does passion. So does a trip to the moon. There are better things to do. Safer, cheaper, more practical. That's not the point.

The next morning, when Eric asked Chhiring whether he really wanted to climb K2, Chhiring didn't look into his wife's face. He didn't pause. He didn't explain himself or describe the sacrifices his family would have to make. He had known the answer for twenty years, and his response was immediate.

Yes.

The Prince and the Porter

Narayanhity Royal Palace, Kathmandu, Nepal
Evening, June 1, 2001

Two hours before he murdered them, Crown Prince Dipendra tried to get his family to relax. He started a billiards game, poured drinks, and joked about turning thirty. The Tarantino-style bloodbath that followed inflamed a civil war that displaced 150,000 Nepalis, including a potato farmer named Pasang Lama.

Pasang's trajectory toward K2 started around 8 p.m. on June 1, 2001, as two dozen members of Nepal's royalty strolled into Kathmandu's Narayanhity Palace, a bubblegum-pink sprawl guarded by soldiers, high gates, and mildew-streaked walls. Together, the family formed the last of the Shah dynasty, the absolute rulers of Nepal since 1768.

The crown prince, a stocky playboy who went by the nickname Dippy, was a practiced host. Educated at Eton, a prestigious English boarding school, he held a black belt in karate and had enjoyed weaponry ever since he received his first pistol at the age of eight. Dippy was also in love with the wrong woman—or at least that's what his family thought.

She was on his mind that night. Watching the billiards game, he downed several shots of Famous Grouse whisky and smoked a joint laced with a black substance, probably opium. As the drug took effect, Dipendra swayed, unable to hold himself upright. He stammered and banged into furniture. Four relatives dragged him to his bedroom.

Sobbing, the prince called his girlfriend, Devyani Rana, who was of lower social standing. Dippy had been ordered to break up with her. He'd have to marry a woman his mother would select or be stripped of royal status. The prince's words to Devyani were slurred. He hung up, dialed, and hung up again.

Devyani Rana called back, reaching his aides, and warned them that Dipendra might injure himself. The aides rushed to the bedroom and found the prince on the floor, squirming and tearing at his clothes. They propped him up and helped him to the bathroom, where he vomited. They splashed cold water on his face and got him into bed.

Alone, the prince called his girlfriend again. He told Devyani he loved her and would try to sleep. Instead, he donned combat boots, black leather gloves, and a camouflage jacket and vest. Then he assembled his weapons: a 9 mm Glock pistol; a modified 9 mm MP-5K submachine gun; a Colt M16 assault rifle, with light and scope attached; and an SPAS 12-gauge pump-action shotgun. Carrying at least two of these guns, he stumbled toward the billiards room.

Almost the entire royal family was crowded inside. Among them was King Birendra Bir Bikram Shah, a soft-spoken grandfather with wide amber spectacles. By Hindu tradition, King Birendra was considered a demigod, an incarnation of Vishnu. He stood near the east end of the billiards table, sipping cognac and discussing the risks of high cholesterol.

When his son entered the room in combat fatigues, gripping a shotgun and a submachine gun, King Birendra didn't seem alarmed. The king, perhaps thinking Dipendra had come to show weapons from the royal arsenal, stepped forward. "Isn't the Crown Prince a bit old to be dressing like this?" remarked an aunt.

Then, as the guests watched, the prince pulled the trigger. Two bullets from the submachine gun tore into his father's side. King Birendra crumpled to the ground, blood soaking his dress shirt. "What have you done?" were his last words, according to official reports.

With a gun in each hand, Dipendra couldn't control the recoil. Bullets sprayed into the ceiling and the west wall. Two relatives lunged toward the king and tried to stanch the bleeding. His rounds spent, Dipendra threw down the machine gun and darted out of the room. "There was some screaming initially, but after that everyone was just looking around," recalled Dipendra's brother-in-law, Gorakh Rana.

Seconds later, Dipendra returned with the M16 in his right hand, the pistol in his left. He fired another shot at the king at point-blank range. Diprendra "really looked exactly like the Terminator 2, expressionless but very concentrated," recalled his aunt, Princess Ketaki Chester.

His favorite uncle, Dhirendra, raised his hands, trying to soothe the homicidal prince. "That's enough, Babu," he said. Without answering, Dipendra fired a burst of bullets that tore through his uncle's chest. He shot more rounds at the men applying pressure to the king's wounds. The prince left the room once again, retreating onto the veranda.

Then, as though he had forgotten something, Dipendra returned. Spraying bullets wildly, he kicked bodies to determine who was dead. Finally, the family panicked. Some shrieked and leaped behind a sofa. Others dashed down the hallway and into the botanical garden. Dipendra jogged out the door toward the royal apartments and dove up a stairway.

His brother, Prince Nirajan, raced after him, trailed by their mother, Queen Aishwarya, and from the landing, Dipendra took aim. His brother dropped.

The queen surrendered. "You've killed your father, you've killed your brother. Kill me too."

Dipendra shot her in the face. Aishwarya's body slid down the stairs, coming to rest on the seventh step.

The top royalty were now dead or dying, so the prince wandered through the gardens. It was a muggy night, thick with cicadas. Bats hung from the trees, and condensation dripped from the panes of the greenhouse. Quietly, Dipendra stumbled toward a bridge over the royal frog pond. He raised a gun to his temple and pulled the trigger. A single bullet tore through his head, just behind his left ear, and out the other side of his skull. He was found on the grass, near a statue of Buddha. In less than five minutes, Dipendra had shot himself and fourteen members of his family.

Early the next morning, doctors at a nearby military hospital declared nine of Nepal's top royalty dead. Prince Dipendra, in a coma, lived on. As funerals were arranged, an official spokesman released a statement that the "accidental firing of an automatic weapon" was responsible for killing several family members. Dipendra wasn't named as a suspect.

It was a clumsy cover-up. Nepalis didn't know exactly what had happened, but they had conspiracy theories. Some believed that Indian spies had framed Dipendra and orchestrated the massacre in an effort to install a puppet regime.

Others had supernatural explanations, stemming from a well-known prophecy. The legend held that the Shahs would soon fall because the dynasty's first king, Prithvi Narayan, had angered the god Gorakhnath. About two centuries earlier, the king had offered an ascetic a bowl of rancid curd. The holy man swallowed it and vomited; then, unexpectedly, scooping up the mess, he ordered the king to eat the curd himself. Repulsed, Prithvi Narayan flung the vomit in the man's face. It was the wrong move. Shielding himself with his hands, the ascetic revealed himself to be a god and cursed the Shahs.

Their dynasty, he said, would be limited to ten generations, one for each of his sticky fingers. Ten generations later, "I had known something was coming," said Dr. Raghunath Aryal, the royal astrologer. "But how do you tell your boss that his son is about to commit mass murder?"

Sixteen hours after the massacre, an eleventh-generation member of the dynasty was crowned. The comatose Dipendra ruled for two days. When he was removed from life support, the monarchy was returned to the tenth generation as his uncle Gyanendra became king.

Rioters stormed the streets because they considered Gyanendra a bad seed. Propaganda described how royal astrologers had examined Gyanendra at birth and declared him unfit to rule. The boy, nevertheless, had been king briefly, at age four, when his grandfather Tribhuvan was forced into exile, along with most of the family. When the Shahs returned, little Gyanendra lost his crown. The boy grew up with a scowl; in his second coronation portrait, he is scowling still. Even loyal subjects found him suspicious. Why had Gyanendra's own children been spared? Had the massacre been a plot by Dipendra's uncle?

After investigators had released the crime scene, Gyanendra razed the billiards room, the site of the massacre. By the time the first comprehensive investigation reports were released that summer, the Shahs had lost their credibility, and Maoist rebels were capitalizing on their weakness.

At the time of Gyanendra's succession, the Shahs embodied all that had gone wrong with the Nepali feudal system. The dynasty during its 239-year rule had produced a series of temperamental royals. In the eighteenth century, for instance, Prithvi Narayan had sliced off the lips of his opponents; in the nineteenth, Surendra had dropped his subjects down wells; in the twenty-first, Paras allegedly had run over a musician with his Mitsubishi Pajero because the man wouldn't play his request. Yet the Shahs remained constitutionally immune from prosecution, and the family enjoyed an extravagant and much-resented lifestyle.

The Communists promised to empower the populace, redistribute land, grant women equal rights, and eliminate the caste system. A coalition of Communist parties nearly secured a plurality of seats in the 1991 parliamentary election, and, five years later, the Maoists declared "The People's War" to extinguish the monarchy and bring about a secular republic. Over the next decade they accomplished little, but they had gained strength by recruiting troops, looting police stations for weapons, and hoarding homemade explosives. When the unpopular Gyanendra succeeded the beloved King Birendra, the Maoists knew it was time to strike.

The Maoists invaded remote villages unprotected by the royal army. They burst into classrooms, shot teachers, and abducted the pupils, forcing them to join their ranks as child soldiers. The troops tortured their opponents and displayed their mutilated bodies. They blockaded Kathmandu and gained control of the provinces.

In response, Parliament passed the Terrorist and Destructive Activities Act, allowing ninety-day detentions and aggressive interrogation of Maoists. King Gyanendra suspended the elected government and instituted martial law, assuming command over the military and the press. He censored criticism of his government, imprisoned journalists, and executed suspected terrorists. "Nepal has been experiencing a grave human rights crisis," declared a report from the United Nations General Assembly. Amnesty International and Human Rights Watch condemned the abuse, recording gruesome cases of electrocution, beating, assassination, kidnapping, public execution, and sexual humiliation. Until 2006, civil war raged. The government controlled Kathmandu, but Maoists penetrated nearly every village. More than 12,800 people were killed, and about 150,000 were forced to flee their homes. Unemployment soared to around 50 percent.

The Maoists finally got their way, in part. In July 2008, the monarchy was abolished and Nepal was declared a federal republic. Elections placed the Communists in power periodically, but protests and violence continued.

During the height of the civil war, Pasang Lama was living in Kathmandu in a one-room flat with seven others. His village in eastern Nepal was a war zone: The king's army, trying to root out Maoists, was arresting and shooting young men his age. Pasang couldn't go back home, and his family of refugees needed money.

Despite the violence, die-hard mountaineers kept climbing in Nepal, paying porters about $3 a day to carry loads to Himalayan base camps. The job required little skill beyond brute strength, making it one of the few options for men like Pasang. Cornered by war in a riot-torn city, living under curfew and fear of bombs, the seventeen-year-old potato farmer became a porter.

▲ ▲ ▲

Pasang Lama used a mnemonic to teach English speakers how to pronounce his name. "It's Pah-SONG," he would say, "because I'm always singing." While trekking, Pasang skipped down dirt trails, clapping rocks together and crooning a Nepali tune resembling "Take Me Out to the Ball Game." His high notes even made the *dzos* stop chewing the cud and pay attention.

A sticker on his helmet labeled him "The Joker," and Pasang lived up to it. He smuggled rocks into friends' sleeping bags, pillows, and packs. He wrapped pebbles in Tootsie Roll wrappers and handed them to children begging for candy. At night, he festooned tents with branch-and-trash towers. When the tents' occupants crawled out in the morning and the scaffolds crashed down, Pasang threw back his head, cackling, and galloped off in search of the next victim.

When he wasn't trekking or climbing, Pasang turned into someone else. In Kathmandu, he seldom sang or joked, cloaking his happy-go-lucky personality in an armor of shyness and caution. Men like Chhiring bounded up to newcomers with the enthusiasm of a Labrador, no matter the setting. In Kathmandu, Pasang couldn't do that. He hung back, keeping a safe distance. When acquaintances opened their arms for a hug, they received a handshake. While eating dinner with a group of new clients in Kathmandu, Pasang's body was at the table but his eyes were patrolling the room, ready to alert him of danger. It often took him several hours to crack a smile for a stranger, but when he allowed one, his grin was sincere.

Compact, stretching just shy of five-foot-two, Pasang had hands as rough as a cat's tongue. When he was twenty-four years old, he looked fifteen and accepted his nickname: "Little Pasang." Clients occasionally doubted that he was an adult and asked for "another sherpa with more experience than this baby." To age himself, Pasang rarely shaved, but it made no difference. His chin refused to grow a beard.

Pasang's village, Hungung, lies on the Tibetan border in the Upper Arun Valley along the watershed of 27,765-foot Makalu, the world's fifth-highest peak. For decades, Nepal's government has restricted anthropologists, journalists, and some relief organizations from entering this sensitive border area. But it's easy enough to sneak in. To get to Hungung from the nearest airstrip in the village at Tumlingtar, visitors have to ride for a day in a jeep and then undertake a ten-day trek.

The trails leading into the village fork around rod-shaped mounds of limestone. By custom, all travelers must pass by the mounds on their left; even Hungung's Tibetan mastiffs follow this rule. The residents live in rock-and-mud homes that roost among terraced hillsides, and black pigs dominate the pens. A stream trickles through the center of the village, providing running water of sorts, and rooftop solar panels, installed by a long-forgotten NGO, generate electricity. A health post is stocked with antibiotics, but no doctors.

About 250 people live in the region. It was once the hub of a medicinal plant trade; now a general store deals in flashlights, lollipops, Neosporin, and Communist manifestos that, curiously, are available only in French. The residents speak Ajak Bhote, an endangered language derived from Tibetan, and believe they descend from the Ajak, an ancient priestly class once charged with protecting Tibetan royalty. Most villagers are Buddhists who work as farmers, herders, or blacksmiths.

Growing up in Hungung, the oldest of four children, Pasang was reared without a father. Phurbu Ridar Bhote, a mountaineer, moved to Kathmandu to find work when his son was six. Phurbu visited his family every two or three years. Sometimes Pasang dreamed that an avalanche had buried Phurbu, but Hungung's *lama* reassured the boy. Using clairvoyance, the *lama* updated Pasang on his father's whereabouts—whether Phurbu was bound for Everest or K2 that year—and delivered messages Phurbu sent in prayer. The *lama* told Pasang that his father wanted him to apply himself and study mathematics. Pasang read whatever books he could find and attended school as often as he could, but living was usually hand to mouth. He sowed the millet and barley fields and dug potato tubers. He gathered firewood and swept the homes of wealthier villagers in exchange for rice or a few coins.

When Pasang was fifteen, he received word from his father to join him in Kathmandu. After a decade of saving and a stint on K2, Phurbu had amassed the equivalent of $1,000, plenty to send his son to prep school and university. "I wanted him to stay as far away from mountains as possible," Phurbu said. "Who would climb if he had a choice? It's only a matter of time before you're killed. I didn't want my first-born son to die before I did. He needed to get an education. I climbed mountains so he wouldn't have to."

Before leaving for Kathmandu, Pasang changed his surname from Bhote to Lama because he didn't want his heritage to hold him back.

Pasang is Bhote, a Tibetan ethnicity culturally distinct from Sherpa. Although the two groups have related beliefs and share many rituals, Bhotes frequently face discrimination. Like an immigrant taking the surname Rockefeller, Pasang chose Lama, the highest Sherpa caste, so no one in the city would look down on him.

With a new name and a new life ahead of him, Pasang Lama left for Kathmandu. During the ten-day trek to the nearest road, he planned his future. First he'd earn a degree that would lead to a safe and respectable job. Next he'd get so rich he would send his siblings to prep school in the city. Then he'd buy solar panels for his mother. Maybe he'd build her a new house. By the time Pasang reached the highway and saw a metal creature rumbling toward him, he had convinced himself that anything was possible. The teenager had never seen a bus before, but he confidently climbed inside and left his old life behind.

For several days, as the wheeled machine bounced down the road, Pasang watched a ghastly world appear. Kathmandu's pollution and bustle rattled him. How could a million people cram into such an intolerably tight space? As the bus kept plowing through traffic, he missed Hungung's expansive skies. Finally the vehicle delivered him to Balaju, a densely populated area northwest of the city center. Pasang joined his father and six other relatives in a one-room rental. At night, they all piled onto the same mattress. During the day, they tipped it upward to allow living space. The toilet was a hole dug in the courtyard.

Soon after arriving, Pasang started eleventh grade at British Gurkha Academy, studying commerce. His classmates taunted him. "They pointed at me and shouted, 'Bhote, Bhote, Bhote!'" Pasang recalled. "They were calling me a stupid villager." The teenager struggled to keep pace, unaccustomed to schoolwork in Nepali, a foreign language to him. He flunked the first year, costing his family precious tuition money. Demoralized, Pasang went back to Hungung for a season to harvest the potato crop. He then returned to Kathmandu in September 2000 to give school another shot. This time he was on track to finish, but in June the royal massacre disrupted exams. Kathmandu went into lockdown.

Hungung was worse. The Royal Nepalese Army invaded during a festival, publicly killing three suspected terrorists who were about Pasang's age. Fighting flared. Pasang's mother, sisters, aunts, uncles, cousins, nephews, and nieces fled.

"It wasn't safe to stay, especially as a woman alone with children," said Pasang's mother, Phurbu Chejik Bhoteni. Bus tickets were too expensive. Carrying two toddlers and whatever else she could strap on her back, Phurbu walked the entire way to Kathmandu on a fractured leg. The journey took more than a month. Exhausted and hungry, she and the children arrived in the spring of 2002 at Pasang's one-room flat.

They couldn't all fit inside, so Pasang, his mother, his father, his two younger sisters, his younger brother, and a fluctuating number of desperate relatives moved into a separate room that cost more than they could afford. Food and rent became higher priorities than education. Pasang had to find a job.

Competition was cutthroat. Refugees were flooding the job market. Destitute, they accepted any employment they could get. Wages fell; unemployment rose. After three months, Pasang found work, but it was humble. He received an offer to earn $3 a day carrying pots and pans to Gosaikunda, a holy lake north of the city.

Grateful for this first portering job, Pasang shouldered loads over the undulating terrain between Kathmandu and the lake. Afterward, with one trip on his résumé, it was easier to find the next job, and the next. An American trekker befriended him and offered to pay his tuition, so Pasang attended classes during the slow season between expeditions, but he no longer considered himself a commerce student. School could not support his family; portering could.

Still, he disliked it. Pasang didn't speak the same language as many of the other porters, and he hadn't learned their protocol. One misunderstanding nearly cost him his job. In 2004, Pasang carried a pack stuffed with tinned fruit, Clif bars, freeze-dried soup, and kerosene to the Base Camp of Annapurna, a mountain whose name means "full of food." Pasang had brought nothing of his own to eat, expecting his employers to feed him. They didn't. Pasang scrounged for handouts from kitchen hands, gathered scraps from his clients' plates before washing them, and bartered clothing for rations. When the clients extended the trip, supplies dwindled further. Pasang's peers had no more food to share. Feeling sorry for him, the cook brewed him stew from roots found around camp and offered him three days' worth of lemon-lime Tang. When the Tang ran out, Pasang reeled from hunger.

As he lugged his eighty-pound load, all he could think of was food, food, food. His muscles jittered. His feet kept missing the places he intended to step. "I was going to pass out unless I found something to eat," Pasang recalled. He didn't consider asking the Western climbers for help. "You just don't do that," he said. "Porters aren't hired to beg for things or complain." If he had, other staff would have alerted the expedition outfitter, who'd blacklist him.

Stealing seemed safer. After four days without food, Pasang staggered off the path and hid behind a boulder. Setting down his load, he rummaged through it and pulled out a tin of mandarin oranges and hammered it against a rock. The metal burst and the edge sliced deep into his middle and index fingers. Blood smeared over the can, but Pasang was smiling. He jimmied back the lid, slurped the sweet syrup, and dropped the delicate wedges into his mouth. Sugar coursed through his body. Revitalized, Pasang shouldered his load and tied a rag around his bleeding right hand.

On the trail that day, Pasang had visions of mandarin oranges—luscious wedges, dripping in syrup, melting in his mouth. He craved other tins inside the pack but resisted the urge until that evening, when he stole a can of tuna. If the other porters suspected, they stayed quiet. The thefts continued until his job finished three days later. "Annapurna was the first and last time I was a thief," he said.

After Annapurna, jobs poured in. Clients called him a porter, but Pasang—who eventually was setting ropes, pitching tents, and hauling gear up rock and ice—saw himself as something better. By the time he reached the summit of Everest in the spring of 2006, he was unquestionably a mountaineer. The civil war and its bombing and maiming had slowed that year, and the Maoists called a truce in November, but Pasang's mother doubted the fighting would stop. Refusing to return to Hungung, Phurbu Chejik said she'd seen enough violence. She and the children would stay in Kathmandu. Pasang continued to support them with the wages of what he considered to be a temporary career.

A proposal in May 2008 raised the stakes. Pasang was ushering a South Korean woman named Go Mi-sun up Lhotse, the world's fourth-highest peak. On their return from the summit, "Ms. Go" told Pasang about her ambitions. There are fourteen mountains taller than 8,000 meters, she explained. She intended to be the first woman to climb them all—and to do it faster than anyone else had. With five down and nine to go, K2 was next. Would Pasang help?

He was more than a little infatuated with Ms. Go, who laughed with him, joined him for meals in the kitchen tent, shared her energy bars, and asked whether he had a girlfriend. When her climbing partner, "Mr. Kim"—Kim Jae-soo—lost his cool, Ms. Go smoothed things over. To Pasang, she was angelic, and she had his trust.

Once in Kathmandu, Pasang had only had a few days to decide whether he'd join her. He scoured the Internet to learn more about Ms. Go. She was Asia's sweetheart. After a 200-foot fall shattered her backbone, she'd made a comeback as a star of the Asian X-Games. Go was backed by Kolon Sport, the Nike of Korea, and adored by her fan club.

But critics called her "a woman on the Go." They dismissed her as reckless, swept up in a publicity stunt. Only a handful of mountaineers had managed to climb every 8,000-meter peak, and it had taken Reinhold Messner, widely considered the greatest of all, more than sixteen years to do it. Kolon Sport couldn't wait that long, so the sportswear giant paid Go to replicate the feat in a quarter of the time. Unlike Messner, however, she was using support climbers and bottled oxygen—and simultaneously modeling a clothing line.

Setting aside his crush on Ms. Go, Pasang tried to evaluate a K2 attempt on its own merits. He sought out his father for advice. To Pasang's surprise, Phurbu Ridar saw the climb as a lucky break. True, Pasang could be killed, but Phurbu thought that was unlikely, especially if a beautiful woman were involved. And how could Pasang go into commerce when the Maoists were still halting commerce? If mountaineering was to be his career, he should make it his career, especially while he had no wife or children to hold him back. Pasang should not only load-carry on K2, Phurbu advised, but also shoot for the summit. When Phurbu had attempted K2's North Ridge in 1994, he'd put his clients' success above his own, staying in camp and boiling water as other men climbed to the top. He regretted being passed over. Pasang should have no regrets. A K2 conquest would make the family proud, and it would pay the bills for a year.

Furthermore, Phurbu noted, four of Pasang's cousins would be on the Korean team. Tsering Lama was like Pasang—in his twenties and unmarried. His other cousins were leaving families behind. Jumik Bhote had a wife who was eight months pregnant and expecting to give birth while he was away. "Big" Pasang Bhote had two toddlers. Ngawang Bhote, the team cook, also had a wife and daughter, but K2 was too profitable for any of them to pass up.

Nearly convinced, Pasang went to Big Pasang's house to see what his older cousin had to say. Big Pasang endorsed the expedition, reminding Pasang that K2 meant $3,000 for each of them, plus tips and a summit bonus. As Big Pasang spoke, his wife Lahmu boiled tea. She remained quiet but kept glancing up at the summit certificates proudly fastened above the rice sacks in the kitchen. Mountaineering had provided her children with a good home. Its walls were plywood and the floor was dirt, but a tarp and corrugated tin roof kept rain out, and her toddlers, Dawa and Nima Yangzom, always had enough to eat. Pasang could tell she was supportive of the plan.

He found himself nodding in support of it, too. "Everyone was saying I should go," Pasang recalled. "They said I'd lose my chance, and it meant so much money."

If Pasang doubted whether he had made the right choice, his concerns evaporated when he and his cousins met the rest of the Korean team in the lobby of the five-star Hotel de l'Annapurna in Kathmandu. The hotel features a massage parlor, four restaurants, a casino, and an underground shopping center. It promises in its brochure to "treat guests like gods."

Shy and unsure what to say, Pasang shook hands with the two Koreans he knew, Ms. Go and Mr. Kim. He nodded to other team members and slumped down on a leather couch. He filled out forms, including an insurance document from Highland Sherpa Trekking that amortized his life at $7,500. Ms. Go passed out team bumper stickers. For reasons no one explained, the Koreans called their expedition The Flying Jump.

As the Koreans talked among themselves, Pasang wasn't sure what they were saying, but he liked sitting among such affluent foreigners. The hotel's opulence impressed him. Globes dangled from the ceiling, emanating rose-colored light. Orchids in water bowls purged cigar smoke from the air. Buddhist *tangkas* adorned the walls. Mesmerized by their maze of red and gold paint, Pasang daydreamed until a waiter interrupted him. The man bowed and poured him a glass of chilled mango juice.

When the Korean team dismissed Pasang, he headed toward the glass door. It swung open spontaneously, before he could touch the massive brass handle. Pasang stepped into a wall of noise and traffic. Beside him, a doorman bowed. "*Namaste*," he said, as he did to all the guests, and offered to carry Pasang's duffel to a taxi.

Is he talking to me? It was beyond confusing. All his life, Pasang had been the one to bow, pour tea, open doors, lift bags. That's what people known as sherpas were expected to do, he thought: Serve. Hotel de l'Annapurna, the most luxurious place he had ever entered, showed him another kind of life. Yes, Pasang decided, his father was right. K2 was a golden opportunity. He couldn't overlook the prospect of earning $3,000 in eight weeks, but K2 could give him something he valued more. Respect.

Once he conquered the Savage Mountain, Pasang thought, nobody would consider him a stupid villager. Nobody would think of him as a baggage handler. Maybe he would have the chance to spend more time with powerful people like the Koreans. Maybe he'd drink mango juice again in places like the Hotel de l'Annapurna. Maybe the world would treat him as kindly as the doorman had.

In the driveway, Pasang turned around. He wanted to thank the doorman, but the words would not come out. He was too stunned to speak. Feeling like a prince, he strode out of the five-star hotel and into the chaos of the city.

"After K2, I thought, I'll no longer be treated like a Bhote."

4

The Celebrity Ethnicity

Mountaineers use *sherpa*, with a lowercase *S*, to describe a high-altitude load carrier, and the word is often applied commercially to anything that helps people get around. Haul your terrier in the Sherpa Dog Carrier. Brace your belly with a Baby Sherpa Maternity Belt. Stow your bibs and burp cloths in the award-winning Alpha Sherpa™ or Short Haul Sherpa® diaperbag. "It's no mystery how this pack got its name," reads the promotional website for the Evo-Sport Sherpa Rucksack. "The Sherpa is built to carry all your gear, and you won't feel a thing."

Many ethnic Sherpas tolerate the stereotype because it promotes their skill and unique genetic advantage. The people of the Tibetan Plateau, including Sherpas, have lived at high altitude for at least eleven thousand years, and physiological evidence suggests that they are well adapted to oxygen deprivation. Compared with other groups studied, often acclimatized Caucasian men, Sherpas are more resistant to illnesses and brain damage exacerbated by the thin air, and they sleep more soundly and demonstrate remarkable endurance at high altitude.

What explains their advantage? Contrary to one popular theory, it's not a high red-blood-cell count. Compared with Caucasians, Sherpas actually have fewer red blood cells per liter of blood. Nor is the difference explained by diet, acclimatization, metabolism, iron-deficiency, or environmental factors. At sea level, Sherpas have such a low red-blood-cell count that they are technically anemic, but, curiously, they don't show symptoms. Overall, Sherpas require as much oxygen as anybody else, but they have less of it dissolved in their blood.

Scientists initially found this puzzling. Red blood cells ferry oxygen around the body, and other populations well adapted to altitude, such as the Quechua and the Aymara of the Andean highlands, have veins teeming with red blood cells. How do Sherpas manage with less at a much higher altitude than the Andes?

Probably by circulating blood faster. Sherpas have wider blood vessels. They breathe more often when at rest, providing their blood with more oxygen to absorb, and they exhale more nitric oxide, a marker of efficient lung circulation. There is also a genetic explanation. Sherpas' red-blood-cell count stays low because of Hypoxia Inducible Factor 2-alpha, a gene that regulates response to low oxygen and turns on other genes. In addition, Sherpas have inherited a dominant genetic trait that improves hemoglobin saturation, allowing their red blood cells to soak up more oxygen. Sherpas' thin blood, in turn, may prevent the sort of clotting that crippled Art Gilkey on K2.

This genetic advantage only enhances the Sherpa mystique. Lowlanders clutching the Lonely Planet guide are convinced they want to hire "a sherpa," even if they don't know what a Sherpa is, and, after three generations of gathering tourist dollars, Sherpas now rank among the richest and most visible of Nepal's fifty or so ethnicities. They didn't start out that way.

Ancestors of the oldest Sherpa clans originated in the Kham region of Tibet. In the thirteenth century, Mongols, with their catapults and fast-riding archers, conquered much of Central Asia, and besieged Khampas fled to the Tibetan interior. In the sixteenth century, Muslims from Kashgar invaded Tibet from the west, displacing the Khampas again. Fleeing on foot, they migrated across the Himalaya to a region south of Everest known as the Khumbu. During the journey, they began to call themselves *sharpa* (people from the east), and their new Nepali homeland became *Shar Khombo*. Several immigrant waves followed. Some were driven from Tibet by famine, disease, and war; others moved to establish trading outposts. These newcomers, from various regions and social classes, assimilated into existing settlements or built their own, creating more clans. Steep passes isolated the villages, and unique cultures evolved. With language, for instance, dialects varied by as much as 30 percent—enough to produce misunderstandings and jokes, but not enough to qualify as separate tongues.

Despite the harsh geography, Sherpas from different clans traded and intermarried. The naming system they developed still causes mass confusion. According to custom, an individual's primary name is one of seven weekdays. Boys and girls born on Monday go by *Dawa*; Tuesday babies are *Mingma*; for Wednesday, it's *Lhakpa*; Thursday, *Phurbu*; Friday, *Pasang*; Saturday, *Pemba*; Sunday, *Nima*. Surnames aren't used, and phonetic transcriptions to English vary. When filling out legal forms, most Sherpas put their weekday as their first name and *Sherpa* (or the female version, *Sherpani*) as their last. Occasionally the clan name—such as *Chiawa*, *Lama*, or *Lhukpa*—substitutes for *Sherpa*.

The system works in a close-knit village. In a city, it's dysfunctional. Thousands of Sherpas in Kathmandu have identical names. Phonebooks are useless, and it's impossible to find someone by casually asking around. Gossipers must provide elaborate descriptions of the person they wish to malign. Nicknames abound, but they're inconsistent. A growing number of Sherpa parents are giving their children individualized names, but the naming convention may never resemble anything as varied as the Western system.

Making matters more confusing, primary names can be altered or scrapped based on events in a child's life. If a baby falls ill, the parents may change his name to *Chhiring* (long life), to confound the evil spirits. If a child dies, the parents may switch a sibling's name to something inconspicuous like *Kikuli* (puppy), so evil spirits will overlook her. Parents might also turn to a Buddhist *lama* for a new name provided by divine inspiration. Long before he conquered Everest, Tenzing Norgay went by Namgyal Wangdi, but the *rinpoche* of Rongbuk Monastery determined that the child was the reincarnation of a rich and devout man. The *rinpoche* thus renamed him "wealthy follower of religion." Chhiring received *Dorje* (lightning bolt) as his second name. It must have seemed appropriate for a child who set the hills ablaze.

Sherpas can receive virtue names as well, often those of saints. They combine with the primary name to bestow special attributes. Chhiring's wife, Dawa, received *Da Futi* (blessings to conceive a son). Pasang's cousin received *Lahmu* (a protector of temple gates). Virtue names also describe an individual. To distinguish a daughter from a mother with the same name, the child might acquire *Ang* (young). A Sherpa who gave a rousing speech might become *Lhakhpa Gyalgin* (courageous orator). Sometimes the same Sherpa goes by different names depending on context. When addressed by his *lama*, Chhiring goes by *Dorje*. When pronouncing his name for Tibetans, he says *Tsering*.

Sherpas also identify with one of roughly twenty clans that reflect ancestry. Children receive their father's clan name. Sherpas are supposed to avoid romantic entanglements with members of the same clan or anyone from their mother's clan going back three generations. And just as names such as Rockefeller have cachet in the West, some Sherpa clans, such as Lama, are top drawer. Others, such as the Bhote clans, are considered alien and second class—impostors who aren't ethnic Sherpas at all.

So what defines a Sherpa? When Europeans first encountered them in the nineteenth century, the Sherpas introduced themselves as *sharpa*, which was interpreted as *Sherpa*. The word resurfaced in the 1901 Darjeeling census, which classified Sherpas as one of four types of Bhotias, or Tibetans. Nepal's most recent census considers Sherpas to be a self-reported ethnicity, so anyone can claim to be one.

Sherpas from the oldest and wealthiest clans, living near Everest, would prefer a narrower definition. Just as colonial families who arrived on the *Mayflower* claim some special distinction, many old-clan Sherpas claim to be the only authentic members of the ethnicity. Tibetans, they argue, whether living in Tibet proper or in villages in Nepal, do not deserve the Sherpa identity, nor do those who have recently assimilated into Sherpa villages. Pemba Gyalje, a member of the Dutch K2 team, hails from the Solukhumbu region settled by the earliest immigrants. As he put it, "We are true Sherpas."

Chhiring prefers a broader definition. He belongs to the Kyirong clan, which suggests that his father's ancestors were part of a later immigration wave from the village of Kyirong in Tibet. His village of Beding hosts a mix of clans ranging from ancient to upstart. A Sherpa, he says, is anyone who can convince the established Sherpas that he deserves to be one. Good faith is cultivated by living in Rolwaling, adopting a clan name, following the clan-marriage rules, and speaking Rolwaling Sherpi tamgney language.

Pasang, from the Upper Arun Valley, uses the most inclusive definition, which disregards ethnicity. *Sherpa* is a job description, he maintains, so anyone who works on a mountain qualifies. He may favor this interpretation because old-clan Sherpas would never recognize Pasang as part of their ethnicity. To them, he is a Bhote, now and forever.

Bhote, pronounced BOE-tay, stems from *Bhot* (Sanskrit for

"Tibet"), and the Bhotes in Hungung observe many Tibetan customs. With marriage, for instance, the Bhotes of the Upper Arun Valley, like other Tibetan tribal groups, traditionally practice bride abduction. When Pasang's cousin Lahmu Bhoteni was fourteen, the groom's brothers secured permission from her father, seized her in the night, and dragged her to the wedding. This break from her paternal household may have been ritualized, but it was hard on the bride. "I was miserable for years," Lahmu said. It took a long time for her resentment to wear off. "When I was twenty-three," she added, "I finally realized I loved my husband." Sherpa marriage rites, by contrast, are public-relations campaigns. Before betrothal, a Sherpa couple consults all stakeholders—families and gods—and gets a horoscope cross-check. Sherpas widely consider the Bhote approach, which is less common nowadays, a brutal and primitive practice.

Another breach, according to Sherpas, is the Bhote practice of blood sacrifice. Bhotes of the Upper Arun occasionally stray from Buddhist precepts and slaughter animals as large as yaks, pulling out entrails to read divinations. In Pasang's village, the carcass is offered to Surra, a deity who occupies Makalu's eastern spur. God by day, demon by night, Surra charges through the Arun Valley on a black horse and drags a banner jangling with human hearts. Local Buddhist *lamas* have been unable to tame him. Sherpas say he causes epidemics, but Bhotes believe the opposite—that Surra heals the sick—so they make sure he gets all the offal he can eat.

Citing this sacrificial slaughter, some Sherpas describe Bhotes as bloodthirsty barbarians. Sherpas, competing with Bhotes for mountaineering jobs, popularized the use of the term *Bhote* for "yokel" in Nepali slang. According to a popular saying in the Sherpa villages near Everest, every Bhote "has two knives: one in his boot, which he can draw quickly to stab you in the stomach, and another in his waistband to stab you in the back when you embrace him."

But the sharpest knives are reserved for foreigners. Both Bhotes and Sherpas hate how they used to be described by outsiders, and the terms are still politically charged. Well into the twentieth century, Western mountaineers were calling both groups *coolies*, an offensive word that means "unskilled laborer" and, in some contexts, "slave." Now Western mountaineers use *sherpa* or *Sherpa-climber*, which conflates a job description with an ethnicity, frustrating ethnic Sherpas who want to distinguish themselves from Bhote competitors. Pakistanis use *high-altitude porter*, or *HAP*, but sherpas working in the Karakorum reject that term because it includes the word *porter*, and in Nepal, porters don't climb. Nepal's government now promotes the term *high-altitude worker*.

Despite these ethnic and linguistic tensions, coexistence is the norm among high-altitude workers. As Sherpas and Bhotes vie for the same jobs, they still befriend each other, worship the same gods, and intermarry. The life of Tenzing Norgay illustrates this duality: The man who made the Sherpas famous wasn't one, at first.

▲ ▲ ▲

One of *Time* magazine's most influential people of the twentieth century was born in a yak-herder's tent in Tsechu, a pilgrimage site in the Kharta region of Tibet—a three-day walk from Pasang's birthplace. Tenzing Norgay was the eleventh of fourteen children, one of only six who survived infancy. His parents, Kinzom and Mingma, subsistence herders of Ghang La, sent Tenzing to a monastery so he could learn to read, but monasticism didn't suit the boy. When a Buddhist *lama* beat him with a stick, Tenzing quit.

At age seven, Tenzing got a glimpse of his future. In the spring of 1921, the legendary British mountaineer George Mallory pitched several camps in the Kharta region to explore Everest's north side. During his four-month reconnaissance, Mallory spent a halcyon month in the grazing lands of Ghang La. Spreading money around, he hired local scouts and bought yak butter and cream from herders at Ghang La and Dangsar, where Tenzing's family stayed. Mallory would die three years later below the summit of Everest, but Tenzing never forgot the hobnailed boots that his expedition left behind.

Mountaineering was the least of Tenzing's concerns in the 1920s. His family leased the herd they cared for, and one day the yaks erupted in lesions and died, likely during the 1928 pandemic of rinderpest disease. Tenzing's father couldn't repay his debts or support his six children in Kharta, so the family migrated across the border, possibly to Thame or Khumjung, villages in the Sherpa heartland of the Khumbu.

The Sherpas in the Khumbu were relatively affluent, enjoying a monopoly on regional trade. For centuries, Tibetan salt and wool had been carried over the Nangpa La Pass into Nepal and exchanged for lowland products such as bamboo, medicinal plants, paper, rice, and soot-based ink. Tenzing labored as an indentured servant for a more solvent family, and, as a Tibetan among the Sherpas, suffered from ethnic discrimination. Inevitably, he fell in love with a beautiful Sherpani whose family disapproved of him. Tenzing, then seventeen, proposed eloping, and the girl, Dawa Phuti, agreed. The couple left the Khumbu, heading to a new life at the Indian hill station of Darjeeling.

Nepal, then an insular kingdom, forbade foreign mountaineering expeditions, so Darjeeling, with its hot baths and billiards, became the recruitment hub for Everest. When the couple arrived, Englishman Hugh Ruttledge was recruiting porters for his 1933 Everest expedition. "They wanted only Sherpas," Tenzing recalled. As a Bhote, he was turned away. "And you go away wondering if you will never get a job in your life." For two years, expeditions continued to reject him because of his ethnicity.

In the early 1930s, Sherpa mountaineers deployed aggressive tactics to force Tibetans out of the profession. Instead of merely staging strikes when they had to work alongside Tibetans, Sherpas on a 1931 German expedition even threatened to sue their paymaster, Paul Bauer, for refusing to hire and compensate Sherpas preferentially. Most expeditions, including Bauer's, caved. Sherpas dominated the local workforce, and they could halt expeditions that failed to meet their demands. To avoid delays and ethnic conflicts, some expeditions hired Sherpas exclusively, and only local climbers who passed as Sherpa were able to accumulate experience.

In 1935, Tenzing was still in Darjeeling, jockeying for a mountaineering job. Determined to hold out, he milked cows, set mortar, and read Darjeeling's eponymous tea leaves. He finally got a break. A mountaineer named Eric Shipton was about to leave for Everest as part of a British reconnaissance when he made a last-minute decision to hire more men.

At that point, pickings were slim: The most-experienced Sherpas had been killed the year before on Nanga Parbat. In a rush, Shipton decided to broaden his search and encourage Tibetans to apply. Tenzing darted up to the veranda of Darjeeling's Planters Club, where Shipton was inspecting a throng of candidates. "[T]here was one Tibetan lad of nineteen, a newcomer, chosen largely because of his attractive grin," Shipton later wrote. "His name was Tensing Norkay—or Tensing Bhotia, as he was generally called." Tenzing was finally on his way to Everest.

En route, the Sherpas staged a strike, refusing to carry loads, so Shipton had mules and Tibetan porters such as Tenzing lug the gear instead. Later, in a village called Sar, the Sherpas got into a drunken brawl with the Tibetans. Tenzing kept out of it, carried whatever weight he was given, accepted coworkers of any ethnicity, and kept on grinning until the reconnaissance ended with the approach of the monsoon.

Tenzing returned from Everest with new boots, snow goggles, and a recommendation from Shipton. His obsession with the summit may have started then, but the deaths of his wife and son may explain the determination he showed in the years to come. Climbing gave him solace and, with his reputation established, work became easier to find. Eventually, he married again. His new wife was Ang Lhamu, a Sherpani who helped him gain acceptance within her community, something he'd never had with Dawa Phuti.

By 1953, Tenzing had clocked more time on Everest than any mortal, and the British offered him an opportunity he couldn't refuse. During their Everest expedition, Tenzing would work as *sirdar*—chief of the mountain workers—and climb as a full team member, a status the British had never before afforded an indigenous climber. Tenzing quit smoking and started carrying around a rock-filled pack. This would be his seventh Everest expedition, and he was destined for the summit.

Early in the climb, Tenzing became fast friends with Edmund Hillary, a beekeeper from New Zealand. Hillary had tried to jump a crevasse but landed short, breaking off a cornice. He slid with the ice sheet into the chasm. As Hillary grasped for the sides, Tenzing snagged the trailing line, flicked it around his axe, and planted the axe into the mountain. The rope yanked tight. Hillary's ice axe and a single crampon dropped into the fissure. Tenzing, "after positioning himself to gain some leverage, was able to gradually haul Hillary up to the edge of the crevasse, with some help from Hillary's single cramponed foot," wrote Tenzing's son and biographer, Jamling Tenzing Norgay. The rescue forged a friendship that led Hillary and Tenzing to the roof of the world.

During the summit bid, it was Hillary's turn to help Tenzing. Tenzing belayed Hillary as he cut steps toward their final obstacle, a 40-foot protrusion of near-vertical rock now named the Hillary Step. Sherpas call it Tenzing's Back, but, in fact, it was Hillary who led the section, "[t]aking advantage of every little rock hold and all the force of knee, shoulder and arms. . . ." As Hillary "heaved hard on the rope," Tenzing stemmed up a crack in the rock face and "finally collapsed exhausted at the top, like a giant fish when it has been hauled from the sea after a terrible struggle." Hillary was just as tired, but from the top of the Step, the route was straightforward: "A few more whacks of the ice axe in the firm snow, a few very weary steps," Hillary recounted, "and we were on the summit."

It was 11:30 a.m., May 29, 1953, when they became the first mountaineers to reach the highest point on earth. Tenzing felt "[a]t that great moment for which I had waited all my life, my mountain did not seem to me a lifeless thing of rock and ice, but warm and friendly and living. She was a mother hen, and the other mountains were chicks under her wings." Hillary felt emotional too, but expressed it differently: "We knocked the bastard off."

Tenzing left an offering of chocolates in the snow and tried to take a photo of Hillary but didn't know how to operate the camera. So he passed it to Hillary, who snapped Britain's iconic victory image: A Tibetan hoisting an axe strung with a flapping Union Jack, the most visible of his four flags. The men basked in the achievement for fifteen minutes before descending to an alien world.

The sudden stardom that followed caught Tenzing by surprise. "I appeared on television, before I had ever even seen a set." Queen Elizabeth got word of the triumph and invited Tenzing to receive the King George Medal. King Tribhuvan awarded him the Most Refulgent Order of the Star of Nepal, the Shah dynasty's highest civilian award. Mickey Mantle sent a signed baseball bat and cheers from the New York Yankees. Not to be outdone, India's prime minister, Jawaharlal Nehru, offered Tenzing a passport and suits from his own closet.

In Kathmandu, fans mobbed Tenzing, chanting his name and hoisting him aloft on their shoulders. Rumors swirled that Tenzing had three lungs. He and Hillary rode in the Shahs' gilded chariot and tried to ignore the banners overhead: An artist had depicted Everest with a brown man on the summit and a white stick figure sprawled below. Autograph seekers muscled in, and Tenzing, who could neither read nor write, accepted their outstretched pens and scrawled his mark. Far removed from his life in Tibet, he was visibly dazed.

Such wild, postcolonial display unsettled his teammates, and the impropriety intensified when one of Tenzing's autographs suddenly became front-page news. Tenzing had unwittingly signed a statement declaring himself to be the first to summit Everest. Hillary did not want to comment, so the British mobilized. Colonel John Hunt, the expedition leader, called a press conference to deflate the native son. Tenzing Norgay isn't a mountaineer of Hillary's caliber, Hunt proclaimed, and he lacked the technical skill to lead the climb. A Sherpa wasn't first on the summit of Everest; that distinction belongs to a citizen of the Commonwealth.

The backlash in Kathmandu was brutal. Tenzing's supporters smeared Hillary as a buffoon carried to the summit in a sedan chair. Hunt apologized and retracted his statement. Hillary drafted one of his own, declaring that he and Tenzing had climbed to the summit "almost together." The summiters signed it and released it to the press, but they failed to bury the controversy.

"Why Hillary added 'almost,' I have no idea," Tenzing's son Jamling later said. "Ever since that day, my father and Hillary have maintained that they climbed together and reached the summit together. People still ask who was first, and it doesn't matter."

Between Sherpas and Tibetans, another dispute arose. Which ethnicity could claim Tenzing as their own? Various Bhotia groups in India and Nepal, including those claiming to be Tenzing's own relatives from Tibet, noted that Tenzing was born in Tibet and spent his youth there. The Sherpas made their own case. Tenzing had married Sherpanis, spent his adult life in villages with sizable Sherpa populations, and reared his children in the Sherpa language and culture. "Many see my father as the godfather of Sherpas because he was the one who brought the ethnicity into the limelight," Jamling said. "If my father had said 'I am a Tibetan' then there would have been no Sherpas" as the West knows them. The Bhotias of Ghang La in Tibet would be the celebrity ethnicity.

In his autobiography, Tenzing chose to describe himself as a Sherpa from the Khumbu, and that's what the media continued to report. In a passage deleted from the book, he went further, distancing himself from Tibetans: Tibetans "would often pretend they were Sherpas so as to get jobs," he explained, and they would become "very quarrelsome and often draw their knives."

Tenzing also had an exigent reason to identify himself as Sherpa in the 1950s. China had invaded his Tibetan homeland, seizing a cornucopia of mineral wealth. Mao Zedong's Red Army, at the crest of the Cultural Revolution, consigned roughly one-sixth of ethnic Tibetans to prisons, labor camps, and starvation. Tenzing's spiritual leaders were under siege. The Dalai Lama fled to India.

If Tenzing had publicly declared himself Tibetan, China would have claimed him as one of the "Chinese" ethnicities and used the first ascent of Everest in its propaganda—something Tenzing would have deplored. Coming out as Tibetan, as biographer Ed Webster put it, "would only have magnified his nationality problems."

Tenzing had fully assimilated by then. He was the world's most prominent Sherpa. But in his heart he was neither Sherpa nor Tibetan, exclusively; he was both. After Everest, Tenzing honored his complex heritage by founding the Himalayan Mountaineering Institute in Darjeeling, which trains indigenous mountaineers of many ethnicities, including Sherpas and Bhotes. Since 1954, the school has trained more than 100,000 students, excelling in its mission to "produce a thousand Tenzings."

5

Insha'Allah

Shimshal, Pakistan
10,500 feet above sea level

Shaheen Baig warned his son and daughter to look before flopping into bed. A dormouse the size of an apricot pit lived between the cushions where the family slept, and Shaheen refused to trap it. With winter approaching, "the creature has no time to make another burrow," he said, "and if we turn him out, he'll freeze in half an hour."

For an entire winter, his family shared their bed and bread with the rodent. "Shaheen may be the toughest mountaineer in Pakistan, but he can't get rid of a mouse," said his wife, Khanda. "He hates to see anything suffer."

With humans, Shaheen was even worse. Working as a guide, he fretted over clients' headaches, tracked how much they ate and drank, checked and rechecked their harnesses, and filed their crampons with a nursemaid's anxiety. The thirty-nine-year-old had tapered brows that emphasized his constant concern. He had already summited K2 in 2004 without bottled oxygen, and when he returned four years later, many climbers recognized his familiar frown. They turned to him for advice, let him negotiate their labor disputes, and put him in

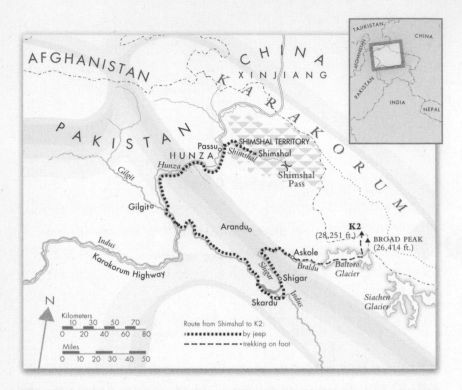

Shimshal Valley, Pakistan Shaheen Baig, one of Pakistan's best mountaineers, grew up in Shimshal and taught two local men, Jehan Baig and Karim Meherban, how to climb. All three Shimshalis worked as high-altitude porters on K2; Shaheen was at one point a leader of the climb.

charge of rope placement on the Bottleneck. Shaheen knew the terrain better than anyone.

"He was an ace," said Wilco van Rooijen of the Dutch team. "I trusted that guy completely. If he had been at the Bottleneck as planned, nothing would have gone wrong on summit day."

▲ ▲ ▲

Shaheen was born in Shimshal, a mountain village in the Hunza region of Pakistan, 76 miles northwest of K2. Shimshal lies beyond a snow-choked gorge that's impassable from November to March.

Nine peaks, each rising higher than the tallest mountain in North America, flank the village; to the east over a pass, the Silk Road meanders through Xinjiang, China. Shimshalis make up the majority of Pakistan's K2 summiters, and three Shimshalis were at the epicenter of the 2008 disaster.

Shimshalis have long been soldiers of fortune. Their ancestors, by some accounts, deserted Alexander the Great as he drove his army through the area in 372 BC on a campaign to conquer the world. Three shield bearers named Titan, Khuro, and Gayar wanted to find a strange creature described by the Greek historian Herodotus. "Northward of all the rest of the Indians," he wrote, live "the great sand ants, in size somewhat less than dogs, but bigger than foxes . . . and very much resembling Greek ants in shape." These ants excavated a deep tunnel network, and "the sand that they threw up was full of gold." Modern scholars suspect that Herodotus mistranslated the Persian word for marmots; the legendary ants were probably the whistling ground squirrels that burrow above Pakistan's Indus River, tossing up gold dust.

Disappointed, the prospectors abandoned their quest and settled in a hundred-mile-long valley that became part of the Kingdom of Hunza. They worshipped their hometown gods at first, but around 150 BC Zeus gave way to Buddha, who was displaced, in turn, by Allah. In 711 AD, General Muhammad bin Qasim invaded the Indus Valley with "the Bride," a stone-launching precursor of the artillery gun. He sheltered those who submitted, disemboweled those who didn't, and introduced Islam. Qasim's faith spread, but not immediately throughout Hunza, which remained predominantly Buddhist and animist until the sixteenth century.

Around the time of the Islamic conversion, Shaheen's village was founded in a remote valley of the kingdom. According to legend, a herder and his wife wandered into the Shimshal Valley and tripped over a slab of slate. As they dusted themselves off, the wife noticed that the slab was vibrating. Curious, she flipped it aside. Water spurted from a hole underneath, soaking the couple, filling the gorge that led out of the valley, and creating the Shimshal River. The couple grabbed their bedraggled sheep and waded to shore. Unable to leave the flooded valley, they collected driftwood to build a hut and waited for the waters to drain. They planted apricot orchards along the river-bank and watched their sheep grow fat in the high grass.

The ewes and rams multiplied each spring, but the herder's family did not grow. The couple lived alone, praying for children but unable to conceive. One morning, when they had become infirm and too weak to feed themselves, the river abruptly receded, revealing a waterlogged saint named Shams. The herder and his wife were over-joyed to see someone after so many years of living in solitude. They offered Shams dry clothes and what little food remained.

Shams appreciated their kindness and took pity on them. He fished deep within his pockets and pulled out a pot and a stick that transmuted water into cream. Shams instructed the herder's wife to drink twelve drafts a day. She had to be strong, he said, if she wanted to start a village. Miraculously, the woman's belly swelled, and, forty-eight hours later, she gave birth painlessly to a son named Sher. Less than a few minutes old, the infant stood up, introduced himself to his parents, bathed, folded the laundry, and cooked breakfast. Sher had many talents, among them an ability to understand the speech of animals.

As Sher grew, he explored beyond the valley and discovered that Chinese merchants from Xinjiang had claimed his father's territory as their own. To settle the land dispute, Sher challenged the merchants to a game of polo, using the entire valley as a playing field. The Chi-nese told Sher he'd lose. After all, the boy rode a miniature yak against a team of expert horsemen. But Sher was resourceful. He discussed game strategy with his yak and carried the saint's stick as his mallet.

When the match started, the Chinese charged down the field in control of the ball, but Sher's yak knew the stakes and pushed himself to keep up. When one merchant tried to hit the ball forward, Sher hooked his mallet to block the swing and whacked the ball across the glaciers, winning single-handedly. Shimshalis trace their ancestry back fifteen generations to this original champion.

If Sher did live for two centuries, as the legend claims, he'd have seen Shimshal's population grow from three to 150, but this increase had more to do with sinners than saints. The Mir, Hunza's ruler, was sending his best thieves to Shimshal. He ordered them to scale the Shimshal Pass into Xinjiang and pillage camel caravans that were plying the Silk Road between the oases of Leh and Yarkand. Successful raids yielded bullion, cannabis, coral, felt, indigo, opium, pashmina, sugar, silk, slaves, and tea bricks, all of which were taken to the Mir. He either rewarded the raiders or, if dissatisfied, dropped their broken bodies into a pit beneath his stronghold, the Baltit Fort.

Faced with this choice—climb and steal or be killed—Shimshalis learned to climb and steal. In the eyes of the British, they served their master too well: slaughtering and enslaving, disrupting British trade, and exposing holes in British defenses. Intelligence officers were alarmed. The British had assumed that Hunza's peaks buffered their Indian empire from Russian invasion, but now raiders were punching through, using a previously unknown pass to slink in and out. Could the Russians use the same breach to launch an attack? The Shimshal Pass, the British determined, had to be secured.

They sent out their smoothest spy to find it. His mission ultimately positioned Shimshalis to become pioneers of Karakorum mountaineering.

▲ ▲ ▲

Francis Younghusband was a nineteenth-century James Bond. With a walrus mustache and hair slick with pomade, he considered marriage "coercive" and could talk himself out of danger in a dozen languages. In 1889, the twenty-six-year-old joined six Gurkhas—elite soldiers from Nepal—and left in search of Shimshal. From the stories traders told him, Shimshalis moved like snow leopards, silently stalking and devouring their prey, then vanishing into the Karakorum. Intrigued, Younghusband trekked in the direction of the raids. Within a month, he had found the Shimshal Pass and, below it, a den of thieves. Younghusband scrambled up the cliff to the raiders' fort, peered inside the wide-open gate, and waved a greeting.

The gate slammed shut. Instantly, "the wall was manned by wild-looking Kanjutis, shouting . . . and pointing their matchlocks" at him. The spy waited, "expect[ing] at any moment to have bullets and stones whizzing about [his] ears," until two henchmen emerged from the gate, sized him up, and left.

Younghusband returned that afternoon on horseback. This time, when he approached the gate, it swung open. Leaving his Gurkha soldiers behind, he trotted inside the fort. Before his eyes could adjust to the darkness, a man sprang from the shadows and yanked the horse's bridle. The startled animal reared, nearly bucking Younghusband off the saddle. In the commotion, the Gurkhas charged, ready to defend horse and rider, but Younghusband kept his cool. He dismounted as though he'd just arrived at a stable, and the Shimshalis burst out laughing. As the spy had guessed, this mock ambush had been their way of testing his mettle. He had passed.

The raiders welcomed him, offered him tea and dope, and showed off their matchlocks, which fired the only slugs available: garnets gouged from the hillsides. When conversation turned to the caravan raids, the Shimshalis said they couldn't negotiate; Younghusband would have to speak to their employer, Mir Safdar Ali. They agreed to escort him to Baltit, the Mir's stronghold down the valley.

Younghusband scaled the Shimshal Pass to map it and continued his reconnaissance. En route, he encountered his archrival, Bronislav Gromchevsky, a spy for the Russians. Although adversaries in the diplomatic duel known as The Great Game, Younghusband and Gromchevsky considered themselves gentlemen, so they shared vodka and brandy, debated imperial policy, and gossiped about the Mir, whom Gromchevsky knew by reputation. Mir Safdar Ali, Younghusband learned, claimed descent from Alexander the Great and a promiscuous fairy. Safdar had ascended the throne by chucking one brother off a cliff, beheading a second, dismembering a third, poisoning his mother, and garroting his father, who had murdered his own father by sending him a smallpox-laced robe. "Patricide and fratricide may be said to be hereditary failings of the royal families of Hunza," contemporary historian E. F. Knight once noted. The Mir, "whose cruelty was unrelieved by any redeeming feature," took personal and military advice from a drum pounded by invisible hands, audible only to him. Younghusband must have wondered how he could negotiate with such a psychopath.

When Younghusband arrived in Hunza, he buttoned up his scarlet Dragoon Guards uniform and, flanked by Gurkhas, strode into the Mir's ceremonial tent. The throne of absolute power resembled a wooden lounge chair, and, when Younghusband glanced around for a place to sit, the Mir motioned for him to kneel in the dust.

Younghusband suspended negotiations. The next day, the Mir visited Younghusband's tent and proposed a compromise. Raids through Shimshal were a legitimate source of income, Safdar declared, and would stop only if Britain provided a bribe.

But "the Queen is not in the habit of paying blackmail," Younghusband replied, balancing on the folding chair his aides had found. He switched tactics and tried intimidation, ordering his six Gurkhas to point their rifles out the tent flap and shoot a rock far down the valley. Every bullet struck the target. But when Safdar told the Gurkhas to shoot an innocent bystander scrambling along a path, they refused. Seeing this as a weakness, the Mir pressed for more money—and "some soap for his wives."

So Younghusband picked up his chair and left. The Mir "was a poor creature," he wrote, "and unworthy of ruling so fine a race as the people of Hunza." Younghusband returned to his handlers, recommended that the British seize Hunza, and in 1891, a thousand soldiers invaded under the command of Algernon Durand.

As the British colonel marched toward the kingdom, the Mir bombarded his enemy with maniacal letters. In them, Safdar promised to defend Hunza "with bullets of gold"; he considered one seized fort "more precious than the strings of our wives' pajamas"; he threatened to hack off Durand's head and serve it on a platter. Nonetheless, Durand kept advancing, snatched the fortress at Nilt, and seized Baltit Fort.

When Durand's troops blasted apart the gate of the Mir's stronghold, they stormed into empty rooms. Instead of exotic concubines, a search of the harem revealed "artificial flowers, scissors . . . toothpowder, boxes of rouge, pots of pomade and cosmetics." Safdar and his wives were gone, enjoying a comfortable exile in China. On Durand's orders, the soldiers dumped Safdar's wooden throne over the embankment, installed the Mir's half-brother as the new ruler, and set up a garrison in the valley.

The new ruler, Mir Muhammad Nazim Khan, kept his pledge to monitor the Shimshal Pass for the British. Shimshalis turned to herding, and the surrounding kingdom of Hunza became a vacation destination. Bestselling 1930s novelist James Hilton modeled his Shangri-la after the region; pseudoscientists claimed that the local apricots helped residents live to 160; *Life* magazine called the kingdom "Happy Land," a utopia "where the ruler sows gold dust with the year's first millet seeds, and where mothers-in-law go along on honeymoons in order to school their newlyweds in the intimate art of marriage." During the turbulent years of Partition, the Mir was so intent on maintaining stability that he refused to take sides with India or Pakistan. He asked to join the United States. Pakistan ultimately administered the region—first called the Northern Areas, sometimes considered part of Kashmir, and now governed by elected leaders as part of Gilgit-Baltistan.

▲ ▲ ▲

The next foreign invasion was by mountaineers. In 1953, Hermann Buhl and the Austrian Embassy sent a telegram to the Mir, asking him to recruit high-altitude porters for Buhl's expedition to Nanga Parbat. Buhl offered to pay the men 20 rupees, or $6 a month, to carry loads.

Aspirants, many of them Shimshali, packed the Durbar, a dusty courtyard below the Mir's Baltit Fort. Wearing a black velvet robe embroidered with gold sequins, the Mir rejected the weak and sent the strongest to a German doctor in the town of Gilgit. With a magnifying glass, the physician examined each patient's chest, mouth, and teeth, and then "he smelled us to see how we would do in altitude," recalled Haji Baig, one of the high-altitude porters selected for Buhl's expedition.

With men like Haji and Amir Mehdi, the sniff test proved accurate. When Buhl struggled down from the summit with frostbitten feet, Haji and Mehdi alternated carrying him on their backs. Impressed, Buhl spread the word about his Pakistani high-altitude porters, and the Italians recruited the same men the following year for the first ascent of K2. This success established a warrior class known as the Hunza Tigers, mountaineers whose political influence grew to rival the Mir's.

One of these Hunza Tigers, Nazir Sabir, later overthrew the Mirs' 950-year rule. Walking to elementary school one morning on the way to Baltit, a holy man waved him down and presented the young Nazir with a pebble of rock salt. Lick this once a day until it is dissolved, the holy man told the eight-year-old, and you will bring fame to these valleys.

The boy finished the rock salt and, decades later, pioneered a new line up K2's treacherous West Ridge with a Japanese expedition. Without using bottled oxygen, he survived a forced bivouac in the Death Zone, four days without sleep and two days without food or water. After K2, Nazir focused his legendary toughness on politics.

In 1994, Nazir ran against Crown Prince Ghazanfar Ali Khan, the hereditary Mir of Hunza, for a seat in the local legislature. With mountaineers as his supporters, Nazir trounced the monarchists, becoming the first commoner to lead Hunza in almost a millennium. Once forced to steal and kill to satisfy their Mir's greed, climbers now controlled Hunza politics. As the region's most powerful leader, Nazir fought corruption and built schools and roads, including a jeep track to Shimshal. He mentored Shimshali climbers and employed them on K2 with his expedition company.

Nazir Sabir Expeditions organized the 2008 Serbian K2 Expedition, and Nazir hired Shaheen Baig as the team's leader. "He's the safest climber around," Nazir said, "one of the best in Pakistan." Nazir breaks down when he thinks of what happened to Shaheen and the other two Shimshalis. "That village will never be the same."

▲ ▲ ▲

Despite the new jeep track, Shimshal seems inviolate. The six hundred residents farm barley and herd goats, which they carry in their arms to the grazing lands to avoid setting off landslides. In spring, Shimshal's apricot orchards explode in a pastel flurry; in winter, snow leopards pad along the riverbank, leaving prints in the frost. After dark, Shimshalis tell mountaineering stories while huddled around yak-tallow candles in a central hall where ancient beams, carved with stars, frame a skylight to the heavens. The village has one satellite phone, which is almost always switched off.

Shimshalis speak Wakhi, a rare language related to Persian. Many of their climbing tales feature Shaheen, but not everyone enjoys them. "These are ghost stories of living men," said Shaheen's wife, Khanda. "I leave the room." She tolerates only one: her husband's failure on Broad Peak. "It gives me confidence that he has the sense to stay alive."

Broad Peak, or K3, juts out of the Karakorum like a giant incisor. A moderate 8000er compared to its neighbor, K2, Broad Peak turns brutal in December. Winds pummel the slopes at up to 130 miles per hour, gouging out tents, shredding ropes, and shooting hail like rounds from a machine gun. No climber has managed a winter ascent. Only a few have been daring enough to try.

On Broad Peak in the winter of 2007, Shaheen started each day with a clean shave, although it was *haraam*, forbidden by Quranic law. The Prophet directed Muslim men to grow beards as a visible sign of their faith, but a temperature of minus 49 degrees Fahrenheit made Shaheen a pragmatist. His whiskers created air pockets between his cheeks and his neoprene mask. At cold enough temperatures, those humid pockets could freeze the mask to his face.

After shaving, Shaheen and his Italian climbing partner, Simone Moro, left for the summit around 6:30 a.m. They made each other a promise: No matter how close they were to the top, they'd turn around at 2 p.m. That way, they'd avoid descending in darkness.

Shaheen felt strong, and at 2 p.m., he could taste the summit. It was perhaps an hour away. Winds were low. Shaheen understood the temptation to continue. If he topped out, the winter ascent would go down as one of the most extreme in mountaineering history, and he would become internationally famous.

"But you can't think clearly in the Death Zone," he said. "You have to do it before you get there, when you have judgment. Climbers die when they ignore a set turnaround time." So he and Simone turned back, reaching their tent before temperatures plunged further at sunset. By getting so close, yet respecting the turnaround time, Shaheen earned his reputation as one of the sanest of the madmen who take on winter ascents. Shimshalis respected his judgment, and if a local carpenter or a shepherd wanted to become a mountaineer, Shaheen was the man to talk to.

In 2001, two such men had approached Shaheen for climbing instruction. Twenty-four-year-old Karim Meherban and twenty-five-year-old Jehan Baig had been scrambling up mountainsides since they were boys, using hemp rope and ibex-horn anchors to reach the grazing lands. Now the two shepherds wanted to earn climbers' salaries.

"Karim and Jehan became my little brothers," said Shaheen. "I set technical routes on the White Horn and made them climb the ice, over and over, until I knew they had the skills."

Shaheen's students proved not only strong but lucky, with Jehan cheating death more than once. When Jehan was crossing an icy pass near Shimshal, the slope slithered beneath his boots as though the mountain were shedding its skin. He couldn't sprint faster than the tons of sliding snow, so he waded to a boulder, wrapped his arms around the granite, and hugged. The rock shielded Jehan, and the flow rumbled around him, leaving him unharmed.

Another avalanche brought Jehan recognition. On July 18, 2007, on K4, or Gasherbrum II, a German pulling fixed lines out of the snow triggered a slide. It partially buried Japanese mountaineer Hirotaka Takeuchi, crushing his rib cage and collapsing a lung. Jehan grabbed a shovel and sprinted more than 600 feet across the wash of the avalanche and made it to Hirotaka. Jehan dug him out of the snow and lowered him down to camp. Hirotaka survived, and Jehan won acclaim and gratitude. He'd seen enough to know that fortunes reverse in a split second on mountains. Now thirty-two, his experience made him seem much older than his friend Karim, whom clients called "Karim the Dream."

Unlike mountaineers who seldom look up from their boots, Karim reveled in the views and seemed unable to conceive of anything going wrong. It never did. In 2005 on Nanga Parbat, sometimes called "The Killer Mountain," Karim reached the summit and earned a hefty tip from his French client, an aristocratic insurance salesman named Hugues Jean-Louis Marie d'Aubarède. Karim returned to Shimshal and told his two children about the climb; his youngest, a three-year-old named Abrar, begged to hear what had happened on the summit. Had Karim entered the magical crystal palace of Nanga Parbat? Was it true that mischievous fairies buzz around the mountaintop, dining at translucent tables and kicking off avalanches for fun?

Karim shook his head. He'd seen nothing supernatural on Nanga Parbat, but he promised to pay better attention on the next climb. That peak, he announced, would be K2. His French client had hired him again for the following summer.

Karim's children cheered and hugged their father; his wife, Parveen, picked at the tablecloth. She asked her husband for more details about this plan. Wasn't his client pushing sixty? Could Hugues handle the climb? Was the money worth the risk?

Hugues brokers insurance, Karim replied. He is too sensible to sell our lives cheaply.

Comforted by Karim's confidence, Parveen congratulated her husband on getting the job and joined the rest of the family in celebration.

Karim guided Hugues on K2 in 2006 and 2007 and returned home both times with a stack of rupees but no summit. In 2008, Hugues hired him again, and Karim told his wife that he'd reach the summit this time. After all, Karim now had experience from two previous attempts, and this summer he'd be climbing alongside his friends, Shaheen and Jehan. The Shimshalis had been hired by different teams—Karim by the French, Shaheen by the Serbians, Jehan by the Singaporeans—but they planned to help each other on the mountain. Maybe they'd even stand together on the top. "Everything seemed so perfect," recalled Shaheen, echoing Karim's sentiments. "We were all so young and strong. I never thought there would be an accident."

Parveen was more realistic. In late May, as her husband prepared to leave for his third attempt of K2, she made a last-ditch effort to stop him. She told Karim that they didn't need the money; she could support him with her general store. Shimshal's most successful female entrepreneur, Parveen had invested her husband's mountaineering earnings in a one-room shop that sold soap, pens, children's shoes, embroidery, and nail polish. The family no longer needed to rely on Karim's dangerous career. "I asked him to stay in Shimshal," Parveen said. "Then I begged."

Karim embraced his wife and his children, grabbed his pack, and left the house he'd built. He walked down the irrigation channel, crossing barley fields cloaked in *waki sholm wush*, a yellow wildflower. Karim's father, Shadi, met him by the jeep track that runs through the village. Shadi also tried to convince Karim to stay.

No Shimshali has ever died on K2, Karim replied. Then, to make the assurance ironclad, he added, "Father, I'm going with Shaheen."

As he listened to his son, Shadi stared at the riverbed and remembered how three glaciers—the Khurdopin, the Virjerab, and the Yukshin—had once conspired to exterminate the village. Slow-flowing rivers of ice, the glaciers drain their summer meltwater through a subterranean channel. A natural ice dam constricts the flow, blocking a torrent. In 1964, the dam broke. Snowmelt gushed down, and the river rose 90 feet. It uprooted apricot orchards, hurled homes down the valley, and washed away half the settlement. Villagers scrambled to higher ground. The water tore through the gorge that leads out of Shimshal and demolished the village of Passu 40 miles downstream. Nature had devastated Shadi's family once. He knew it could happen again.

Shadi looked back at his son and tried to reason with him. "I said, 'You don't need to climb K2 again. What about carpentry?' But Karim smiled and told me: 'Father, I can't stop yet. Just this one summit, then maybe.'"

When Karim left that afternoon, Shadi watched the jeep disappear down the river basin, kicking up sand. He stayed fixed on the spot long after his son was gone.

"Insha'Allah," he prayed—if God wills it.

PART II

CONQUEST

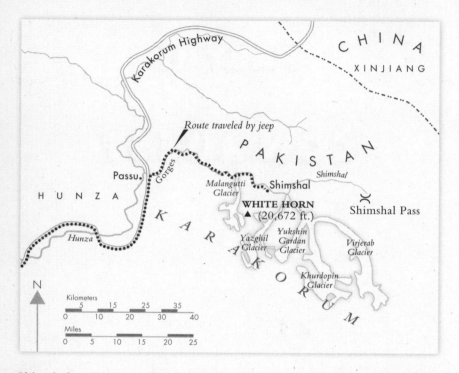

Shimshal to K2: From Shimshal, the climbers drove to Askole, the village where the trail to K2 begins. This trekking path is too treacherous for jeeps, so climbers employ hundreds of low-altitude porters, who ferry food and supplies to Base Camp.

6

The Approach

The Karakorum Highway, barely two lanes wide, rolls through the intersection of the Karakorum, Himalaya, and Hindu Kush. The builders of the original road faced tribesmen who stalled construction by "rolling down avalanches of rocks upon them." Blasting a modern highway from the cliffs was nearly as treacherous. It took twenty years and cost nine hundred lives—about a life a week. Today, jeeps bumping down the highway dodge pits and boulders, swerve around hairpin turns, and squeeze between trucks tricked out like pinball machines.

In June 2008, Karim Meherban left Hunza in a baby-blue Jeep Scrambler and jostled down the Karakorum Highway. He passed miners scraping rubies from the hillsides, children panning for gold along the river, and guards flaunting Kalashnikovs at military checkpoints. Near the town of Skardu, he passed an airfield and military compound best known as the home of the Fearless Five. Its hangar was emblazoned with a snarling snow leopard and a pentagram, signifying the squadron's five tenets: sacrifice, courage, devotion, pride, and honor. The Fearless Five command a fleet of helicopters used to defend Pakistan's borders and to airlift injured soldiers and avalanche survivors. Karim hoped he'd never need them.

Splashing through the milky-green water of the Shigar River basin, his Jeep then moved onto a rutted track, joining vehicles from other expeditions. Eight hours after leaving Skardu, Karim stopped at a dirt patch in Askole, the village at the end of the road. As the driver switched off the engine, local men mobbed the vehicle. Shouting welcomes and stirring a dust storm with their feet, they pulled supplies to the ground, unloading the cargo into snaking rows of stoves, tables, lawn chairs, blue plastic barrels, and duffels crammed with mountaineering gear.

These laborers are called *low-altitude porters*, or *LAPs*. Less expensive than mules, they ferry supplies across terrain too treacherous for jeeps. Pakistan's Ministry of Tourism estimated that, in 2008, low-altitude porters were hired to carry 5,600 loads from Askole to peaks such as K2, Broad Peak, Trango Towers, and Gasherbrums I and II. A seven-member expedition to K2 might hire 120 LAPs a season, spending $10,000. Low-altitude porters "are your umbilical cord during a climb," said Rehmat Ali, a porter coordinator for Nazir Sabir Expeditions. "Mountaineers don't have a shot at the summit without them."

In 2008, the low-altitude porters carried all kinds of things to K2: ropes, tents, orthopedic pillows, Cajun popcorn, chickens, skin mags, hand warmers, raspberry liqueur—whatever their clients paid for. The Flying Jump had its porters bring in a jug of pickled seaweed; Nick Rice, a climber from California, had porters shoulder a seventy-pound generator so he could power his laptop and access his blog—which, by the end of the climb, would receive two million hits. The porters weighed the loads on a hand scale and, when possible, divided them into fifty-four-pound piles, the limit established by their union.

With strips of fabric, they bound the loads onto wooden frames and hoisted them onto their backs, beginning the ninety-six-mile slog to K2.

As the low-altitude porters weighed in and left, the climbers exchanged satellite-phone numbers and audited each other, counting the peaks they'd bagged and the friends they'd lost. They told each other to quit climbing, but not yet. Some Serbians who had been soldiers compared leaving Askole with marching off to war. Beyond this outpost, there would be no more orchards, no more children, no more laws.

The hundreds of porters, trudging one behind the other, formed human trains stretching for miles. At noon, nearly everyone stopped while the Muslims dropped their packs to perform *salat*. Turning southwest toward Mecca, they pressed their foreheads to cloth laid on the scree, bowing to praise Allah. Then the work continued.

Thrashing through an undergrowth of scrub and wild rose, the porters brushed against spines as long as sewing needles. When temperatures scorched to 115 degrees, the men doused their heads in the side creeks and balanced along tracks cut in the cliffs. After two days, the poplars vanished, then the grass. The Baltoro Glacier, a thirty-five-mile tongue of ancient ice, rippled ahead. To the north stood the earth's tallest rock walls, the Trango Towers. Beneath the ice, a rush of subglacial melt could be heard, feeding the Braldu River. Sometimes the sun punched through the clouds, and from a single point in the sky, amber beams radiated downward in columns.

Within a week, the climbers had reached Concordia, where the Baltoro Glacier collides with the smaller Godwin-Austen Glacier. As the buckling ice cracked like rifle shots, K2 stood before them, a dusty carpet of ice and scree rolling off its slopes. Framed by lesser peaks, the pyramid seemed to prop up the weight of the sky.

On this, his third attempt of the mountain, Karim must have

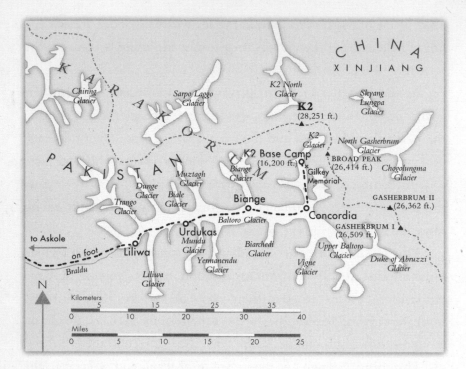

The Approach to K2: The week-long trek from Askole to K2 runs up the icy tongue of the Baltoro Glacier. Near Base Camp, 18,000 feet above sea level, a makeshift cairn known as the Gilkey Memorial commemorates those claimed by the mountain.

admired K2's symmetry and dreamed of the summit. At Concordia, still a day and a half's walk from K2, he pitched his tent next to the Sherpas'. Buddhist chanting was audible. As an Ismaili Muslim who believed in no god but Allah, Karim would never have prayed to a vacant mountaintop. To him, K2 wasn't a goddess—just a vicious piece of rock.

▲ ▲ ▲

The low-altitude porters and the foreign climbers spent a week together but kept their lives segregated. "I don't remember any of their names," said Marco Confortola, a climber from Italy. It was a challenge even to discuss practical issues with them, such as work he wanted done. Most porters spoke uncommon languages, such as Balti, Khowar, Wakhi, Shina, and Burushaski. Marco spoke Italian. Cultural barriers, such as Marco's appreciation of salami, made matters worse. Keeping *halal* according to Quranic dietary rules, the porters avoided pork and its by-products. As Muslims, some considered it immodest when Western women wore shorts and were disconcerted when the climbers showed a gay romance on DVD. "*Brokeback Mountain* shocked me," said Yaqub, a twenty-seven-year-old porter from Gulapur. He watched it anyway.

Like most of his peers, Yaqub ate and socialized away from his clients and slept out in the open. The porters even had their own latrines. "It felt a lot like separate but equal," recalled Nick Rice, "but I preferred the porter toilets. The white guys got sick and made a mess in theirs."

Low- and high-altitude porters found the cultural exchange educational and downplayed their employers' transgressions. "I was amused," said Shah Jehan, a fifty-three-year-old from the village of Kuardo. He had overheard a couple from the Flying Jump having noisy sex in their tent. "We don't encounter that kind of thing in Pakistan, but why should I mind? That's how they do it in Korea."

The expedition was also paying him good money. The average Pakistani worker earns $2.81 a day; Shah Jehan and other low-altitude porters made $9 a day, or about 90 cents an hour, assuming that every day they crossed two camps and worked ten hours. The porters could earn even more by pocketing a cash allowance for boots, socks, and shades. Expedition companies used to provide their porters with this crucial equipment, but many porters resold it the same day. "If you don't scratch the sunglasses, you can get 100 rupees [$1.20] for them at the bazaar in Skardu," said Shujaat Shigri, a thirty-six-year-old low-altitude porter from Gulapur. "That's a lot of money."

Now all porters receive the equivalent of a signing bonus intended for gear. Some buy adequate equipment. Some buy the minimum. Some buy nothing at all. Porters often walk barefoot or use cheap flip-flops to preserve the soles of their better shoes. Others wear mismatched sneakers discarded by former clients. When snowstorms hit, expeditions hand out charity supplies on a last-minute, as-needed basis, but there's never enough, and some porters would rather suffer and resell the gear than actually use it. Toes freeze and eyeballs, seared by ultraviolet rays bouncing off the snow, flush to the color of pomegranates.

Low-altitude porters can earn more by moving quickly. If they're fast and the weather cooperates, they can manage five or six round trips to K2 in a season. "If I carry three loads, I can earn enough to last the whole year," said Zaman Ali, a nineteen-year-old low-altitude porter from Tisar village, where he farms barley, peas, and wheat. Some loads, he explained, are better than others. "Tents and pots are the most prestigious" because they are needed throughout the trek in, he said. He carried the mess tent for the Serbian team in 2008. If he had carried rice, it might have been consumed en route, and he would have been sent back early and earned less.

Although porter strikes used to be routine, they were rare in 2008, because "all the expeditions agreed to our pay scale and standards," said Jaffer Wazir, president of the porters' union, Khurpa Care. To discourage expeditions from renegotiating these terms, porters carried laminated Khurpa Care ID cards and brochures that explained their civil rights.

Nonetheless, two-thirds of the porters heading to K2 were uninsured, despite Pakistani regulations that say expedition outfitters must insure them all, said Syed Amir Raza, general manager of Islamabad's Alpha Insurance, the only company that insures Pakistan's porters. The policy costs the equivalent of $1.75 per month and pays out $1,200 for deaths due to "visible accidents." If no one witnesses the death—as commonly happens when porters are spread out or lost in a crevasse—

the policy is void. On average, two insured porters die a qualifying death every year. Nobody tracks the deaths of the uninsured.

The foreign climbers also had to take their chances: Their lives were uninsurable. Even specialized insurers, such as Patriot Extreme, decline to extend coverage to climbers for accidents and deaths above 14,760 feet. That's lower than K2 Base Camp.

Medical evacuations for the critically injured aren't automatic, either. Pakistan used to provide emergency airlifts for the injured whenever Fearless Five pilots could land, but nobody reimbursed the army for these trips. It cost Pakistani taxpayers an arm and a leg so foreigners might save a toe, said Brigadier M. Bashir Baz, chief executive of Askari Aviation, which dispatches the choppers. Now the government requires every mountaineering expedition to register with Askari and to deposit a $6,000 refundable bond, but only three-quarters of the 2008 expeditions did this, he said. "And if you don't pay the deposit in advance," he said, "we won't pick you up."

In his office in Islamabad, Brigadier Baz displays a bumper sticker beneath the glass on his desk and directs climbers to read it: "Good judgment comes from experience, and experience comes from bad judgment." When climbers refuse to pay, he shakes his head in disgust, visualizing the quixotic legions, unbonded and uninsured, marching toward the Savage Mountain.

▲ ▲ ▲

The 2008 expeditions pitched Base Camp on a rocky glacier two miles from the foot of K2, a safe distance from avalanches. Green and yellow domes sprouted from the ice like mushrooms, sponsorship banners flanking their sides. By late June, Base Camp had swelled into a multicultural tent city, population 120. Laughter and rock music piped out of the tent flaps. Generators whirred amid snarls of power cables. Damp socks steamed in the sun. Solar panels baked.

Many found it a cheerful place, but Chhiring Dorje's first impression was the stench. It wafted over from a communal grave to the south, on a rise between the Savoia and Godwin-Austen Glaciers. The Gilkey Memorial, a cairn of rocks piled eight feet high, is K2's Tomb of the Unknown Soldier. Family photos and unread letters feather the monument. Threadbare scarves wrap around its base like the bindings of a mummy. These scarves, Buddhist offerings called *katas*, beat in the wind, petitioning the gods. On hot days, the cairn stews with the scent of defrosting flesh, and the odor clings to mourners' hair and clothing. Tin plates, fastened to the rocks, glint in the sunlight. Engraved with names of K2's victims, they display dates from 1939 onward, June to August, the climbing season.

The Gilkey Memorial is a grisly necessity because corpses rarely make it down the mountain in one piece. For Everest losses, families sometimes send a recovery team. This doesn't happen on K2. The Savage Mountain devours its victims during the long winter between climbing seasons. It encases the torsos in ice and grates them against the rocks, only to spit out the digested remains decades later, scattering limbs among avalanche debris.

When Art Gilkey's team gathered stones to honor their friend in 1953, they started a morbid tradition. To keep their campsites sanitary, climbers began using the memorial as a place to dispose of the fingers, pelvic bones, arms, heads, and legs found in the glacial melt. Burying these scraps under the Gilkey Memorial felt more respectful than leaving them to the ravens. For more than half a century, the memorial has been a place to caution the living and consecrate the dead. Mountaineers attempting K2 visit the site to remind themselves of what they are getting into.

Chhiring considered the memorial a travesty. In 2008, he was among the first to arrive at Base Camp for the season, and he felt sick sleeping and eating so close to corpses. Why, he wondered, would anyone pin these people under rocks? All they do is freeze at night, defrost in the morning, simmer in the day, then freeze all over again. Such mistreatment, he worried, trapped the souls inside the bodies when they were suffering for release. He assumed that the mountain goddess suffered along with them. "I would not go near the memorial," he said. He urged his friend Eric Meyer to stay away from it, too.

Chhiring believed the bodies deserved better. Sherpas and many other Buddhists prefer to cremate the dead. The smoke carries the spirit to the sacred realm above, as it did with Chhiring's mother. When someone dies above the timberline and it's hard to find firewood, a sky burial substitutes for cremation. Although outsiders consider sky burials barbaric—China outlawed the practice in Tibet from the 1960s to the 1980s—to Chhiring this was the sacred way to free the soul. During a sky burial, Buddhist *lamas* or others with religious authority carry the body to a platform on a hill. While burning incense and reciting mantras, they hack the corpse into chunks and slices. They pound the bones with a rock or hammer, beating the flesh into a pulp and mixing in tea, butter, and milk. The preparation attracts vultures, and the birds consume the carcass, carrying the spirit aloft and burying it in the sky, where it belongs. Souls inside the Gilkey Memorial receive neither cremation nor sky burial, and this troubled Chhiring.

He decided to find out more about the temperament of K2's goddess, so he approached another Sherpa to discuss it—Pemba Gyalje, a devout Buddhist on the Dutch team. Pemba belonged to the Paldorje, an ancient Sherpa clan of the Solukhumbu. At the top of the ethnic pecking order, Pemba had also summited Everest six times and trained at the prestigious Ecole Nationale de Ski et d'Alpinisme in Chamonix, France. Like Chhiring, he was a Sherpa climbing as an equal member of a Western team. They were natural allies but had opposite personalities. Pemba usually observed discussions in silence, offered some austere logic, then withdrew into silence again. That style put Chhiring on edge, so he ended up consulting someone else. He called his *lama* on speed dial from his $2-per-minute Thuraya satellite phone.

Ngawang Oser Sherpa picked up on the eighth or ninth ring. The *lama* told Chhiring he was praying at the Boudhanath *stupa* in Kathmandu. "I can't gauge Takar Dolsangma's mood long distance," he said. He advised Chhiring to perform a *puja* ceremony and pay attention to the mountain's reaction. "And don't climb on Tuesday," he added. "It's an inauspicious day for you."

Chhiring switched off the phone and began hauling rocks to the center of camp, building a *chorten*, a sacred mound to honor the goddess. He attached a string of Buddhist prayer flags to it. The red, blue, white, and yellow squares of calico, stamped with sacred verses and strung along a line, were his *Lung Ta*, Tibetan for "wind horse." Eric and other mountaineers joined him at the *puja* ceremony as the breeze picked up. The flags whipped, purifying the air and spreading blessings around camp. Chhiring knew Takar Dolsangma was present. Mindful, he recited mantras, asking the goddess for counsel and forgiveness. He leaned his ice axe and crampons against the *chorten*, balancing a plate of rice beside it and hoping she would accept the offering, bless his equipment, and forgive the injury they were about to cause her. Burning incense, Chhiring dusted the faces of his friends with flour to signify that he wished them to live until they were old and gray. Finally, he asked the goddess for permission to climb.

The ceremony failed. The goddess was still restive. Avalanches roared down her slopes that night, and the jet stream scoured the summit. For a week, she hid behind the clouds. When the Flying Jump arrived in Base Camp on June 15, Chhiring recognized the problem: Pasang Lama's boss.

Others saw Mr. Kim as an omen, too. "I was also praying the mountain wouldn't recognize Mr. Kim," said Ngawang Bhote, the Korean team's cook.

Although Kim had made sure the Flying Jump was one of the best equipped teams at Base Camp, he hadn't been welcome among the Sherpas since a scuffle at Everest in 2007. That year, a member of Mr. Kim's team discovered a quartz rock with the Korean symbol for Everest naturally ingrained in the crystal. According to the expedition organizer, Mr. Kim had declared the stone holy, and his team erected an altar in the kitchen tent. They believed the quartz would protect them as they climbed Everest's Tibetan flank.

But the stone disappeared and the Flying Jump panicked. For four days, the Koreans suspended climbing operations, combing Base Camp for their talisman. On the fifth day, the Chinese liaison officer—Base Camp's equivalent of a sheriff—arrived to investigate allegations that a Korean climber had assaulted a Sherpa for misplacing the rock. Jamie McGuinness, a New Zealander who had organized Kim's expedition, got into a shouting match with his client.

"I told Kim I'd pull his entire Sherpa staff if they were going to clobber someone over a missing rock," recalled Jamie, who consulted with the liaison officer about revoking the Korean team's permit.

Mr. Kim apologized and successfully climbed Everest with his teammates and Pasang's cousin Jumik Bhote. After Everest, Jumik joked privately that working for the Flying Jump was like jumping off a cliff and expecting to fly. On K2, the Koreans boasted to Chhiring and Eric that the Flying Jump "had sponsors to impress and would reach the summit, whatever the cost."

Chhiring stayed away from the Flying Jump just as he kept away from the Gilkey Memorial. Still, Mr. Kim's presence weighed on him. A few months earlier, Chhiring had been consumed with K2, but now he was beginning to think his wife may have been right; maybe K2 wasn't worth the risk. He spoke with Eric about going home. He asked Pemba for his opinion. He called his *lama* again by satellite phone and asked him to perform another *puja* ceremony at Boudhanath. For a week, Chhiring kept hauling rocks to his *chorten*, which grew seven feet tall, becoming the largest in camp. Climbing the mountain still felt wrong. Ngawang Bhote also sensed it. "I could feel the weather change every time Nadir Ali"—the Pakistani cook for the Serbs—"butchered an animal and served its ground flesh," he said. Chhiring agreed and stuck to rice and noodles.

Most of the others in camp ignored the goddess. They scarfed down Nadir's cheeseburgers, played poker, hoarded porn, licked Nutella from the jar, debated the Bonatti Bivouac, updated their blogs, complained about the weather. Chhiring saw that the young man hired by the Flying Jump, Pasang Lama, wasn't praying much, either. He was too busy leveling tent platforms and digging holes for the Flying Jump's latrine. Concerned, Chhiring watched him closely. Pasang worked hard and lacked fancy gear. That meant he needed this job and was ready to do whatever the Flying Jump asked of him, no matter the danger. Pasang reminded Chhiring of himself when he started out: eager but oblivious.

Chhiring hoped Pasang would acknowledge Takar Dolsangma soon. If Pasang was going to be on K2 with the Flying Jump, he would need her. Chhiring also recognized something Pasang didn't: Pasang and his cousins hadn't landed their jobs because of superior luck, strength, or skill. The Bhotes were climbing K2 because ethnic Sherpas did not want to work for the Flying Jump.

One evening, just before the weather cleared and the teams began their assault on the mountain, Chhiring saw Pasang kneeling next to the *chorten*. Chhiring hadn't spoken with him yet but decided to join him in prayer. He bent his knees, pressed his hands together, and leaned forward. Instead of directing his prayer toward the goddess or his wife and children, he prayed for Pasang, asking the mountain to protect him.

When he opened his eyes, Chhiring looked up and scanned the horizon. Hidden behind storms for weeks, K2's summit materialized and seemed to swallow the sky.

7

Weather Gods

Rawalpindi, Pakistan

On June 2, 2008, the day Shaheen's clients arrived in Pakistan, a white Corolla packed with sixty-five pounds of fertilizer, diesel, and TNT rolled through a security checkpoint in Sector F-6/1, near Islamabad's diplomatic enclave. The driver, an eighteen-year-old jihadi named Kamal Saleem, turned left at Street 21 and parked in front of the Danish Embassy. At 12:10 p.m., Kamal's car exploded.

The bomb blasted a four-foot crater into the road, incinerated Kamal, flipped the Corolla, caved in the embassy's metal gates, pulverized most of the embassy's front wall, blew out the windows, and punched through a quarter of the building next door. Dozens of cars shot off the road and rubble blanketed Sector F-6. "Bodies are littered all over the place," Al Jazeera reported. "The blast could be heard all over the city, and it has literally taken the leaves off the trees." Eight people died, including an unidentified child, and twenty-seven were wounded.

Al-Qaeda called the attack retaliation. Danish newspapers had published a series of cartoons satirizing Islam. One ridiculed the

Prophet by depicting a bomb concealed in his turban. After the explosion, journalists made it sound as though jihadis were on the verge of taking over Pakistan, seizing its nuclear arsenal, and annihilating civilization. But foreigners heading to K2 considered it a routine delay. As Serbian climber Hoselito Bite put it: "In Islamabad, Armageddon is nothing special."

Shaheen Baig, however, took the bombing personally. Waiting for his clients' cargo, he questioned the sanity of the world outside Shimshal. Al-Qaeda was slaughtering children over a cartoon. He instructed the Serbian team to stay inside the hotel. "I will show you the real Pakistan," he told them. The country Shaheen knew was peaceful, most of the time, and he wanted foreigners to see past the threat of terrorism and behold Pakistan's beauty.

So did the mountaineering industry. To persuade skittish tourists, the Alpine Club of Pakistan had successfully lobbied for climber-friendly incentives. By 2008, the Ministry of Tourism, using a sliding scale based on altitude and season, had slashed fees for 8,000-meter peaks to half their pre-9/11 rates. Some lesser peaks were on sale at 95 percent off. A K2 permit was $12,000, while Everest cost seven times more. At the same time, the ministry stopped enforcing caps on the number of expeditions to K2 and other peaks. In practice, anyone with ready cash could attempt any Pakistani mountain, at any time, by any route.

Most mountaineers appreciated the reduced fees and climber-friendly deregulation. " 'Pay to play' is how we want it," said the Alpine Club president, Nazir Sabir. "The government has no business deciding who can or can't climb." Nepal has policies similar to those of Pakistan. The United States is more restrictive. Although the summit of North America's highest peak barely reaches the altitude of K2's first mountain camp, climbers heading to Denali in Alaska must submit a climbing résumé before securing a permit. If prospective mountaineers don't appear to have enough experience, "I'll call them and say, 'I see you've been on Grasshopper Glacier for a few days, but Denali is different," said Joe Reichert, a National Park Service ranger. "We'll try to talk them out of it, tell them it's too dangerous."

The Park Service can't turn away mountaineers from public lands, but it reviews applications sixty days in advance and requires climbers to attend a PowerPoint presentation about avalanche risk, crevasse rescue, environmental impact, fixed-line etiquette, and sanitation. The Park Service installs and maintains fixed lines on Denali, and U.S. taxpayers pay for helicopter rescues. Injured climbers are airlifted to hospitals regardless of whether they can pay.

In the Karakorum, the bargain price for climbing has had the intended effect. After the September 11 attacks, tourists and mountaineers avoided Pakistan; in 2008, more than seventy foreign mountaineers arrived to climb K2, although half would be culled by illness before a summit bid. Hundreds more were attempting nearby peaks. Instead of cancellations, K2 had a crowd.

Shaheen wanted to give the climbers a good impression of his religion and his country, and when he arrived at Base Camp with the Serbian team, he tried to be an ambassador. "Part of my job is to keep harmony," he said. Still, diplomacy was tough when expeditions made unreasonable demands. The Singaporean team, for instance, ordered Jehan Baig, their Shimshali high-altitude porter, to carry loads through what Jehan believed to be an avalanche zone. Jehan balked. The team fired him.

Afterward, Shaheen found Jehan another job. Jehan's new employer, Hugues d'Aubarède, the sixty-one-year-old French insurance salesman, paid well, and he had already hired another Shimshali, Karim. But Shaheen soon had misgivings about Hugues. Hiking along the moraine near Base Camp, he and Karim had spotted Hugues crouched down as though tying a shoelace. On the rocks in front of him lay a gray forearm, chopped at the elbow, fingernails intact enough for a manicure. The empty shoulder socket was fringed in tendon. Hugues snapped several photos, aiming his lens at the man's desiccated lips.

Shaheen and Karim were sickened. Muslims consider the mouth, which recites the Qur'an, to be the holiest part of the body. Upon death, as Allah sends an angel to coax the soul from its body, Muslims traditionally close a corpse's mouth, shut its eyelids, and comb its hair. The body is bathed in scented water, shrouded in clean sheets, and lowered into the earth on the right side, facing Mecca—all before night falls on the day of death.

Shaheen gestured toward the dead man. "That could be any of us," he told Karim.

Karim asked what they should do.

"Let me handle this," Shaheen replied.

Several hours later in Base Camp, Shaheen intercepted Hugues. "What do you plan to do with those pictures?" he asked.

"Nothing," Hugues replied. Plenty of climbers photograph human remains along the glacier, he said. When Hugues climbed Everest, he had nearly tripped over a frozen cadaver. Death is part of this sport, Hugues noted, and he was simply "documenting it, as usual."

Shaheen knew what that meant: "Are you going to post those photos on the Internet?"

No, absolutely not, Hugues said. He vowed to keep the images to himself. "Exposing a body like that would be obscene. The dead man's family might even recognize him online."

Shaheen left satisfied. On July 11, he invited the Frenchman to a party. The celebration was in honor of the fifty-first anniversary of the Aga Khan's coronation, a day of solidarity for Ismaili Muslims who accept this direct descendant of Muhammad as their spiritual leader. Nadir, the Serbian team's cook, slaughtered a goat, set up a line of tables in the sunlight, and spread out a buffet of almond cakes and meat skewers. Shaheen, meanwhile, corralled guests into a circle, clapping his hands as Karim and Jehan sang in Wakhi. A dance

Chhiring Dorje Sherpa (left) became one of the most respected Sherpa mountaineers. A trekker passing through the village of Na in 1980 took the only known photograph of him during his childhood. (*credit Dr. Klaus Dierks*)

A decade later, Chhiring had begun working as a porter. In 1991, at the time this photograph was taken, he was sixteen years old, carrying loads for a French Everest expedition. (*credit Jean-Michel Asselin*)

To many devout Buddhists in Rolwaling, mountaineering is an offense to the gods. Chhiring's grandfather, Pem Phutar, carried loads for a British expedition to Gauri Shankar but never spoke about it. Although he received a recommendation letter from the expedition, he hid it from his family. (*Courtesy of Chhiring Dorje Sherpa*)

MERSEYSIDE HIMALAYAN EXPEDITION
GAURI SANKAR MASSIF

Leader: ALFRED GREGORY

Expedition Secretary
CHARLES P. BOOTH,
20 SHREWSBURY AVENUE,
LIVERPOOL, 23.

TO WHOM IT MAY CONCERN.

The bearer, Pem Phutar, has been employed by the above Expedition from the 31st. March until the 18th. June 1955. He has carried heavy loads over difficult country and has proved to be a safe and steady porter under the most adverse conditions. It should be placed on record that he descended the Tesi Lapcha Pass by himself on one occasion to bring up more food for the Expedition.

In addition to being of great value on the mountains, he was of the utmost assistance in recruiting coolies in the valley and in obtaining the necessary supplies of local food. At all times, he was cheerful and helpful and we have no hesitation in recommending him to any Expedition.

FOR MERSEYSIDE HIMALAYAN EXPEDITION
C.P. Booth.

Phurbu Ridar Bhote (left), a mountaineer, left Hungung to find work when his son, Pasang, was six. When he had saved enough money from expeditions, he sent for Pasang to attend school in Kathmandu. (*Courtesy of Pasang Lama*)

Pasang's brother, Dawa, and sister, Lahmu, in front of the house that their father built with his mountaineering wages. Climbing was more lucrative than farming; most families in Hungung couldn't afford a corrugated tin roof. (*Courtesy of Pasang Lama*)

During school vacations, Pasang sometimes returned to Hungung from Kathmandu to help out at the house and with the potato harvest. (*Courtesy of Pasang Lama*)

Serbian climber Dren Mandić shoulders the load of a low-altitude porter. Depending on the weather, the 96-mile slog to K2 Base Camp might take a week. The climbers and their low-altitude porters must carry all necessary food and equipment over the Baltoro Glacier. (*credit Iso Plani / Predrag Zagorac*)

Many mountaineers got their first glimpse of K2 from Concordia, a camp en route to the mountain where three glaciers meet. (*credit Lars Flato Nessa*)

Although paying mountaineers and the low-altitude porters rarely hang out together, Serbian climber Hoselito Bite made a point of getting to know the men he'd hired. (*Courtesy of Hoselito Bite*)

Pakistani high-altitude porter Karim Meherban (top) shears Serbian climber Iso Planić. Although the weather was often clear in Base Camp, the jet stream was pounding K2's summit, making it impossible to climb to the upper reaches of the mountain. (*credit Qudrat Ali*)

For twenty-seven days, the climbers waited in Base Camp for the weather to improve. To pass the time, Cecilie Skog knitted a cap for her husband. She and Rolf Bae (right) had been married just a year. (*credit Lars Flato Nessa*)

French climber Hugues d'Aubarède (right) hired Pakistani high-altitude porter Jehan Baig (left) after another team fired Jehan for refusing to carry loads through an avalanche zone. Here they display one of Hugues's gourmet dinners, freeze-dried chicken breast. (*credit Nick Rice*)

Pakistani high-altitude porter Karim Meherban guided Hugues on K2 in 2006 and 2007. In 2008, Hugues hired him again, and Karim believed they would reach the summit that time. "I can't stop yet," Karim told his father before leaving for the mountain. "Just this one summit, then maybe." (*credit Qudrat Ali*)

Shaheen Baig, who had previously summited K2, was appointed leader of the advance team. "We were all so young and strong," he recalled. "I never thought there would be an accident." (*credit Simone Moro*)

During the final logistics meeting at Base Camp, Muhammad Hussein wrote up the list of the lead team members who would break trail and place ropes through the Bottleneck. Only Pakistani and Nepali climbers were to lead; the Korean climbers volunteered to play an administrative role. (*Courtesy of Hoselito Bite*)

Muhammad Khan (left) and "Little" Muhammad Hussein worked as high-altitude porters for the Serbian team. They had previously summited K2 in 2004. (*credit Peter Zuckerman*)

Before their summit bid, the mountaineers took a group photo. Dren Mandić, Eric Meyer, and Chhiring Dorje Sherpa are in the second row, second, third, and fourth from the left. The French climber Hugues d'Aubarède leans forward directly above them, with Pemba Gyalje and Marco Confortola to his left. Standing in the front row is Korean leader Mr. Kim. Kneeling in the front row, third and fourth from the left, are Ms. Go and Karim Meherban. Kneeling front and center, with blond hair, is Dutchman Wilco van Rooijen. (credit Hoselito Bite)

Seracs loom above the Bottleneck, the deadliest stretch of K2. Giant blocks of ice routinely calve from the sheer ice wall. (credit Iso Planić / Predrag Zagorac)

The Bottleneck, a thirty-story ascent, is only wide enough for a single-file line of climbers. (*credit Lars Flato Nessa*)

Climbers want to move quickly through the Bottleneck and the Traverse to reduce the amount of time they spend below the seracs. Unfortunately, the line moves only as fast as the slowest mountaineer. (*credit Chris Klinke*)

Basque climber Alberto Zerain made it up through the Bottleneck before everyone else and topped out at 3 p.m., hours ahead of the other climbers. Chhiring took this photo of Alberto descending as seventeen climbers were still going up. (*credit Chhiring Dorje Sherpa*)

Upon reaching the summit of K2, Chhiring unfurled Nepal's double-pennant flag in celebration. He topped out at 6:37 p.m., too late to avoid heading back in the darkness and cold of night. (*credit Pemba Gyalje Sherpa*)

From the summit, the climbers surveyed the entire Karakorum range.
(*credit Lars Flato Nessa*)

By 9:58 the next morning, at least five men had died. Marco Confortola and Ger McDonnell remained with three distressed climbers, trying to free them from a tangle of fixed lines. The detail shows Marco leaning over Jumik Bhote's head as Ger kneels beside him. Above them lie two members of the Korean team, hopelessly entangled. (*credit Pemba Gyalje Sherpa*)

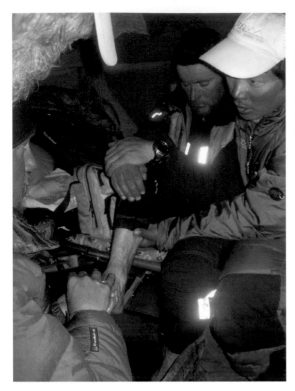

Marco Confortola (center), the last survivor to return to Base Camp, had feet consumed with frostbite. Chhiring (right) helped treat him in a tent converted to a field hospital. (*credit Roberto Manni*)

The survivors mourned the dead by incising their names on metal dinner plates and placing them around a cairn known as the Gilkey Memorial. This plate, for Jehan Baig and Karim Meherban, notes that the men were HAPs—high-altitude porters—from Pakistan. (*credit Hoselito Bite*)

Some of the injured survivors were airlifted to Skardu's Combined Military Hospital, where the mortuary overlooks the children's park and helipad. (*credit Amanda Padoan*)

Dawa Sangmu, the widow of high-altitude porter Jumik Bhote, holds Jen Jen, the son Jumik never met. Behind them, rolled inside a duffel, is the Kolon Sport sleeping bag that Jumik used on K2. (*credit Amanda Padoan*)

Nazib, the mother of high-altitude porter Jehan Baig, holds a photo of her deceased son and his family. Without his wages and mourning their loss, Jehan's family in Shimshal struggled to make ends meet. (*credit Amanda Padoan*)

Karim Meherban's father, Shadi, and four-year-old son, Rahmin, in Shimshal. Rahmin still believes his father will return from K2. (*credit Amanda Padoan*)

pit formed and Hugues boogied into the center. Dressed in slacks, a button-down shirt, a sportsman's cap, and a cashmere sweater, he hopped and flopped his arms to the music like an injured seagull. The crowd adored him. Amid catcalls, Hugues ceded the dance floor to Karim. "I've got rheumatism," Hugues announced. Laughing, Shaheen decided he'd misjudged the good-natured Frenchman. He hadn't. Shortly after their conversation on the glacier, Hugues had downloaded the images onto a laptop. He composed an entry for his blog, speculating about the identity of the pieces. Then he tapped *SEND*.

▲ ▲ ▲

In many ways, the climbing community is like high school. The number of high-altitude mountaineers is small enough that almost everyone knows one another. With the added stress of death and dismemberment, cliques form and peer pressure builds. Mountaineers swap allies, trash-talk, tussle, hook up, and show off. In the weeks before the tragedy, some even squabbled like tweens.

Dutch expedition leader Wilco van Rooijen, for example, "did this, like, 13-year-old-girl thing to me," recalled Nick Rice, the climber from California. "Cold shoulder, completely bitchy, he wouldn't say 'hi' if I said 'hi.'"

"Because I couldn't believe what he was wearing!" Wilco explained. Nick wore only a lightweight Petzl Meteor helmet, too flimsy for K2. "A plastic bicycle helmet."

"Wilco just hates me," Nick said. "I don't know why."

"And he didn't bring his own rope," Wilco continued.

"The American team brought my rope."

"He surfed the 'net all day and mostly brought petrol so he could run his generator."

"Wilco had generator envy."

Such spats ranged from essential to existential, and when Chhiring overheard them, he drew into himself. Compared with those who climbed Everest, the K2 mountaineers more blatantly blurred the line between crazy and courageous. Many were hoping to bag all the 8000ers—the fourteen peaks taller than 8,000 meters—and their swagger sometimes overshot their skill. The strong resented the weak, the weak resented being discounted, and the arrogance unsettled Chhiring. Anticipating that they'd all have to work together, he sized up the most ambitious of the group.

Chhiring found the Basque climber Alberto Zerain astonishing; he had never seen a European who could climb like a Sherpa. Alberto had struck a deal with Shaheen, agreeing to work as a high-altitude porter in exchange for a tent spot.

In addition to Alberto and Shaheen, Chhiring considered Wilco among the most capable mountaineers at Base Camp. A knight of the chivalric Order of Orange-Nassau, Wilco was on his third crusade. He had attempted the Savage Mountain twice before and failed. In 1995, a rock smashed his arm "so the bone was jutting out through the skin." During the 2006 season, bad weather had beaten him back.

This time, Wilco was the first to arrive at K2, setting 3,000 meters of rope along the Cesen route. But when the knight abandoned chivalry and tried to charge the customary toll for use of these lines, his popularity tanked. On most days, he wanted to go home and see his wife and seven-month-old son. "I wanted to feel love," he recalled. "I was crying inside my tent, thinking, 'I'm done with this mountain.'"

Chhiring recognized Wilco's homesickness, but he rarely spoke to him. He preferred the company of Wilco's Irish teammate, Gerard McDonnell, who got along with everyone. A musician and engineer, Ger had acquired the nickname "Jesus" because of his messianic beard and his role as the camp peacemaker. He had also experienced a resurrection of sorts and had a dent in his head to prove it.

In 2006, climbing K2 with Wilco, Ger was at about 23,000 feet when a rock slide hissed down the slope. As Ger ducked behind a boulder to shield himself, a gneiss hockey puck spun at him and smashed into the left side of his Kevlar helmet. Climbers use Kevlar because it is tough—it's a common component of bullet-blocking body armor. Nevertheless, the helmet dented, and the impact chipped off a shard of Ger's skull, exposing his brain.

Ger's climbing partner, Banjo Bannon, tore a wool sock from his pack and wadded it over the peephole. Delirious and losing blood, Ger stumbled down the mountain. After several desperate hours, he staggered into Base Camp and passed out. Storms kept the helicopter from landing that afternoon. The next day, Ger was airlifted to Skardu's Combined Military Hospital.

Chhiring would have retired if he had a hole in his head, but this was a minority view. Base Camp was crawling with adrenaline junkies. Extreme skier Marco Confortola was in the vanguard, amusing his friends with videos of himself zipping down vertical drops in an aerodynamic catsuit. A tattoo of gothic script scrawled across the back of his neck cautioning, *Selvadek* (Wild Thing). His right bicep sprouted a row of edelweiss tattoos, each one signifying an 8000er that he had climbed. A Buddhist mantra was etched into the flesh of his wrist: *Om mani padme um,* a meditation for benevolent attention. The thirty-seven-year-old Italian lived with his mother. When anyone asked about his long-term plans, Marco said he refused to be tied down: "I am married to the mountains." K2, however, wasn't his type. "She is not a lady like Everest," he said. "K2 is a surly and disagreeable man." Marco was positive about the mountain's gender because women coddled him, and no female, not even a goddess, could reject him the way the Savage Mountain had. In 2004, a windstorm on K2 had slapped Marco's tent off the slope, taking his gear with it. Determined to succeed this time, Marco paraded around Base Camp wearing a patchwork of corporate logos and pumping hands with anyone he came across.

In contrast to the voluble Italian, Serbian mountaineer Dren Mandić spent his free time away from the crowd. Chhiring often watched him pacing the moraine, photographing birds or stooping to admire a clump of moss. At home in Serbia, Dren volunteered at an orphanage, and over the years he'd cared for a menagerie of strays and pets, including dogs, fish, geese, a goat, hamsters, parrots, pigeons, a squirrel, snakes, spiders, and turtles. As a child, Dren even refused to step on the grass. "How would you feel if someone stomped on your neck?" he had told grown-ups. Named after a medicinal tree whose sharpened sticks are used to lance boils, Dren was now thirty-two and in love with a woman who worked at the zoo.

Chhiring sometimes wandered the moraine as Dren did, but when he needed a retreat, Chhiring usually sought out the happiest people around, the newlyweds Cecilie Skog and Rolf Bae. They invited Chhiring to lounge on their inflatable IKEA couch and watch the comedy *Borat: Cultural Learnings of America for Make Benefit Glorious Nation of Kazakhstan.* The lack of oxygen made the film's antihero more hysterical than he might normally have been, and they played and replayed it.

Cecilie, who had once called climbing a "male-dominated affair," was the first woman to complete the Explorer's Grand Slam, reaching the top of the tallest mountain on every continent—the Seven Summits—and the North and South Poles. K2 was a kind of honeymoon for her and Rolf. They had been married only a year. After K2, they were planning a more conventional adventure: They wanted to have a baby.

Chhiring admired the newlyweds, and seeing them made him miss Dawa. He sometimes felt alone in a swarm of strangers. His friend Eric helped him practice reading English, and Chhiring helped Eric dispense medicine to the sick. They treated everything from bronchitis to appendicitis, stocked camps, and waited for the weather to improve.

For twenty-seven days, storms prevented anyone from going far. Shaheen flexed his diplomacy, Nick stoked his generator, Wilco cried in his tent, Ger told cautionary tales, Marco flashed his tats, Dren studied moss and birds, Rolf and Cecilie watched *Borat*, and Pasang set ropes for the Flying Jump. The jet stream battered the mountain, and snow flurries buried the camps. Until the weather cleared, the climbers could only wait.

▲ ▲ ▲

Around the planet churns an invisible sea of waves, swells, and currents. Alfred Russel Wallace, codiscoverer of evolution by natural selection, called it "The Great Aerial Ocean." Gas expands and contracts, rises and falls, warms and cools. Solar rays zip through atmospheric layers and strike the land, transforming into heat. Jet streams, cyclones, and ocean currents traffic the earth's energy.

Stuck in Base Camp, the teams monitored a raucous layer of atmosphere called the troposphere. The stakes were sky-high: Windless days deliver the summit; unpredicted storms kill. As Buddhists perform *pujas* and Muslims kneel in *salat*, all denominations worship the meteorologist. Well-funded expeditions engage one for the entire season at $500 per day.

Nothing predicts weather with absolute precision, but infrared photos, satellite images, weather-station data, and an ensemble of statistical models run through supercomputers can foretell the future up to ten days in advance. For most of the year, the models predict the same thing for K2. Week after week, the jet stream blasts the summit. Yet, in summer, for a few hallowed days every few years, the winds die. This weather window is brief and precious. Until it opens, climbers acclimatize so they can bolt up the mountain when the forecaster calls.

Acclimatization hinges on genetics. Some mountaineers can

adjust to altitude in two weeks; others will never get used to it. No matter how much they train, they can't climb high mountains without bottled oxygen. These different physical responses help explain why climbing is rife with theories about how best to acclimatize. Climbers will tell you to eat bananas, meditate, practice yoga, sleep on your left side, swallow Diamox, or avoid it and instead chew *yarsagumba*, a mummified caterpillar with a mushroom spore shooting from its brain.

Almost all altitude-adjustment routines involve climbing in order to stock camps, followed by a period of recovery at lower altitude— ideally, below 18,000 feet. Mountaineers ascend in the morning and descend before nightfall. Doing this seems to jolt the body into faster adjustment until about 27,000 feet.

Above that is the Death Zone. Nobody can adjust to it. At this extreme altitude, the percentage of oxygen in the air is the same as at sea level, but the air pressure is much lower—the same volume of gas has fewer molecules in it. As a result, the body can't extract enough oxygen from the air. The more time spent in the Death Zone, the weaker and sicker a climber becomes. The digestive system fails and the body devours its own muscle tissue. "It's living hell. You feel your body deteriorating," said Wilco. "Ever tried to run up a staircase while breathing through a straw?"

Acclimatization increases the amount of time climbers can survive in the Death Zone. During acclimatization, the kidneys excrete more bicarbonate ions, acidifying the blood, which quickens respiration. The bone marrow revs up red-cell production so the blood can transport more oxygen. Blood flow surges in the brain and lungs. Without acclimatization to altitude, someone dropped off at the summit of K2 would black out within minutes. Those who have acclimatized can last several days.

These adjustments nevertheless come with dangers. A higher concentration of red blood cells thickens the blood. Clots form more easily and the heart has to pump harder. The rise in blood pressure can dislodge the clots, which then travel up the legs and clog the coronary artery, causing heart attacks; or the clots can cut off oxygen supply to the brain, causing strokes. There is also the specter of edema, or fluid buildup. Desperate for more oxygen, the body's cells release nitric oxide and other chemical signals to the capillaries, directing them to accept more blood. As the capillaries expand, they expose themselves to higher blood pressure and tear. Fluid leaks, pooling in places it shouldn't.

Capillaries in the eyes explode like fireworks, and this hemorrhaging blurs vision in severe cases. When the fluid collects in the lungs, which have the body's greatest concentration of capillaries, climbers suffer from high-altitude pulmonary edema. Instead of breathing normally, victims of high-altitude pulmonary edema can only pant. The cough resembles the bark of a sea lion. The pulse races. Lungs cannot deliver oxygen. Death comes within hours unless the climber descends fast or is entombed within an inflatable pressure bag.

Like the lungs, the brain, which draws in an enormous supply of blood, can also leak fluid. When this happens, it's called high-altitude cerebral edema. Its first symptoms are often mild; they may be what causes acute mountain sickness. However, victims can deteriorate fast. The headache feels as though a sadist is testing a jackhammer on your cranium. Balance wavers and speech slurs—almost as though you've downed ten martinis. Half the body may go numb. Unreal smells, sounds, tastes, and visions appear. During an altitude-induced hallucination on the 1954 K2 expedition, "I found myself inside an ice cream parlor in Padova," recalled Italian scientist Bruno Zanettin. "I told myself, 'This can't be real. I'm alone inside a tent in Pakistan,' but I could still taste the flavor of the ice cream."

It's hard to predict whom these afflictions will strike. They can break even the best climbers, ones who have always excelled in thin air. Bizarrely, the dying commonly fail to notice how sick they are.

And even those handling the altitude well or breathing bottled oxygen can feel the drain. Viagra can help. The drug relaxes the vessel tone of the pulmonary arteries and can increase exercise tolerance, so mountaineers commonly take it.

Experts debate whether altitude causes permanent brain damage, but oxygen deprivation certainly impairs judgment. In 2008, for example, Roeland van Oss of the Dutch team nearly gassed himself. On July 1, at 23,000 feet, he was melting a pot of ice inside his tent without adequate ventilation. "On the burner there's a big sticker: 'Only use this outside,'" explained Wilco. Carbon monoxide filled the tent, and Roeland fell flat. He would have died if his teammate, Court Haegens, hadn't immediately dragged him into the open air. Although Roeland's mistake was just an oversight, the Savage Mountain had nearly claimed the first victim of the summer.

▲ ▲ ▲

Climbers call him "The Weather God," but meteorologist Yan Giezendanner is an atheist—"to the point of eating priests." Multiple sclerosis consigns him to a wheelchair, but his reach extends six miles into the troposphere. From his ground-floor apartment in Chamonix, Yan was responsible for choreographing the movements of Hugues, Karim, and Jehan.

On July 22, Yan studied two screens streaked with yellow slashes and green waves superimposed on the contours of Kazakhstan. A cyclonic circulation was blowing east. As the eye moved into China, a ridge of high pressure developed over the Karakorum on the cyclone's west side. In this ridge, right over K2, winds would become preternaturally calm for three to four days. "In ten years, I had never seen such a beautiful window," Yan recalled. He didn't pick up the phone right away. "I sat in my kitchen, stalling. I knew August 1 would

be perfect. I also knew my prediction might cause a friend to die."
Reluctantly, he dialed Hugues's number. When the Frenchman's satellite phone chirped at Base Camp, Hugues, Karim, and Jehan were
packing to go home. Hugues had no sponsors to impress. After four
dreary weeks stuck in Base Camp, he could catch a flight to Paris
without disappointing anyone but his dentist, who wanted a photo of
Hugues's teeth gleaming from the summit.

But once he heard the news about the weather window, Hugues
resolved to stay, and so did many others. That day, Thuraya phones all
over camp were bleating, and ecstatic climbers were zipping from one
tent to the next. "Base Camp turned upside down," said expedition
manager Maarten van Eck, who had received an earlier forecast from
the Dutch weather god. Although they still had nine days before the
window opened, climbers lined their axes, ropes, and pickets across
the moraine like butchers primed to gut a hog. They huddled around
laptops. They filed their crampons. And soon the problem became
obvious: With so many mountaineers planning to climb the mountain at once, crowds would pack the slopes. Nobody wanted to miss
this one chance, and forecasters had only predicted four days of good
weather. The teams decided to work together.

Four days after the news came in, about two dozen mountaineers crowded into the Serbian mess tent for the last logistical meeting
of the summer. A jaundiced light filtered through the nylon fabric.
A Warhol-style collage of food labels hung from a string overhead.
Climbers drinking sugar-laced tea fidgeted as though waiting to be
strapped inside a roller coaster. They discussed the siege of the Savage
Mountain. Teams would advance along two routes, the Abruzzi and
the Cesen, which converge at high camp, or Camp 4. Twenty-six
climbers had claimed the Abruzzi; ten had chosen the Cesen.

▲ ▲ ▲

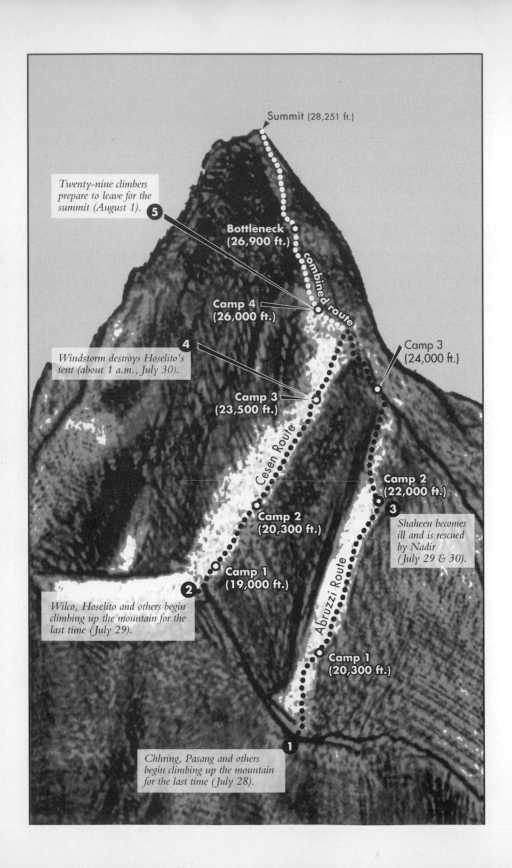

Summit (28,251 ft.)

Twenty-nine climbers prepare to leave for the summit (August 1). **5**

Bottleneck (26,900 ft.)

combined route

Camp 4 (26,000 ft.)

Camp 3 (24,000 ft.)

Windstorm destroys Hoselito's tent (about 1 a.m., July 30). **4**

Camp 3 (23,500 ft.)

Cesen Route

Camp 2 (22,000 ft.)

3

Camp 2 (20,300 ft.)

Shaheen becomes ill and is rescued by Nadir (July 29 & 30).

Camp 1 (19,000 ft.)

Abruzzi Route

2

Wilco, Hoselito and others begin climbing up the mountain for the last time (July 29).

Camp 1 (20,300 ft.)

1

Chhring, Pasang and others begin climbing up the mountain for the last time (July 28).

The Abruzzi, the most popular route, traces the mountain's southeast spur. It has four camps: at 20,300 feet, 22,000 feet, 24,000 feet, and 26,000 feet. Past Camp 1, a 45-degree slope rains rocks. This stretch almost killed Wilco in 1995 and Ger in 2006. Climbers must clear it in the early morning when the ice is firm. Next, they face House's Chimney. Free-climbing this rock flue with a pack is impractical, so mountaineers ascend using a rickety ladder and a loom of fixed lines. Camp 2, above, is a wind-scoured platform that backs into a headwall. The route then claws toward the Black Pyramid, a 2,000-foot wall of granite-gneiss, with Camp 3 perched on top. Approaching the Death Zone, the route flattens onto the Shoulder, a glacial saddle reserved for high camp.

The Cesen route is longer and more technical but safer. It avoids some rockfall areas. From Base Camp, the Cesen follows a ridgeline that initially seems as gentle as a ski slope. The first camp, at about 19,000 feet, is jammed behind a butterfly-shaped outcropping. From there, a rock wall at 20,300 feet shelters Camp 2 from wind and avalanches. Snaking around the wall, the route plows upward, fanning into a monotonous incline called the White Desert. Camp 3 is pitched above a hump of gneiss at 23,500 feet. A steep ice field and a rock spire are the last obstacles before the Cesen joins the Abruzzi.

From Camp 4, the common camp on the Shoulder, the combined routes approach the Bottleneck. Seracs hulk above this channel like prows of tanker ships. Lines of climbers crowd the narrow passage. Once through the Bottleneck, the route swerves diagonally across K2's southeast face along the Traverse. A massive lump of ice called the Snow Dome bridges the Traverse with a crevassed snowfield. From there, a ridge leads to the summit.

Abruzzi and Cesen Routes (*opposite*): The weather on K2 allowed a climbing window of just three days, forcing a crowd of mountaineers to try for the summit at once. They took one of two routes, which converged at Camp 4.

During the logistical meeting, the group chose Shaheen Baig to supervise the men who would break trail and fix ropes through the Bottleneck. Each large team contributed support climbers. The Koreans volunteered Pasang Lama and Jumik Bhote. The Serbians assigned two Balti high-altitude porters, Muhammad Hussein and Muhammad Khan. Chhiring Dorje represented the American team; Pemba Gyalje represented the Dutch. This advance team of Pakistani and Nepali climbers would start from Camp 4 at midnight and scale the Bottleneck before dawn.

A second wave of climbers planned to set off an hour behind the lead team. If all went well, the fixed lines would be in place by the time they reached the Bottleneck. Another six hours of breaking trail and they'd be on the summit. "We should turn around by 2 p.m.," Shaheen said. If deep snow clogged the Bottleneck, the climbers might take an extra hour, "but no one should continue up after 3."

Everyone would set their radios to frequency 145.140 MHz. The teams agreed to share willow wands used to mark the route, as well as rope, ice screws, and pickets. Mr. Kim anointed his teammate, Park Kyeong-hyo, as equipment manager. He would check in with each team and confirm that they had brought the necessary gear. "Everything was decided in a systematic way, every small detail," recalled Pemba Gyalje. He felt confident about the plan.

Few recognized the cultural crevasse beneath the slick organizational surface. The advance team was dangerously diverse: Shaheen spoke Wakhi; the two Muhammads, Balti. These Pakistanis communicated in Urdu, a third language, which Shaheen translated into English for the Nepalis to understand. The Nepalis, in turn, played their own linguistic hopscotch. Pasang and Jumik's first language was Ajak Bhote; Chhiring's was Rolwaling Sherpi tamgney; Pemba Gyalje's was Shar-Khumbu tamgney. They used Nepali to communicate among themselves. Information could easily become garbled as it passed through four linguistic layers, not to mention the crackle of a radio. Furthermore, only Jumik could communicate with Park, the equipment manager, who spoke Korean. If one link in the linguistic chain broke—Shaheen, for instance—the Pakistanis would be completely unable to talk to the Nepalis.

The liaison officer of the Serbian team, Captain Sabir Ali, recognized the potential for breakdown. He made a list of the equipment the teams promised to carry and proposed a contract, insisting that each leader sign his name on the paper. But even after that, several climbers were still unsure of the particulars.

"I speak Tarzan English," Marco said to Shaheen after signing. "I hope I understood."

Shaheen shrugged.

Wilco soon regretted the decision to join ranks with all the other climbers. "I signed for it," he recalled, "but I should have said, 'I've never climbed with any of you. Why should I trust you based on nothing but your blue eyes?'" He didn't voice this concern at the time. No one did. The summit was waiting, and the teams felt ready. As the meeting broke up, Ger switched on a boombox. It blasted Biffy Clyro's rock ballad *Mountains* into the clearing sky.

8

Ghost Winds

Base Camp to Camp 4
Up the Abruzzi. Up the Cesen
17,388 feet to 25,800 feet
July 28 to July 31

Two hours before he left Base Camp, Chhiring blessed his ropes, smoking them with incense. He stuffed the coils in his pack below a cylinder of oxygen, stashed for emergencies. He placed a *mala* rosary of 108 gnarled bodhi seeds in his jacket. He'd use them for meditation at high camp. Beside the beads he put a Ziploc bag of *tsampa*, barley flour that his *lama* had blessed. He planned to scatter grain through the Bottleneck as an offering to the goddess.

Deep in his pack, beneath strata of energy powder and butane canisters, he carried an envelope of rock salt. His *lama* had told him to sprinkle it on his last meal before the summit—it would give him strength. Around his neck he wore a crimson thread called a *bhuti*. A gift from his *lama*, the *bhuti* had three charms attached. The most potent, a silver amulet, concealed a mantra stamped on rice paper. Lama Ngawang Oser Sherpa had forbidden Chhiring to open the amulet's casing and examine the mantra inside. If exposed, the mantra's power would evaporate, reversing Chhiring's fortune. The *bhuti*'s second charm, an oblong bead cocooned in black electrical tape, prevented cerebral and pulmonary edema. The third, a cluster of knots, halted avalanches and deflected falling rocks. Chhiring tucked the *bhuti* and its charms under his Capilene shirt, next to his heart.

Like Chhiring, other climbers deliberated over what to carry. Provisions supplied warmth, orientation, and motivation, but everything added weight, so they packed needful things first: altimeters, batteries, cameras, candy, crampons, downsuits, duct tape, goggles, headlamps, helmets, ice screws, ice axes, lighters, nose guards, radios, ropes, sleeping bags, stakes, stoves, sunscreen, tents, toothpaste, and satellite phones. But everyone had different ideas of what was essential.

The Nepalis wore *bhuti*s similar to Chhiring's, but charms differed. Pasang's older cousin, Big Pasang Bhote, wore a pendant of red coral, symbolizing eternal life. He hoped it would relieve him of his recurrent nightmare in which a horned demon came to gore him in the stomach. Pasang's other cousin, Jumik, wore a *bhuti* with a special weave to protect his teenage wife, Dawa Sangmu. Their baby was two weeks overdue.

Pasang usually kept two *bhuti*s: one to wear around his neck and another to slip beneath his pillow to dissolve nightmares. But as he left Base Camp, Pasang realized that he'd forgotten them both. At least he remembered the lucky ring. Its soft gold, soldered into a snake, coiled up his middle finger. The ring belonged to his mother, Phurbu Chejik Bhoteni, who lent it on the condition that Pasang return it to her in person.

Many climbers brought reminders of people they loved and hoped to return to. Serbian climber Hoselito Bite carried a photo of his four-year-old daughter, Maya. "I've grown a lot in two months," she had told him via satellite phone before he left for the summit bid. "When you come back, you won't recognize me." Hoselito kept her photo in a locket wrapped in waterproof tape.

Marco kept his grandmother's rosary inside the top lid of his pack. It was a peculiar inheritance. She had died when Marco was a child, and, on the day of her funeral, Marco had tiptoed to where her body lay. "The rosary was laced between her fingers," he explained, "and I stole it."

Dren carried a miniature Snoopy that his girlfriend, Mirjana, had given him at the airport in Belgrade. He bound the doll to the right strap of his pack. It reminded him of his pretty zookeeper and their home filled with reptile tanks.

Rolf wore a blue-gray cap his wife had knitted at Base Camp. His bride, Cecilie, wore her wedding ring on a chain, so she wouldn't have cold metal around her finger, increasing the chance of frostbite. It was a replacement for the first ring Rolf had given her. En route to the South Pole, Rolf had removed his skis, knelt in the snow, and presented her with a ring fashioned of steel wire from a repair kit. With tears freezing on her face, Cecilie had agreed to marry him. She had worn the ring, which dug into her finger, until they returned to Norway, where Rolf replaced it with a white-gold band.

Nick, the climber from California, brought an iPod filled with a motivational mix of Coldplay, Radiohead, and The White Stripes. He liked to lip-synch, infuriating Wilco. Wilco carried a Thuraya satellite phone with fresh batteries and raised buttons that he could punch even if he were snow-blind.

Others carried intangibles. Hugues climbed with faith in Yan, his weather god; Hugues's high-altitude porters, Karim and Jehan, who believed "no atom's weight in earth or heaven escapes Allah," both shouldered seventy-pound packs filled with Hugues's food and bottled oxygen. Hugues's dehydrated meals were not *halal* by Islamic dietary law but luxurious by mountaineering standards. The most appetizing was a silver packet of freeze-dried Bumble Bee chicken. With boiling water, it would swell into a juicy fillet.

At least one climber, Mr. Kim, itemized his gear with military precision, rejecting all items of superstition except for a single object. The leader of the Flying Jump was rumored to be carrying the lost quartz, the same rock that had caused a scuffle with the crew on Everest.

Chhiring's friend Eric packed a portable pharmacopoeia. Aside from diuretics, steroids, antibiotics, and antivirals, the anesthesiologist carried several doses of alteplase, a clot-busting tissue plasminogen activator, designed to reverse severe frostbite. Each 50 milligram shot cost $1,375. The doctor wore a Capilene undershirt silk-screened with the motto: "K2: A Little Shorter/A Lot Harder." A climber who asked not to be named brought JWH-018, a synthetic marijuana with ten times the punch of THC. The drug's street name was "K2."

Irish climber Ger McDonnell carried a crucifix, his grandfather's pocket watch, an eighty-five-year-old whistle that had called four generations of McDonnells to the dinner table, and a vial of holy water mixed from Lourdes, Knock, and St. Bridget's. Just before he departed, Ger assured his mother in a final blog entry that he had not misplaced the holy water, adding in Gaelic: "*Tá an t-am ag teacht*"— The time is coming.

▲ ▲ ▲

Climbing an 8,000-meter peak resembles a siege, and over the years, two campaign strategies have emerged: expedition style and alpine style.

Expedition-style climbing is akin to trench warfare. High-altitude workers scout the route, break trail, fix lines, and establish fixed camps, each higher than the last. Returning to Base Camp, they scoop up supplies and climb the mountain again, stocking the tents with food and fuel. Then, on the summit push, they climb to the camps again, escorting the clients through crevasse fields and up the slopes. With expedition-style climbs, clients frequently use oxygen during the long and expensive assault on the mountain, and many have no compunction about taking drugs to aid acclimatization.

Alpine-style climbing is like a blitz. Elite teams with as few as two people sprint up and down the mountain as fast as their bodies allow; speed is safety. They pack light, only the bare essentials, and carry their tent between camps. They also adhere to a protocol called "fair means," which rejects acclimatization drugs, high-altitude porters, and bottled oxygen. Alpine-style climbers who adhere to fair means are the real rock stars of mountaineering. They generally are highly skilled and experienced, and they attract considerably more attention and respect than expedition-style climbers.

True alpine style forgoes fixed lines, but hardly anyone attempts the purest form on K2. Mountaineers on K2, regardless of style, need to fix ropes. To do this, a lead climber, with a rope attached to his harness, starts up a pitch and creates a protection by driving in a snow picket, twisting in an ice screw, hammering in a piton, or looping a sling over a solid rock. Then the climber clips the rope through the protection, continues up, and adds more hardware as required by the terrain.

A well-placed anchor should hold on rock, but snow and ice are harder to predict. If the lead slips and the anchor holds, the belayer can quickly brake the rope, and his partner will only fall twice as far as the last anchor. To absorb some of the shock of a fall, ropes are designed to stretch, but that's not always enough to avoid pulling out an anchor. The astute belayer knows whether to stop a fall instantly or to slow it more gradually, thus reducing the yank on the line.

With alpine-style climbing, the leader climbs to a suitable spot, puts in a solid anchor or two, and prepares to stand nearby to belay. The second climber then ascends. With expedition-style climbing, the ropes stay in place. The followers clip onto the fixed ropes with a jumar—a D-shaped device that bites the rope like a ratchet, sliding up but not down—and winch their way along the lines. If a climber slips, the jumar, leashed to the harness, stops the fall immediately. On descent, fixed ropes serve as a convenient hand line, and, on steep terrain, they provide an easy way to rappel down.

Expedition-style climbing might appear safer, but it isn't necessarily. Hanging from knots that strangers have tied, many commercial expeditions' clients don't have lead-climbing experience or a clear understanding of climbing mechanics. Faster clients get caught behind slower ones, or climbers set out in groups, placing the weight of several bodies on a single anchor, which "increases the chance that somebody is going to blow up the whole thing," as Wilco put it. Overloaded anchors pull out and then everyone goes down, initiating a death train. In 2008, all the climbers approached K2 in expedition style, but each team imposed its own ethos. The Flying Jump relied heavily on fixed lines, support staff, and bottled oxygen; the Dutch team abstemiously followed the fair-means rules of engagement.

▲ ▲ ▲

Early on the morning of July 28, Chhiring, Pasang, and Shaheen left Base Camp as part of the lead team on the Abruzzi route. The snow was pitted and pocked, Chhiring recalled, "as though the goddess had swung a hammer" along the route. Ice screws had melted out or vanished. Fresh snow slides covered the bamboo stakes that marked supply caches, and sections of fixed lines, now buried, had become useless. Pulling them out could trigger avalanches. The climbers strung new ropes.

Pasang, breaking trail, stomped out bucket steps for the climbers to follow, testing for hidden crevasses and marking weak snow bridges with purple flags. When he reached camp, he realized that the jet stream had sent some tents sailing, leaving lonely platforms. So he pitched new tents.

Once the lines were reset, the rest of the climbers followed, using jumars attached by a line to each climber's harness. The followers stepped in the lead climbers' tracks to reduce the chance of setting off an avalanche or dropping down a crevasse. "You take a step. You breathe. You take another step. You breathe again," explained Wilco. "Your whole mind is occupied with taking each individual step." Using just an ice axe or a ski pole to balance, they climbed a distance roughly the equivalent of three Empire State Buildings on the first day.

To overcome the exertion, mountaineers use several tricks to stay strong at altitude. One method is to inhale deeply, pursing one's lips and exhaling forcefully, as if blowing up a balloon. This is known as pressure breathing; physicians call it positive end expiratory pressure, or PEEP. Patients with emphysema or other breathing difficulties use this technique reflexively, and research shows that it improves gas exchange and prevents fluid buildup in the lungs. The pursed lips and forceful exhalation increase air pressure, which resuscitates the lungs' air sacs, or alveoli, so they can expand, absorb more oxygen, and expel more carbon dioxide.

Many climbers also take rest steps, a gait with a momentary pause and knee lock. Greater weight rests on the leg when locked, not bent, and spares the calf and thigh muscles. The gait looks stiff, as though the climber were wearing stilts, but it postpones "Elvis leg," or uncontrollable muscle twitching.

Some members of the teams were professional guides who knew the safest and most efficient ways to climb; others floundered, wasting energy. Based on how they moved, "it became clear that not everyone was as skilled at mountaineering as they had made out," recalled Marco, who had been a mountain guide for eighteen years. This worried him and many others. "Some of them were ignorant of basic safety," recalled Fredrik Sträng, a Swedish mountaineer on the American team. "Kicking off rocks [that could hit climbers below], stepping on ropes with crampons, yanking fixed lines, clipping six people to a rope that should only hold two. When I saw the crowd climbing, I thought, 'What the hell? They're going to get us killed.' " Fredrik was so frustrated he started climbing at night to avoid the crowds. He hoped that by the time the two major routes converged at Camp 4, exhaustion and altitude would have culled the weak, forcing many to turn back.

Alberto Zerain sometimes avoided fixed lines altogether. He took the advice a friend had given him after attending an organizational meeting at Base Camp. "K2 is set for tragedy," Jorge Egocheaga had told Alberto, suggesting he avoid "the circus" and climb the mountain independently. With this in mind, Alberto broke a trail of his own, hauling everything he needed on his own back. He pulled ahead of the crowds, caught up with Shaheen, and helped him break trail to Camp 2.

For safety, if not comfort, mountain camps are often wedged underneath rock outcroppings, away from avalanche trajectories. These few protected spots are usually cramped and crowded, as was the case with Camp 2. "Tents were on top of each other," recalled Eric. By the evening, "more than 30 people were there, and it was just too dangerous to go far to take a crap, so the space between the tents turned into a sewage canal." When melting snow for dinner, the mountaineers scooped up the whitest stuff they could find in the darkness, dropping iodine tablets into the pot. Many smeared their fingers with Purell before handling food. But it takes just a speck of stool to infect climbers with campylobacteriosis, or some other digestive illness.

In Camp 2, Shaheen drank two cups of Balti milk tea and fell asleep. A few hours later, he doubled over at the threshold of his tent, vomiting uncontrollably. "It was clearly bacterial gastroenteritus from contaminated water," recalled Eric, who treated Shaheen. "He could have gotten it from the tea"—as Shaheen suspected—"but might have picked it up even earlier than Camp 2." Eric gave Shaheen six gray-green tablets of Compazine, which reduces vomiting and nausea, and six chalky pills of Cipro, an antibiotic. He advised Shaheen to descend in the morning.

Shaheen had no intention of going down. He'd never left his team midclimb and wasn't going to start on K2. He willed himself to feel better by daybreak and retreated into his tent. Tossing, he tried to sleep but spent the night heaving, trying to vomit out his empty stomach.

In the morning, something else was wrong: his lungs gurgled. As other climbers prepared to leave, Shaheen managed to yank on his boots. He weaved 10 feet across camp to where Alberto was about to strike his tent. "Leave your tent up and use mine in Camp 3," Shaheen said. He handed Alberto dried apricots, about 40 yards of lightweight rope, three ice screws, and a Ziploc bag of oatmeal.

"Can you get down?" Alberto asked him.

Shaheen waved off discussion. He needed Alberto to forget about him. Describing the precise location of his tent in the two highest camps of the Abruzzi, he instructed Alberto to take his place on summit day and supervise placing ropes through the Bottleneck.

Alberto stuffed Shaheen's vital gear into his pack and left to face House's Chimney and the Black Pyramid.

"We shook hands, said good luck," Alberto recalled. "He said goodbye to his friends, and that was it."

As Camp 2 began to empty, Shaheen heard Iso Planić of the Serbian team radio Base Camp. "Shaheen Baig needs an evac on the Abruzzi," Iso said. Shaheen interrupted on the same frequency. "I am fine," he insisted. Iso left camp, and soon Shaheen was alone.

Furious with himself, Shaheen decided to rest for an hour and catch up to the others once his health improved. As the hours passed, his stomach burned and kept trying to empty itself. He spat pink froth into his glove. His wheezing became shallower, and he coughed so hard he expected to crack a rib. Shaheen could ignore the nausea, but not the telltale gurgle in his lungs. Pulmonary edema had set in, and he'd drown in his own fluids if he didn't drop altitude fast.

He sat there thinking about it for the rest of the day. As the sun sank behind Broad Peak, Shaheen realized it was too late. Getting down on his own felt impossible. He could barely move. He refused to radio the climbers higher up the mountain, which would jeopardize their summit bids, and he couldn't imagine that anyone left in Base Camp could reach Camp 2 in time to save him.

Sullenly, he picked up the radio and called Nadir Ali Shah, the Base Camp cook for the Serbian team. "Shaheen asked to be left on the mountain," Nadir recalled. "He didn't want anyone to risk dragging down a dead body."

▲ ▲ ▲

Around the same time, Wilco sat inside a tent anchored to a pinnacle at 23,600 feet. Unaware that Shaheen had fallen ill, the leader of the Dutch team was on a different part of the mountain, the Cesen route.

Wilco was having a bad day. Most of his frustrations came from things he couldn't control. For example, he had just missed a $500 shipment of Mars candy bars, ferried by nationalistic Dutch trekkers. The sixty pounds of chocolate, intended to power him to the summit, sat melting in Base Camp. His main gripe, however, was Serbian climber Hoselito Bite. Wilco couldn't shake him. "I was telling him straight," recalled Wilco. "I said, 'Hoselito, we want to be friends with you, but you can't climb with us. You're too slow. . . . You are not going with us to the summit because you are not capable of it.'"

Wilco disliked being K2's bouncer, but someone had to do it. The altitude had debilitated Hoselito, who had spilled a can of sardines in one of the tents, saturating the fabric with fish oil. The close quarters of the tent now carried the stench of low tide. What would happen if Hoselito failed to buckle his harness or crampon correctly? Wilco wanted him to turn back before he hurt himself and needed an evac, endangering his rescuers and costing them the summit.

But Hoselito pushed himself to keep going. He told Wilco he was feeling fine and would soon be climbing faster. He had oxygen cylinders in his pack, and he'd start using gas at Camp 4. "I have my daughter to return to," Hoselito told him. "I'm not going to get killed."

▲ ▲ ▲

When the radio crackled at Base Camp, Nadir Ali was in the Serbian mess tent, scrubbing dishes in a tub of glacial melt. The static made it hard to hear the details, but Nadir understood enough.

"It had something to do with Shaheen's lungs, and he was in Camp 2," along the Abruzzi route, Nadir recalled. "He didn't want a rescue, but he needed one, and I knew he was too proud to ask. I figured he'd be conscious if I got there fast enough."

Nadir, a thirty-three-year-old with a pompadour of black hair, usually fried cheeseburgers at the Chancery Guest House in Islamabad, chatting with tourists. He had little formal training as a mountaineer but aspired to be a climbing guide, and Shaheen had helped him break into the business, finding him work as a cook and, occasionally, as a high-altitude porter on mountains lower than K2. A devout Muslim, Nadir believed that he had an obligation to help those in need and that Allah had meant him to hear the radio call. "We couldn't let Shaheen stay at that altitude with a lung problem," he said. "You can die overnight."

Others in Base Camp apparently didn't see it that way. Nadir sought help, but no one would take the risk. Mountaineers higher up the mountain said they never heard a call come through, and those remaining in Base Camp told Nadir he was overreacting. With the wind picking up, a late-night rescue two camps up the mountain began looking more and more irrational.

Still resolute, Nadir didn't have much climbing gear of his own, so he scrounged for a parka, an axe, and whatever else other climbers would donate. It took two hours to gather the equipment. Most climbers refused to part with their gear and discouraged Nadir from going up. There was nothing he could do, they said, especially with what looked like an incoming storm. Nadir managed to get through on the radio to Eric, who was near Camp 3. Eric offered his extra gear and told Nadir which drugs and shots to grab from his medical kit.

Around midnight, wearing mismatched socks, Nadir left Base Camp alone to rescue Shaheen. Before starting, he radioed up to inform Shaheen he was coming. The only response was static.

"I figured he had passed out," Nadir recalled. He knew this meant he had to climb fast with the drugs. A few minutes could make the difference between life and death.

With no stops for meals, Nadir chewed tea leaves and chocolate, pulling himself up the fixed lines. He passed three Western climbers who politely declined to assist. Nadir justified their refusal by assuming that these climbers probably lacked the energy to help and were descending with ailments of their own.

Would they have helped if Shaheen were, say, Australian, not Pakistani? "I don't want to answer that out loud," Nadir said later. "They don't work for us. We work for them, and I want to keep working for them. They pay good salaries. Most of them are good people, and we need them to keep coming back to Pakistan, so please don't make them look bad in your book." It's unfair to judge people when they're oxygen-deprived and exhausted, he said.

When Nadir got to Camp 1, he tried to contact Shaheen again on the radio. No answer. Was he alive? Nadir knew that if he sat down to rest and think about it, he might quit. He kept heading up, praying to Allah for strength as he slid his jumar up the ropes, ignoring the quiver and burn in his calves and the pain in his throat from the dry air. Around noon, after twelve hours of frantic climbing, Nadir arrived at Camp 2.

It was deserted. Sun soaked the scrim like bleach, blazing the landscape ultrawhite and blistering his face. He called out for Shaheen. Nothing.

Where was he? Nadir shook one of the tents, unzipped a flap, and leaned inside. All he saw were empty sleeping bags. He eyed one of them and considered collapsing into the soft down. Even if he found Shaheen now, how would they descend? Nadir couldn't carry him—Shaheen was almost a foot taller and forty pounds heavier—and, in his condition, the sick man wouldn't be able to do more than slither.

Nadir sat down to collect himself. About to shut his eyes, he spotted a lump between the tents. It was Shaheen, curled up in a fetal position on the snow and surrounded by "something that looked like Pepsi."

▲ ▲ ▲

At Camp 2 along the Cesen route, Wilco and Hoselito waited out a blustery day in their tents. Hugues, with his high-altitude porters, Karim and Jehan, kept moving up. Hugues's weather god in Chamonix had predicted windless days ahead, and the Frenchman wanted to position himself for the summit.

Yan's forecast was right—at first. The weather stayed calm on July 29, and the men arrived at Camp 3 that evening. At sunrise, they continued up, enjoying the fine weather, but by late afternoon, winds began shrieking down K2's Shoulder. Karim and Jehan worked fast, stomping out a platform and staking the tent. Cramming inside with Hugues and Nick Rice, they heard the rising growl of the wind. As gusts buffeted the tent, they supported the poles by pressing their shoulders against the fabric dome.

The Shimshalis, who had less faith in Yan's statistical model, tried to rest as Hugues grabbed a sat phone and punched in the thirteen numerals for Yan's home in Chamonix. Shouting above the wind, he kept asking the voice at the other end of the line to repeat the message.

"The winds don't exist," Yan said.

"What?"

"I said, 'They don't exist.'"

"What do you mean they don't exist?"

Yan explained that he was at his desk, studying two monitors that undulated with waves and darts. They showed a gentle breeze blowing across K2's Shoulder. That meant the seventy-mile-an-hour wind blasts pummeling Hugues, Karim, and Jehan were katabatic, ghost winds that the supercomputers of Météo-France could not see. Katabatic windstorms form when air at higher altitude cools, becoming more dense, Yan explained. Pulled by gravity and a lower pressure gradient, the air pours down the mountain like water.

These ghost winds were dangerous, but they materialize and vanish so suddenly that they only terrorize climbers for brief periods. Yan told Hugues that if the three of them would sit tight, the gusts should stop within an hour or two.

Straining to catch the words, Hugues listened without saying much. "OK," he screamed into the receiver. "You have my trust."

▲ ▲ ▲

Lower down on the Cesen route, Wilco was having another bad day. He'd been enjoying the view in Camp 3 until he saw Hoselito trudge in, his six-foot, three-inch frame bent over in exhaustion. Hoselito pitched a flimsy tent beside Wilco's. "It looked like a doghouse," Wilco decided, "and I doubt he even anchored it."

But Wilco decided against lecturing Hoselito about the tent. He couldn't force Hoselito to stop climbing. If Hoselito wanted to risk being blown away inside a poorly secured tent, that was his problem. Wilco had already been explicit enough—he would not babysit a straggler. Those who were weak needed to climb down; those who were strong needed to conserve energy. Wilco ducked into his sturdy North Face VE 25 tent, anchored with aluminum snow pickets, and went to sleep.

He woke a few hours later to the sound of howling. The ghost winds from the Shoulder had sheared down the Cesen route to Camp 3, scouring snow and plastering the sides of Wilco's tent. The gusts were threatening to turn his tent into a kite.

Huddled in his tent, Wilco pulled out his satellite phone and called the *Archimedes*, a canal barge docked in Utrecht. On the other end of the line, he heard the voice of Maarten van Eck, the liaison for Ab Maas, a forecaster at the Royal Netherlands Meteorological Institute. Wilco demanded a scientific explanation for the weather and listened as van Eck assured him that the satellite and infrared photos all showed that the jet stream had pulled off K2. The weather would soon improve, Maarten said.

"Fuck you and your predictions!" Wilco shouted into the receiver.

Maarten told Wilco to put on his downsuit and be prepared to descend. "If your tent rips, that's your only option," he said, "but I promise you, tomorrow morning will be gorgeous."

▲ ▲ ▲

"It's something inside me," Shaheen said between gasps and coughs that sounded like gravel in a garbage disposal.

Nadir knelt down. He pulled Shaheen out of the pool of dark vomit, propped him against his pack, and fished for a brown glass vial. He cracked open the sterile seal and poured the liquid into a syringe. Stabbing the tip into Shaheen's deltoid, he pushed the plunger until it hit the number 3 on the barrel, just as Eric had explained. Nadir hoped this injectable steroid, Dexamethasone, would help Shaheen.

He pushed three Tic Tac–shaped antibiotics into Shaheen's mouth, tipped back his jaw, and dribbled some tea onto his tongue, forcing him to swallow.

All this movement was too much. Shaheen vomited and passed out.

"You must get up," Nadir said. He shook Shaheen's shoulders, slapped his cheeks. No response.

At least Shaheen was still breathing. Nadir searched the camp for stragglers but found no one. Radioing down to Base Camp, Nadir reported Shaheen's status to the Pakistani liaison officer, Captain Sabir Ali. "I need help," Nadir said. Shaheen couldn't walk and was too big to carry.

Nadir was on his own. Most climbers were higher up the mountain, and nobody lower down seemed eager to help. Fortunately, the ghost winds over the Cesen ridge stayed off the Abruzzi. Nadir wasn't about to blow away, and the steroid seemed to be working. Shaheen recognized Nadir, said he was feeling better, and tried to stand.

Although Shaheen could walk, he needed help clipping onto the fixed line and barely had the dexterity to use the simple Figure 8 rappel device. After rappelling a steep section and reaching more level ground, Shaheen collapsed. "I tried to motivate him," Nadir recalled. "I told him his clients wouldn't be mad if he made it back alive."

That failed to get Shaheen moving. Praying to Allah, Nadir attached a rope to Shaheen and dragged his body across the snow as though the man were a sled. It was slow going, and, after perhaps an hour, Shaheen awoke. He tried to stand but toppled over, so he inched down the slope on his rear.

When they reached an icy gutter that didn't have a fixed line, Nadir attached a rope to Shaheen, paying it out as Shaheen slid. As the slope steepened more and that tactic became too dangerous, Nadir pounded a snow picket into the slope and lowered Shaheen down.

Shaheen passed out so many times he barely remembered the descent, and Nadir described it as a blur. Nadir's focus was so intense and the exhaustion so pronounced that hours went by like minutes. He refused to let himself rest because he knew he'd never get going again. When he considered how much his legs burned and how far they had to go, he prayed and once again was able to focus.

At one point, Shaheen begged him to quit. The pain was too much, and he was tired of being swung around like a gunnysack. He asked Nadir to leave him. Then, passing out, Shaheen went limp.

Nadir prayed to Allah, injected the last of the steroid into the meat of Shaheen's shoulder, and kept pulling. Shaheen's body scraped against rocks, and he eventually woke again and stood, teetering.

The two were on their own until they reached Advanced Base Camp at the foot of the mountain. By then, Nadir had been awake for more than thirty hours. He collapsed inside an empty tent beside his friend, choked down an energy bar, and passed out. He was too exhausted to check whether or not Shaheen was even alive.

▲ ▲ ▲

Leaving a tent during a gale is generally a bad idea. Mountaineers don't even step outside to relieve themselves—it's too easy for the tent or the climber to get blown away. But Hoselito had no choice. Around 1 a.m. in Camp 2 on the Cesen route, a ferocious blast peeled his "doghouse" from the ice. Hoselito spread his arms and legs against the tent's sides to keep the walls from collapsing. This worked, but not for long. Another gust snapped the poles, and the fabric ripped. All his gear—burner, down jacket, food, fuel, and helmet—flew away. Hoselito squirmed out from the ruins, hunching against the wind. Despite the snow and darkness, he managed to get his bearings and weave a few yards to the nearest tent, a three-person heavy-duty dome staked onto relatively level ground. The wind blasted it and the poles shuddered, but this tent stayed secured.

Hoselito shook the dome, hugging it for balance. He felt for the entrance, unzipped the flap, and craned his neck in. Frigid air and snow spat in behind him. Inside, he saw two men, Wilco and his climbing partner Cas van de Gevel. They were doing their best to sleep. "I knew Wilco disliked me, but even a half-human would let me inside," recalled Hoselito. "I was going to die."

The circumstances did not allow for much conversation. If they had, Hoselito might have heard Wilco explain himself. Wilco might have noted how his tent clung to a platform that barely supported two bodies, that he'd been straightforward about what help he could offer, and that he had wanted Hoselito to turn around for his own safety. Instead, as flurries swept through the open flap, Wilco got right to the point: Get out.

"Of course, I would have helped him if he had no alternative, but for me it was too easy to say, 'Of course, my dear Hoselito, you can sleep with us.' . . . I had warned him before."

Hoselito crawled backward, zipping the flap behind him. He felt his way above Wilco's tent to another staked above it. When Hoselito unzipped the flap and stuck his head in, he saw three men crammed inside: Irishman Ger McDonnell, Sherpa Pemba Gyalje, and Dutchman Jelle Staleman. The men pulled Hoselito's shivering body inside, knowing they'd all have to sleep sitting up.

"He was blue, so we made him tea, and he relaxed," Pemba recalled. Nobody slept much that night.

Through the Bottleneck

Shoulder to Summit
26,000 feet to 28,251 feet
Evening of July 31 to August 1

Planets blinked on one by one. The night before the summit bid was moonless and cloudless, with constellations sprinkled across the sky like loose gems over pitch. Most of the mountaineers were too miserable to notice.

More than thirty men and women had pitched their tents on K2's Shoulder, the frost-tipped saddle of ice where the Abruzzi and Cesen routes converge. Camp 4, the final camp, offered space to spread gear, scoop fresh snow, and shovel platforms, but the altitude was agony. Burning more oxygen than their lungs could draw in, the climbers felt hung over and strung out. Nobody spoke or moved more than necessary.

Crowd control had failed. Delayed by windstorms, most mountaineers now planned to summit in one wave instead of two. If they deferred, the weather window might close, ruining the chance of a lifetime. Twenty-nine people were now aiming for an August 1 summit. Only a handful of climbers had decided to hold back. Among those who remained in the thicker air of Camp 3 were Pasang Lama's cousins, Big Pasang Bhote and Tsering Bhote, and several Koreans.

With crowding came disorganization. Crucial gear had been left behind, including the Italian team's 100-meter rope. When questioned at Camp 4, the Italians' high-altitude porters said they'd misunderstood instructions to carry the coil up. Others besides the Italian team had also failed to bring the supplies they'd promised to carry, but exactly who was responsible and what they'd left behind was unclear. Park Kyeong-hyo had agreed to lead an inventory once everyone arrived at the Shoulder, but he fell asleep instead.

"Rope was missing, ice screws were missing, and I was thinking, 'What the fuck? We're at 8,000 meters' [about 27,000 feet] but we don't even have the essentials," recalled Swedish climber Fredrik Sträng, who had come to make a documentary. With the summit bid due to start at midnight, nothing could be done anyway, so Fredrik tinkered with his video camera. "It was a beautiful night. We were a big team, and I thought, 'We can probably do this. We can probably do anything.'"

Pasang spent the evening preparing oxygen canisters, which were carrot-colored and had the Russian word *poisk* (search) scribbled across the side. Each three-liter aluminum cylinder contained 720 liters of oxygen, weighed five pounds, and cost $385. When turned on, the odorless gas hisses out of the can, past a regulator, and into a face mask originally designed for fighter pilots. Pasang set the flow rate to one liter a minute. He rubbed moisturizer on his clients' cheeks and fitted the masks onto their faces. That night, as his clients sucked bottled oxygen, every inhale and exhale sounded mechanical, a Darth Vader-ish *pwuh-kwah*. Pasang told his clients to turn up the flow from one to two liters per minute when they started climbing in the morning, and each planned to consume three bottles during the twenty-hour trip to and from the summit.

Chhiring wasn't using bottled oxygen, which made his summit gear simpler. In his tent, he slurped two liters of tea and sprinkled sacred salt in his soup. The excitement quivered to his fingertips. With a grin, he asked Eric whether he was ready for the Bottleneck. Sure, Eric replied.

As Eric nodded off to sleep, Chhiring remained awake, anxious, as though he'd never climbed a mountain before. He leaned to his side and cupped his *mala* prayer beads. Blowing on them, rolling them in his palms, he tried to interpret the mood of the goddess. If all went well, he would reach the Bottleneck before sunrise, tag the summit before 2 p.m.—Shaheen's suggested turnaround time—and return to his tent in Camp 4 before dark. Chhiring recited a mantra under his breath. The Death Zone distorted his sense of time, and it seemed as though only minutes had passed when his Suunto wrist altimeter glowed a quarter past midnight. Time to move.

With a rustle, he slid out from the warmth of his sleeping bag and, sloughing off the ice crystals, zipped up his downsuit. Stomping his feet into the heels of his boots, he scooted toward the tent flap, stuck out his legs, and strapped on his crampons. Hoisting his pack, he left to find the rest of the lead team.

They were waiting: Pasang and Jumik of the Korean team; Pemba Gyalje of the Dutch; Muhammad Hussein and Muhammad Khan of the Serbian team; and someone else, a Basque climber Chhiring didn't recognize. Who was this stranger, and where was Shaheen, who had promised to supervise rope placement through the Bottleneck?

The stranger introduced himself as Alberto and explained that he had climbed from Camp 3 in the night. "Shaheen is sick," he said. "He won't be coming."

Chhiring was indignant. "Right when we needed him, Shaheen was gone," he recalled. "We did not like [Shaheen]. All the sherpas were saying things about him that we probably should not have said." Their voices brittle in the dry air, they wondered whether Shaheen had feigned illness to avoid the toughest climbing. They questioned whether the truant had actually summited K2 before.

Even though the Pakistanis didn't speak Nepali, they understood enough from the conversation's tone and a few familiar words: The Nepalis were ridiculing them. "It was unjust," recalled Muhammad Hussein. "K2 is our mountain, and Shaheen is our brother, the greatest climber in the region. He taught us to show respect to Buddhists and other foreigners, but the sherpas didn't respect me." Nobody bothered to ask him, but Muhammad had summited K2 in 2004 and was familiar with the route and the rope-setting in the Bottleneck. "They assumed I didn't know where I was going," he said, "and dismissed what I had to say."

Or they would have, if they understood him at all. With Shaheen gone, nobody could translate from Urdu to English. Discussion was disjointed, split between Nepali and Pakistani factions, and when Alberto tried to take charge, he was not recognized as their leader.

Resentment, language barriers, and oxygen deprivation all contributed to the flawed decision-making that followed. The lead team members carried willow wands, but nobody used them to mark the trail. Worse, the lead team squandered rope. Jumik directed the Pakistanis to set lines along moderate terrain, where climbers could use their ice axes to arrest a fall. Unaware of the rope shortage, the Bhotes were accustomed to the procedure on Everest, where, on the north side, new rope is laterally fixed from the bottom of the North Col to the summit, with only a single break at Camp 1. Jumik probably didn't realize that trying to set rope all the way up to K2's summit was a mistake.

Muhammad Hussein did. "Save the rope for the bad places," he tried to tell Jumik. But nobody could translate his warning, and "nobody cared until our situation was obvious," Muhammad recalled. The lead team didn't have much line to begin with, and soon it was gone.

"All of a sudden we were asking each other, 'Do you have any more rope?'" recalled Pasang. "We did not understand. How could we run out? Where had it all gone?" They checked their packs, argued, and backtracked, plucking out line already set and anchoring it higher up. They'd hoped to reach the Bottleneck before sunrise. When the barbed horizon flushed red, the lead team was still climbing along the Shoulder.

Back at high camp, the mountaineers tracked the progress of the lead team with binoculars and radio calls. The climbers had planned to leave camp before dawn, but, seeing that the lead team was off to a bad start, several delayed their departure. By sunrise, Nick Rice still hadn't left his tent. He had spilled a pot of snowmelt on his gear and was drying a soggy sock over a burner. By the time he had finished, Nick decided that August 1 wasn't going to be the day he would reach the summit of K2. He'd lost too much time. The mountain would still be there next season. "I wanted to make sure I would be, too," he recalled. A simple mistake—sloshing a pot of water—probably saved his life.

▲ ▲ ▲

Above the Bottleneck of K2, a restless glacier appears to be lunging off a cliff. For centuries it has inched forward, midleap, creating formations known as *seracs*, massive hunks of ice that frequently calve. The mountaineers had been training their binoculars on these seracs for weeks, evaluating the gutter below.

American mountaineer Ed Viesturs calls this section The Motivator, because the seracs overhanging the gutter inspire climbers to get the hell out of there. Nazir Sabir, who pioneered K2's West-Southwest Ridge, calls the channel below the seracs Death Throat, because it resembles a giant's gullet. Most people call this narrow passage the Bottleneck. The Bottleneck is not the end of danger. Above it, the route turns left onto the Traverse, a steep, exposed slog up K2's southeast face. But the Bottleneck's nearly vertical, 30-story rise is the

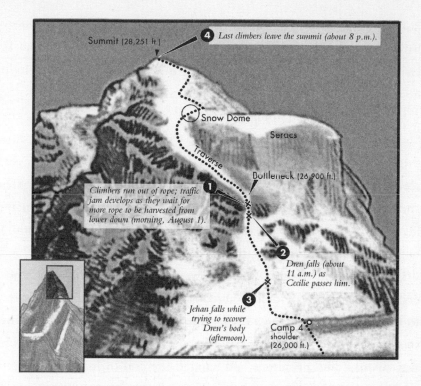

Summit (28,251 ft.)

④ Last climbers leave the summit (about 8 p.m.).

Snow Dome

Seracs

Bottleneck (28,900 ft.)

Traverse

Climbers run out of rope; traffic
jam develops as they wait for
more rope to be harvested from
lower down (morning, August 1).

①

②
Dren falls (about
11 a.m.) as
Cecilie passes him.

③

Jehan falls while
trying to recover
Dren's body
(afternoon).

Camp 4
shoulder
(26,000 ft.)

Camp 4 to Summit: A lead team of Balti, Bhote, Sherpa, and Shimshali climbers broke trail and set ropes toward the summit. Language gaps and miscommunication led to problems with the ropes, which caused a deadly delay in the Bottleneck.

most stomach churning section of the climb. Falling ice and traffic are the killers. The Bottleneck only lets climbers squeeze through one at a time, in a queue that moves only as fast as the slowest legs will allow.

By the time the lead team had reached the Bottleneck, an impatient, single-file line had formed behind them. "I was waiting and waiting, and everybody was waiting," Wilco said. "And the Bottleneck is not the place where you want to wait."

▲ ▲ ▲

Several stories above Wilco, Alberto stood near the front of the line; around 9 a.m., he pulled ahead of the pack. Hard, blue ice, its air bubbles expelled by compression, rejected his pick, and loose snow balled beneath his crampons, but Alberto advanced up the Bottleneck, twisting in ice screws and tying in rope until he had climbed so high he vanished from view.

Skeptical about clipping onto the lines Alberto had set, the Sherpas on the lead team hung back. They were accustomed to the thicker lines for the Everest crowd. Alberto's Endura five-millimeter seemed recklessly thin, unable to support the weight of several bodies and unsuitable for jumars rated for eight-millimeter rope. Chhiring decided to set a secondary rope. He placed it parallel to the Endura but ran out after about 50 yards.

So Chhiring backtracked, weaving through the line of climbers and once again plucking out rope from lower slopes. He waved to some stragglers on the Korean team. They were squatting in the snow, unclipped, observing his gyrations. Chhiring then made his way up, past the spectators, and handed the coil to Jumik. This line went another 75 feet, more than halfway, but another 100 feet would be needed to reach safer ground.

Chhiring turned back to collect more rope, but when he looked down, he saw that fifteen climbers had clipped onto the lines directly below him. They were advancing through the steepest area of the Bottleneck, forming a head-to-toe snarl. Chhiring wasn't sure why they were advancing. Without fixed lines, they wouldn't be able to get far.

Chhiring knew they shouldn't all be weighing on the same anchor. One falling block could bowl everyone over. He stepped to the side, twisted in an ice screw, and clipped himself onto it, hanging to the right of the oncoming train. Others saw Chhiring's logic. Pasang, Wilco, and three others followed, unclipping from the main line and free-climbing toward a rock ramp.

The climbers waited, hanging in place. More rope was needed, but nobody seemed to know who might pass it forward, and the lead climbers couldn't navigate the gridlock below. As the sun beat down, the men peeled their jackets to their waists. They praised the weather gods for bringing such a glorious day and whined about the holdup. The men sucked in the moistureless air and changed their oxygen cylinders. Those climbing without oxygen tried to ignore the drumming inside their skulls. Every once in a while, an ice chunk fell from the seracs and bounced down the slope.

Eric had turned around hours earlier, giving up on the mountain and his dream of reaching the summit. Without his friend, Chhiring became restless. "Instead of sweating, I started to shiver," he recalled. It felt as though the goddess were breathing down his neck. He had to get moving, but where? About to free-climb, he noticed that Wilco was already giving it a try.

The Dutchman soon slipped, and he whisked toward Chhiring. "I didn't have time to blink," Chhiring recalled. His left hand shot out to grab Wilco's harness. His right hand seized the collar of Wilco's downsuit. Then, out of hands, Chhiring body-slammed him, pressing Wilco into the ice.

Wilco slid only six feet. His right crampon nicked Chhiring's side. The left ripped into Iso Planić, a Serb below them, and released a flurry of feathers from Iso's down jacket.

Swiveling, Wilco heaved his axe into the ice. The pick sank in and held. Wilco clenched the axe and leaned hard, pulling himself to a stop. Winded, the men could only nod. The slide had been harmless.

The next one wouldn't be. Below them, the newlyweds, Cecilie and Rolf, were maneuvering around the clog of climbers, carrying about 50 yards of rope harvested from the lower slopes. Cecilie, pushing herself up the Bottleneck, passed Chhiring, Wilco, and Iso to her right. Continuing, she reached Dren Mandić, who unclipped. "He was being a gentleman," said Hoselito, Dren's friend, who thought he'd unclipped to let Cecilie pass. If so, it was a fatal courtesy.

Cecilie asked Dren to stow the loose rope in the top of her pack.

She ducked down and around; he pivoted up and over. This choreography jerked the fixed line, according to Chhiring and Muhammad Hussein, who were a few yards away. The rope slapped into Dren, pushing him off-balance. He lost his footing, then his grip. Both he and Cecilie plunged.

Cecilie shrieked. Her jumar caught, and she fell only a few feet. Dren, with no rope to stop him, tried to bear-hug her. Unable to hold onto her, he dropped, feet first on his stomach, his face raking the Bottleneck. Frantic, he flailed at the snow with his arms, trying to self-arrest.

For two stories, Dren slid. Then his crampons snagged a rock and spun him around like the second hand of a clock. When he had turned a full 180 degrees on his stomach, his leg released and he took a nosedive down the Bottleneck. His helmeted head crunched into a rock ramp, launching him into the air. Somersaulting, he plunged another 10 stories and smacked into a spongy mound of snow, off-route.

Above him, the mountaineers froze. It happened so fast that some barely saw it. Stunned, Chhiring watched Dren's legs squirm, sticking out of the snow.

Chhiring had never seen anyone die on a mountain before. Dren had to live, Chhiring rationalized. A week earlier, he'd watched this man kneel on the moraine to admire tiny flowers sprouting from a clump of moss. The goddess would never exact revenge from a sentient being who appreciated even the smallest life, a man with Snoopy strapped to his pack.

Chhiring radioed Eric in Camp 4, telling him an injured man needed a doctor. After the call, he shut his eyes and looked away from the mound where Dren lay. Chhiring visualized Dawa and his daughters and thought of Dren's family somewhere, not yet knowing. It was past 11 a.m., and Chhiring knew he'd have to climb well past the planned turnaround time. Contemplating his options, he gazed at the seracs above, "softening like yak butter in the sun."

▲ ▲ ▲

Acoustics distorted Cecilie's scream into a maniacal wail that echoed off the Shoulder. The noise startled Fredrik in Camp 4. Clutching his thirteen-pound Sony video camera, the Swedish filmmaker opened his tent flap and peered through the zoom lens, using it as a telescope. Focusing on the Bottleneck, he could see the line of climbers proceeding, one by one, like an ant army. Fixing the coil of line that Cecilie had delivered, they were "continuing on as if nothing had happened," he recalled. Fredrik scanned for something crumpled in the bright snow and shouted to Eric, who was on the radio with Chhiring.

"I grabbed an oxygen set, water, and a survival bag," along with the video camera to shoot footage, Fredrik recalled. Eric took a medical kit. Only midway up the slope did they confirm the fallen man's identity over the radio. "Dren was my friend in Base Camp," Fredrik recalled. "We were always laughing, cracking jokes." Fredrik climbed faster, pulling ahead. "I wanted to see my friend alive."

After climbing for about ninety minutes, Fredrik saw two Serbs, Iso Planić and Pedja Zagorac, dragging a body in a red bivy sack. "You don't want to know what his face looked like," Fredrik recalled.

Iso and Pedja explained what had happened. It had taken them fifteen minutes to climb down to Dren. By the time they'd reached him, he was no longer breathing. Iso had pumped Dren's chest and forced air into his mouth, but CPR couldn't revive him. Dren's pulse was now long gone. The least they could do was take his body back to his mother in Serbia.

Fredrik, pressing a finger to Dren's carotid artery, confirmed that his friend was dead. "I was mad as hell. I was going to bring him back alive. I was committed to that. It was a perfect day, and I was staring up at that blue sky thinking this should not be happening on a day like this."

Iso and Pedja wrapped the Serbian flag, intended for the summit photo, around Dren's battered head. "I was aware that it would be way better if someone cold-blooded took over the recovery," Iso recalled. "We were in shock. Fredrik had experience in rescues. He was fresh and rested." The Serbians wanted his help.

Fredrik wavered. "I do not support the idea of trying to recover a body from the Death Zone," he said. Transporting the dead puts the living at risk. Still, Dren deserved a dignified burial, and it was hard to say no to that. "I was asked to help to bring down my friend to Camp 4, and I agreed."

He stowed his camera in his pack, leaving the audio on, and bound Dren's ankles. He coiled more line around Dren's torso like a corset. From this makeshift harness, he tied two towlines, which radiated from Dren's body in a *V*. Pulling these leashes, the men sledded Dren's body along the ice toward the Shoulder.

As they inched the bundle forward, they spotted Jehan Baig rappelling toward them. The Pakistani "seemed disoriented," recalled Fredrik. He moved like a man in a squall, stumbling but somehow staying on his feet.

Jehan shook his head when he caught up with the others and extended a hand, grabbing the towline. He joined Fredrik to pull the front line; Iso and Pedja pulled the back.

Soon they reached an icy slope that might have been a blue-square ski run, except that it flattened before a sheer cliff. Fixed lines had been strung through this stretch in the early morning. Now, the ropes were gone, removed for use in the Bottleneck.

Trying to lower Dren's body and simultaneously keep it on the route, the men payed out rope a few feet at a time. The corpse had made it roughly halfway down the slope when several things happened at once.

Jehan lost his footing and crashed into Fredrik's right side, knocking him off-balance. Without saying anything, Jehan slid down the slope on his rear and hooked an arm around Dren's body, holding fast.

Meanwhile, Fredrik tipped forward, and his shin slapped into the rope as though it were a tripwire. He flipped, face first. Fredrik righted himself and dug in his crampons to gain purchase on the ice. It worked—Fredrik didn't slide—but the twist of his body wound the rope around his right calf, cinching it like a butcher's wire.

Fredrik clawed the slope. He couldn't hold the position. The rope sawed into his leg as the combined weight of Dren and Jehan pulled down on him.

"Release the rope!" Fredrik yelled.

Jehan said nothing.

"Release the rope!"

Jehan kept silent.

"We're screaming at the Pakistani in three different languages—Swedish, English, Serbian—and I'm panicking," recalled Fredrik. "If [Jehan] had let go, all he would have to do was use his ice axe to self-arrest, but he wouldn't let go."

After roughly one minute, Jehan finally did as he was told. He released his grip around Dren's body and started to slide, as still as a corpse.

Limp and silent, Jehan gained speed until his crampons caught, and, in a sickening reprise of Dren's choreography, he spun around headfirst. He began to slow down as the slope flattened, and it looked as though he might stop on his own before the edge.

Eric and Muhammad Hussein, who had arrived to help, shouted at Jehan, ordering him to wake up and save himself. All he had to do was fan out his body. But still he crept forward. "Maybe it was a heart attack," recalled Muhammad. "Jehan had placed himself in God's hands."

The rink at the bottom was slick. Jehan had just enough momentum when he reached it to go sliding across the ice, barely moving forward. His head went over the ledge first. As his legs followed, he seemed to wake from his trance. He kicked and yelped, disappearing over the precipice.

The men kept shouting after he was gone, and the screams captured on Fredrik's tape suggest that they had trouble believing what had just happened. "What the hell is this?" Fredrik cried. "I came up here to help you guys." Unable to see where Jehan had landed, they knew the drop was about 1,000 feet. Trying to recover one corpse had already produced a second. Stupefied, Iso and Pedja swaddled Dren in extra clothes. Fredrik pounded a stake into the slope and tied the towlines to it. Dren's body was left to hang there until the mountain claimed it.

Returning to the Shoulder in the direction of camp, the men broke down, sobbing in the snow. "The summit wasn't worth it anymore," Iso said. "Everything seemed so senseless."

▲ ▲ ▲

At 2:21 p.m., the moon, cruising through space, barged between the earth and the sun. Its dusty body whittled daylight into a crescent. Jehan's mother, Nazib, was in Shimshal. Around the time of her son's death, a symbol of her faith was branded on the sun. The horizon glowed tangerine. Far to the north, a perfect corona gave the illusion of a hole in the sky.

Above K2, the eclipse wasn't total. A small slice of sun darkened for 121 minutes. Some mountaineers, still in the Bottleneck, wore yellow-tinted goggles and missed the change in light. "A solar eclipse is an omen," said Chhiring, "but I didn't see this one." Most were unaware that K2 had claimed a second victim. They only knew that their pace was too slow. To reach the summit, they would need to descend in darkness. Nonetheless, the nineteen climbers in the Bottleneck continued upward.

Each came up with tactical reasons for disregarding the 2 p.m. turnaround time. Marco, the Italian, mentally compiled a list of mountaineers who had gotten away with a late summit, including K2's original Italian conquerors, Achille Compagnoni and Lino Lacedelli. He considered how his mentor, Agostino da Polenza, had survived an overnight bivouac in the Death Zone. Sure, some of these legendary mountaineers had lost digits, but all had survived, and Marco was convinced that he, too, could make it down in one piece.

Wilco used applied physics to justify his decision. Descending at night, he concluded, would actually be safer—the sun wouldn't be heating the seracs and causing them to calve. "It seemed almost illogical that ice chunks would cleave off [at night] when the temperature was decreasing." He'd spent years preparing for K2, had done everything he could to reduce the risk, and wasn't going to turn around just because the weak were holding him back. "I knew I'd regret it if I came home without a successful climb."

Chhiring felt comforted by the crowd. If scores of less able climbers were heading to the summit, why shouldn't he? The weather was stable. The fixed lines would guide him down in the dark. "I'll never get another shot at K2," he told himself. But Dren's death had persuaded him that the mountain goddess was no ally. He tried to ignore the queasiness that radiated down his throat and pooled in his stomach.

Thinking about the goddess reminded him of the rice and barley in his pocket. Still suspended from an ice screw beside the Bottleneck, he removed the Ziploc bag and flung the contents into the air. They shimmered in space. Suddenly a gust of wind grabbed the grains and spat them back in his face. The offering had been rejected.

▲ ▲ ▲

It took until 2 p.m.—the planned turnaround time—for the members of the Flying Jump to break through the Bottleneck. "We were too slow," Pasang recalled, "and we were burning through our oxygen too fast." But he didn't raise these concerns with his boss. Mr. Kim had already been clear enough: Pasang wasn't hired to retreat; he was hired to lead. In this spirit, Pasang, now in front of the pack, blazed the trail above the Bottleneck. Seventeen people followed him.

Trying to make up for lost time, Pasang pushed himself but struggled with the terrain. He was now on the Traverse, the steep, exposed ridge that cuts under the seracs, tracing the mountain's southeast face. As he climbed, his crampons scraped and clicked against the granite. To maintain purchase, Pasang had to deliberate over each step. "I told myself concentrate, concentrate, concentrate. Only think about the next step."

About two hours later, he reached the Snow Dome, the lump of ice that bridges into snowfield below the summit. Pasang waded in and sank to his hips. Plowing forward, he checked his oxygen pressure gauge and turned the flow to low, below one liter a minute. He climbed faster, probing for weak snow bridges. It was 4 p.m.

His legs pumped forward, making a deep furrow in the snow, but he wasn't on solid ground. One of Pasang's boots punched through the crust, the ice around the ankle broke away, and his leg dropped into a crevasse.

His reactions were quick. As he sank, Pasang fanned out his elbows, spreading his weight. He dropped slowly, and by the time he stopped sinking, he'd been swallowed only to the waist. One boot dangled into space. Keeping his weight on his arms, Pasang wriggled left and right, flipped his knees to his chest, and belly-flopped over the lip of the crevasse. He clawed himself out and away.

Once standing, he patted his body to see if he'd lost any gear. It was all there, but his thoughts were scattered. The dip into the crevasse had left him shaken. If the crust he'd stepped on had been any thinner, he'd have fallen inside a splinter of ice and shattered his limbs. Unable to clamber up or make himself heard, he might have waited in the stillness to die.

Pasang wanted to ensure that this didn't happen to anyone, so he pulled out a wand with a flag, marking the snow bridge he had broken. Before starting the climb again, he scanned his surroundings. Ahead of him, a solitary red suit was tromping down the mountain. Pasang recognized Alberto Zerain, the Basque climber on the lead team who had surged ahead of everyone at the Bottleneck. Alberto flashed a zinc-oxide–streaked grin, and Pasang recognized the look: summit glow. "I was thinking, 'How is this possible?'" Pasang recalled. Alberto had soloed up the rest of K2, topping out at 3 p.m., hours ahead of everyone else. Now he was on his way down. "That guy made K2 look easy."

Alberto dug his heels into the slope, advancing on Pasang, but he was approaching a crevasse. "I tried to get his attention," Pasang recalled. "I waved my hands and yelled, 'Not this side! Crevasses! Not this side!'"

Alberto waved back but also stepped forward. The buttress beneath the snow bridge gave under his weight, and he lurched in. Unfazed, he wriggled out like a worm, and, a moment later, was descending again, digging his heels into the slope just as before.

When the two men met, Pasang shook Alberto's hand, congratulating him for a successful summit. Although there had been radio chatter, Pasang didn't brief him about the deaths in the Bottleneck. It would have ruined the moment. "If I had witnessed those falls, I wouldn't have cared about the mountain anymore," Alberto later said. "I'd have lost the pleasure." Both men were in a hurry, and they went in opposite directions.

Pasang envied Alberto, who was heading down to hot soup and a sleeping bag. Pasang watched him weave through the pack of climbers. As Alberto passed, several Flying Jump members motioned to him as if asking directions on a motorway. They wanted to know how many more hours to the top. Alberto shrugged, barely slowing. "I wasn't going to try to predict how long it would take them to reach the summit," he recalled. Climbers move at different speeds. Alberto assessed their pace and wanted to suggest a U-turn, but he hesitated. Turning around was a personal decision, he decided, between a mountaineer and his maker.

It was 4:45 p.m., and Pasang realized he was wasting time watching Alberto. Annoyed with himself, he turned away and resumed kicking steps. The summit reared ahead of him like a cobra's hood. Sundown would bring a temperature plunge that wouldn't stop until dawn. Pasang was late, at a time when every second counted. The slower he went, the deeper he would climb into the night.

▲ ▲ ▲

After so much fantasy and anticipation, the summit was unglamorous. When he summited at 5:30 p.m., Pasang stood atop the pinnacle of a 100-foot snow ramp, with a ditch to the west where exhausted climbers had defecated. That was it. Unlike the summit of Everest, no prayer flags lay in weathered clumps. The snow beneath his boots looked like any other snow. Nevertheless, Pasang recalled, "it was the most perfect place."

Stepping to the highest point of the ridge, he slung off his pack, crowed and whooped. For an instant, exhaustion evaporated. The panorama dizzied him. The sun was slipping like a brass coin into a pocket behind K2, which cast a triangular shadow into the dark hills of Asia. A dusky band of purple swept around the horizon, and shadows snuffed out the lacy cornices of Chogolisa and Masherbrum. Down the Baltoro Glacier, the scree-paved glaciers at Concordia merged like a freeway interchange. At his back was China; to his face,

Pakistan; and above, infinity. At 28,251 feet, Pasang was the highest human on earth.

He pulled a Sony camcorder from his pack and switched it on. He panned over the violet shoal of clouds and peaks and focused on the climbers marching up the summit ridge: his cousin Jumik; his boss, Mr. Kim; and the rest of the Flying Jump: Ms. Go, Park Kyeong-hyo, Hwang Dong-jin, and Kim Hyo-gyeong. Just ahead of the Flying Jump were two Norwegians, Lars Nessa and Cecilie, who had climbed the last stretch without her husband. In all, eighteen people topped out on August 1. As the sun set, the celebrations continued for as long as ninety minutes.

Wilco, the irritable Dutchman, replaced his pout with a beatific grin. He bear-hugged his teammate Ger, who howled: "We are on the summit of Kay-Toooo!"

Mr. Kim lit a cigarette, took a drag, and passed it to Jumik. Lars put on bunny ears and hopped. Karim prayed, taking in the divine sweep of earth and sky.

"I'll never leave you again," said Hugues, into a satellite phone. His girlfriend was listening. "I'm finished now. This time next year, our family will be at the beach!" He trained a camera on his teeth to satisfy the dentist in Lyon. Both Karim and Hugues were losing it. "They had used up their bottled oxygen and barely responded to our congratulations," Wilco recalled.

Coughing and crying, the climbers yanked pageantry from their packs. Ger, the first Irishman to summit K2, dropped on one knee and hoisted Ireland's tricolor flag in triumph. Chhiring, who summited at 6:37 p.m., unfurled his flag, kneeling with the double pennant before him like an apron.

Last on the summit, Marco waved a ski pole strung with the flags of Italy and Pakistan, plus two pennants representing his sponsors, the Métis temp agency and Credito Valtellinese bank. In the weak light,

Marco removed the shell of his glove and punched twelve numerals into his sat-phone keypad. Battery life was short, so he kept it brief as he told his banker, Miro Fiordi, general director of Credito Valtellinese, the news. The bank's sponsorship investment had paid off.

Like Marco, others felt similar obligations to sponsors who had subsidized their climb. Mr. Kim and Ms. Go modeled Kolon Sport, high fashion for 28,251 feet; Chhiring promoted ColdAvenger face masks; Wilco's mango-colored downsuit displayed the triangular logo of Norit Group, a water filtration company that had provided a healthy six-figure contribution. Nearly every summit photo contained a logo or product placement. These mountaineers documented their triumph not only for posterity but also for publicity. The photos advertised their businesses, their skills, and their sponsors.

Fredrik, part of the team sponsored by ColdAvenger, had once estimated how much summits could be worth. On his website—under the heading "The Value to You!"—he explained to potential sponsors that a $120,000 investment could generate a $4.3 million public-relations value and brand recognition. "We can guarantee a PR ratio of 10 times the invested money," he wrote, basing his estimate on the value of the resulting advertising. Corporate interests had been speculating on a K2 summit. On August 1, they hit pay dirt.

The high-altitude porters and the sherpas also cashed in when their clients topped out. For each mountaineer they ushered up, they earned a bonus of $1,000 or more. This money encouraged them to push clients who were unfit to continue. "When your family needs that money," Pasang acknowledged, "sometimes you don't insist a weak climber turn back."

But summits also have a cost, and by 7:45 p.m. on August 1, the human price was becoming apparent. The Flying Jump started lurching down the mountain like lushes leaving a bar—reveling, swearing, and puking on their boots. The summit party was over. Now they needed to find the way home.

PART III

DESCENT

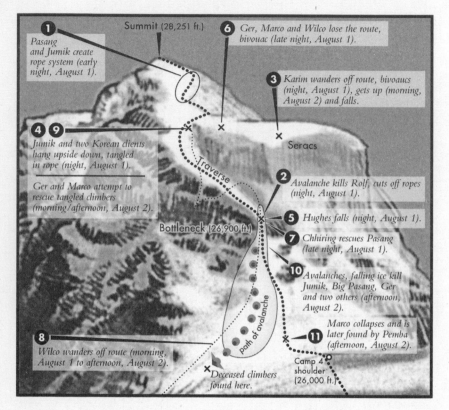

1 Pasang and Jumik create rope system (early night, August 1).

Summit (28,251 ft.)

6 Ger, Marco and Wilco lose the route, bivouac (late night, August 1).

3 Karim wanders off route, bivoaucs (night, August 1), gets up (morning, August 2) and falls.

4 **9** Jumik and two Korean clients hang upside down, tangled in rope (night, August 1).

Ger and Marco attempt to rescue tangled climbers (morning/afternoon, August 2).

Seracs

Traverse

2 Avalanche kills Rolf, cuts off ropes (night, August 1).

Bottleneck (26,900 ft.)

5 Hughes falls (night, August 1).

7 Chhiring rescues Pasang (late night, August 1).

10 Avalanches, falling ice kill Jumik, Big Pasang, Ger and two others (afternoon, August 2).

Marco collapses and is later found by Pemba (afternoon, August 2). **11**

8 Wilco wanders off route (morning, August 1 to afternoon, August 2).

Path of avalanche

Deceased climbers found here.

Camp 4 shoulder (26,000 ft.)

Summit to Camp 4: As the climbers descended in the gathering darkness, an avalanche severed the ropes through the Bottleneck. Some climbers tried to make it down without the fixed lines; others spent the night in the Death Zone.

10

Escape from the Summit

As Pasang left the summit, his head throbbed so relentlessly he could hear his pulse in his ears. Ahead of him, Mr. Kim squatted in the snow, waving his arms like a wizard casting spells. He had run out of oxygen.

Going off the bottle is harder than never having been on it at all. In the best case, you're slammed by extreme exhaustion. The thin air can knock you out, just as it does to a fighter pilot with a failing oxygen mask. Cerebral or pulmonary edema can set in, filling the brain and lungs with fluid. In a worst case, the body revolts with acute vasospasm as arteries constrict, cutting blood supply to the organs. Within three minutes of acute vasospasm, cells wither in the heart, lungs, kidneys, liver, and brain. Within twenty minutes, the organs degrade to medical waste, and the climber does too.

Pasang could see headlamps fanning out below. Sucking a guilty breath from his regulator, he trudged forward and crouched beside Mr. Kim. Pasang's boss was too tired to waste words. Kim tapped the side of his oxygen canister and pointed to the gauge, which registered empty. Pasang understood what was expected. He gestured for Mr. Kim to hold still. Kneeling down, he detached Kim's empty cylinder and swapped it with his own.

His oxygen now gone, Pasang braced for the shock. It hit, but he remained functional, still able to climb and think. It may have helped that he was Bhote—a carrier of genotypic variants for NOS3, a gene that codes for an enzyme that helps modulate blood flow to the lungs—and was perhaps less susceptible to acute vasospasm. His clients, however, were at higher risk.

He and the rest of the Flying Jump had at least three hours to go before reaching the fixed lines on the Traverse, so Pasang decided to take a shortcut. He descended in a straight shot toward the Snow Dome, the massive lump that signaled the start of the Traverse and the fixed lines. The new route allowed the climbers to bypass the summit ridge, but the Snow Dome also had a sheer drop on one side. With no moonlight or stakes for direction, there was no discernible path. Climbers scattered in the darkness.

Pasang spotted a man veering left above the Snow Dome. It was Karim. He never turned around. Now heading away from the Traverse, he would end up on top of the seracs; instead of descending toward the Bottleneck, he'd climb high above it.

If the descent continued like this, Pasang knew delirium would pull his team apart. He herded the Flying Jump together and devised a plan to keep them from stumbling and falling. Pasang tied a Figure-8-on-a-bight, the first climbing knot he'd ever learned, and looped it over his axe. Plunging his axe into the snow, he handed the rest of the rope to Jumik, who uncoiled it while descending ahead of the group. When the line payed out, Jumik tied it to his axe, anchored in the snow. The rope, now strung between two axes, resembled a clothesline.

It led in the direction of the Traverse. The climbers gravitated toward this rope, clipping in and clutching on. Once they'd reached Jumik's end of the clothesline, Pasang pulled out his axe, coiled the slack around his elbow, and raced ahead of the pack. Pasang and Jumik created and re-created this rope system about a dozen times, lower and lower toward the Snow Dome.

It served to guide the group, more or less. The rope caught the climbers when they slipped and kept them from making the disastrous left turn that had led Karim to the crown of the seracs. "It was saving lives," said Chhiring, who used it. But the system was slow. After each step, men slumped over their ice axes or ski poles to rest and shivered for warmth. By sea-level standards, the night was frigid, about minus four degrees Fahrenheit; by K2 standards, it was moderate. On an ordinary evening, the jet stream would have tossed them to China, but August 1 was relatively windless, so the cold merely seared exposed flesh.

As Pasang anchored the last stretch of rope, he thought about his axe. More climbers, all clearly in need, had attached their Figure 8s to the line dangling from it. Pasang couldn't recover his axe without dismantling a rope system that was serving as a lifeline.

Shivering, he waited, punching his fists out for warmth. More figures materialized in the darkness and attached to the line. Occasionally one climber stalled, forcing those behind him to wait. Pasang's headlamp dimmed, and he was no closer to getting his axe back. "I had to make the decision: Take the axe or leave it." He radioed his boss for approval to ditch the axe and descend.

Mr. Kim agreed that the axe wasn't crucial: With fixed lines through the diagonal ridge, the Traverse, and the Bottleneck, Pasang could manage without one. Pasang started down and soon overtook Jumik, leaving him behind with several clients. Descending without an axe would be tough, Pasang thought, but not deadly.

▲ ▲ ▲

Rolf was shivering uncontrollably when his wife reached him, but he smiled when he saw her. Debilitated by altitude, he had waited 300 vertical feet below the summit as Cecilie reached the top at 5:45 p.m. Now, about an hour later, the newlyweds were reunited. Lars, the third member of the Norwegian team, videotaped their exchange, one of their last:

"Are you freezing?" Cecilie asked.

"Not especially," her husband replied.

Lars had removed the bunny ears he'd worn on the summit. He zoomed in on Rolf's face. "Long day?" he asked.

They'd been climbing for seventeen hours, but Rolf's tone sounded as though he were denouncing a desk job: "More than average." With shaking fingers, he manipulated a chalky tablet of Dexamethasone, trying to bring the steroid to his lips. He dropped it, and the tablet hit the ice. "Oh, hell," he said, "it broke."

The newlyweds were the first to start down after Alberto. Behind them, Hugues seemed to be applying risk assessment: Out of oxygen, in pursuit of thicker air, he was moving down rapidly. Next in line was Cas van de Gevel, of the Dutch team, who, climbing even faster, caught up with Hugues along the Traverse. "It never occurred to me to ask Hugues, 'Where's your porter? Where's Karim?'" Cas recalled. "When you see two people climbing together, then one is descending alone. . . . I would have known to ask if we'd been at sea level." But the problem eluded him in the rarefied air.

Hugues stepped aside. "You are quicker," he said. "You go first."

Cas nodded, slid around Hugues, and resumed his descent.

When Cas arrived at the mouth of the Bottleneck, he was 30 feet in front of the Frenchman. That's when he heard a noise—a scratching, like a rat in a wall. Cas looked back. Hugues, who had probably snagged a crampon, shot toward him. "I couldn't see his face at such high speed," Cas recalled. He only recognized the yellow-orange blur of Hugues's downsuit whizzing past within an arm's length. The insurance salesman with dazzling teeth was gone.

▲ ▲ ▲

Just as a sealed glass jar full of water shatters when left in a freezer, refreezing meltwater in the seracs' fissures was expanding, wedging apart the glacier's interior cracks. As the pressure built, the seracs let off slow, elastic, electrified *zoings*. A percussion of pops, snaps, creaks, and booms accompanied the breaking ice. These sounds—high and low, short and long, soft and loud—overlapped in rhythm.

Pasang's cousin Jumik was tied to two exhausted clients, wading through snowdrifts. As he approached the Traverse, the seracs hulked above him. As the *zoings* amplified, Jumik would have moved as fast as possible, frantically dragging his clients along, urging them to rush. But the two Koreans with Jumik could barely walk. Speed wouldn't have mattered much, anyway. To avoid the falling ice, the three men needed a miracle.

The mountain announced its intentions with a drum roll: *Crrrrrk-crrrrk-crrrk-crrk-crk-ck.* The men would have looked up as the seracs crumbled, dropping chunks large enough to transform the terrain. One of these chunks sped toward Jumik, gouging out fixed lines. The three men, still attached to these fixed lines, were yanked downward.

Jumik's boot tore off. His gloves flew away. One Korean's German Rollei camera split open and his skull crunched. Down jackets ripped open, snowing feathers. Jumik may have thought he was going to die and been surprised when he didn't. One of the anchors above him held. The rope cinched tight. The three men jerked to a standstill, coming to rest on a precipitous snow slope.

Dangling from the line's end, Jumik hung upside down, blood pooling in his lungs and head. The rope had wound around Jumik's trunk, binding him, and he was too tangled to adjust his clothing or cover his bare hands. Squirming free would have been impossible, and he would have only been able to see the ice two inches in front of his face.

▲ ▲ ▲

At 9 p.m., about 50 yards from the Bottleneck, Rolf was hit by a serac fall. As chunks of hard ice sailed over the Traverse, one came so fast he had no chance to shout. It must have hit him head-on, severing the rope and burying him under tons of ice.

Twenty yards behind him, the tremor knocked his wife flat. Cecilie slid several feet, but the fixed line caught her. As she scrambled to stand again, the batteries shot out of her headlamp. Cecilie clutched the rope with a gloved hand, felt the limp end, and realized it no longer linked her to her husband. She scanned the slope for the glow of his headlamp. It had disappeared.

Cecilie was stunned, too horrified to move. This was supposed to be her honeymoon. From behind, Lars touched her shoulder. Cecilie stayed frozen. Lars said something as he stepped around her, but Cecilie heard him as though she were underwater. Dazed, she watched him shuffle in front. Lars examined the cord cut by the ice fall, pulled a 50-meter coil of thin rope from his pack, and secured it to one of the surviving ice screws. Then he rappelled down until his headlamp dimmed to a pinpoint.

Cecilie remained fixed in place. Without Lars's light, darkness enveloped her. The ice creaked and the breeze whistled. She wondered why she was there. "I hadn't seriously prepared myself for coming home alone without Rolf," she recalled. "It was not something I could have prepared for. It's a pain you can't simulate." She couldn't climb—she didn't want to. The desolation was complete and unbearable.

Lars's voice jolted her out of contemplation. "Come here!" his cheerful tenor exclaimed from below. Had he found Rolf? Cecilie knew that climbers had survived worse falls. Maybe her husband had landed relatively unharmed.

"Rolf?" she yelled. "Rolf!" Her hope revived, she rappelled down the Bottleneck, repeating her husband's name and shouting at Lars to tell her more. When the rope ended, Cecilie focused on climbing so she could reach her husband sooner. Axe, front point, front point. Axe, front point, front point. *Chuck, shink, shink. Chuck, shink, shink.*

She couldn't see her boots without the headlamp. Slipping once, she heaved her weight onto the axe and stopped herself. As she got closer to Lars, he shined his headlamp to guide her down. Finally, she could see Lars's face. He looked crushed.

"Where's Rolf?" she asked him, out of breath.

Lars wouldn't lie to her now. "Rolf is gone."

Despite the pain, Cecilie appreciated what her friend had done: "He had tricked me into descending." Still, she held out hope that Lars was mistaken. Maybe Rolf was alive, somewhere below the Bottleneck. She kept calling for him and hoping, praying that he might be limping to camp on his own.

Shattered blocks of ice littered the mountain, and the trail made earlier that day had been obliterated, but she saw a red strobe blinking in Camp 4, far below. Lars took a compass bearing in case they lost the beacon, and he and Cecilie continued toward the Shoulder.

When Cecilie reached camp at 11 p.m., she went directly to her tent. Crawling inside, she hoped to see her husband. His sleeping bag was empty.

"It was quiet," she later wrote. "No wind. Just stars and loneliness."

▲ ▲ ▲

Pasang Lama squinted into the darkness as three lights streaked down like shooting stars. What had happened to the headlamps behind him? They had turned a corner or dipped below a rise, he told himself. Pasang waited for the lights to reappear, but they didn't. "I knew what it was, but I didn't want to know," Pasang recalled. Too tired for analysis, he suppressed the thought of an avalanche. He told himself he was losing his mind, and for a time he found that idea reassuring. Perhaps the streaks of lights were a hallucination of his oxygen-starved brain? Trying to ignore the loose ice, scuttling like insects, he waded blindly toward the Traverse.

Soon Pasang felt his boots breaking fresh powder. The terrain, once so familiar, now seemed alien. K2 was another mountain. The route to the Bottleneck had disappeared, along with every landmark. Cursing under his breath, he concluded that he'd missed a turn, just as Karim had, and strayed into China. Disoriented, Pasang backtracked, miserably plodding over the steps he'd just made. Pasang recognized nothing around him.

Finally, he squatted in exhaustion and studied his tracks. The ruts were too deep, the steps too varied, to have been trod by his boots alone; obviously others had climbed along the same route. Pasang decided he had been following the path to the Traverse all along. This meant that fixed lines were nearby. He patted the slope above the track, dug around, and felt something snaking through the ice: ropes, dusted in snow. He excavated them and attached his Figure 8, sliding along a diagonal ridge leading into the Traverse.

As the slope steepened, Pasang rappelled down and across slick ice. Then, unexpectedly, the rope frayed and stopped short.

This seemed inconceivable. The fixed line shouldn't end here. Pasang stared at the tattered end. Confounded, he dropped the rope and glanced around for another section. To his right, he spotted a slender line dangling from an ice screw. The original fixed lines had run horizontally; this one dropped vertically. Pasang didn't know where this strange rope led or how it had gotten here, but he loved the sight of it. Relieved, he threaded his Figure 8 through and rappelled down another 50 yards into the mouth of the Bottleneck.

This rope stopped short too, delivering Pasang to a landing no wider than a shoebox. Once again, his intuition rebelled against the reality. Where was the rest of the rope? Why did the lines keep vanishing?

As he sifted through his thoughts, the rope above him whipped to the side. Another headlamp was making its way down, smoothly and quickly. The glow approached. Beneath a halo of light Pasang could see the silhouette of Pemba Gyalje, the Sherpa on the Dutch team. Pemba stopped beside Pasang on the shelf.

Above, stars dappled the sky but offered only faint light. Shining their headlamps in wide sweeps, Pasang and Pemba hunted for the next section of line. To Pasang, the channel below seemed to extend infinitely. Ice cubes rained down on him, dinging his head harmlessly. Like the plucks of a rubber band, the seracs above chirped and *zoinged*. Soon they would calve blocks the size of Buicks.

Pemba seemed calm, but fear gripped Pasang's chest and gummed inside his throat. He looked below. Mist glided off like fingers goading him to jump. Pasang would have to free-climb the Bottleneck without an axe, which he knew was nearly impossible.

Nonetheless, Pasang tried, clawing and pounding the ice to create holds. He hooked his fingers in and shifted his weight, kicking his front points into the slope. He could barely grip the wall, and as he started to step down, his hands skittered across the wall's surface, searching for soft spots. The ice was as hard as a skating rink.

Shaking, he shuffled back to the ledge and grabbed hold of the rope's end. Pasang was stranded. He tried to say something to Pemba, but his throat, like a corroded pipe, only sputtered. The glacier responded in a cacophony of creaks and *zoings*.

Pasang had no hope. An avalanche or falling ice would certainly kill him before sunrise. Neither Pemba nor anyone else could help him unless that savior carried extra rope. Pasang thought this unlikely—he was certain that all available rope had been located and requisitioned for the fixed lines in the Bottleneck.

"It's over," Pasang told himself. His time to die had come. Trying not to move, he swore and prayed that his next life would be better.

▲ ▲ ▲

Following the freshly excavated line along the Traverse, Chhiring recognized his wife's face. The visitation came on gradually and intensified as he approached the Bottleneck. Dawa appeared to him as he'd first seen her, a teenager driving yaks toward a stream in the Khumbu. Clucking and prodding her animals to drink, she paced the bank.

Suspended between dream and memory, Chhiring felt this stream swell into the river that flows below Beding, the village where he was born. Chhiring's father, Ngawang Thundu, flickered on. With fingers gnarled from years of gripping a plow, he pointed to a boulder, smoothed by millennia in the rapids. He pressed a bony shoulder against its side and rolled the stone homeward to shore up a collapsed wall.

Chhiring's visions continued like a series of celluloid clips: his older daughter, Tshering Namdu, at the family altar, filling copper bowls to the rim with water; his younger daughter, Tensing Futi, emptying them into a flowerpot; his brother, Ngawang, singeing juniper branches at a rooftop *puja*; Ngawang Oser, his *lama*, blessing the charms on his *bhuti*.

Of all the faces he needed, his mother's was the one Chhiring couldn't summon. All he could see were her ashes, billowing in the sky. Chhiring imagined that Lakpa Futi was speaking, but he couldn't make out her words. He squatted, nodding off in the snow, but woke when he understood her. "She was telling me I had to live."

Chhiring focused his attention on the mountain. Studying the plowed ice, he realized what Pasang had not: The seracs had calved, transforming the icescape. "The goddess had timed it for maximum impact," Chhiring recalled.

He slid down the rope in small hops, and, when the first line ended, he quickly spotted the auxiliary rope that Lars had secured to the slope. Chhiring peered down the Bottleneck, wondering how far this slender line would go. Clipping on, he heard a weak cry. A headlamp switched on. Someone was below him. Chhiring rappelled down 50 yards and maneuvered himself next to two men, one of whom clung to the line's end like fish bait. Chhiring shone his headlamp into their faces.

Pemba looked worried. Pasang, his cheeks raw from cold and tears, looked defeated. "No axe," he said.

Chhiring had no idea how to respond. As the three climbers huddled together to speak, their breaths sent puffs of condensation into the air, giving the impression of a smoky backroom. Discussion was stilted. Pemba shaded his headlamp with a finger so it wouldn't shine in the others' faces. After a pause, he excused himself. "I'm going to look for some rope," he said. Old lines might still be strung to the slope. Pemba hacked his axe into the ice, and his headlamp dropped into the murk.

"What do you see?" Chhiring yelled after him.

Pemba kept descending.

"Any rope?" Pasang called down.

If Pemba responded, Chhiring and Pasang couldn't hear him.

"He went fast, and I couldn't blame him," Chhiring recalled. Pemba had a wife and a three-year-old daughter waiting for him, and he'd been climbing for twenty-four hours. Pemba's headlamp disappeared.

Pasang turned to Chhiring and spoke without emotion. "You can go, too," he said.

Chhiring considered it. Taking responsibility for Pasang—stranded without an axe, on the deadliest pitch of K2, on a moonless night, without a rope, beneath crumbling seracs—wasn't rational. But Chhiring never doubted that it was the right thing to do. *Sonam*, the Buddhist concept of virtue, is nonnegotiable, particularly on K2, so near a goddess who could influence his next reincarnation. She was watching and expected him to show compassion. He expected it of himself.

The seracs creaked.

"It's better if the mountain only takes one of us," Pasang continued. "Go."

Chhiring clipped his safety tether onto Pasang's harness and sank his axe into the ice. "If we die," he said, "we die together."

11

Sonam

Chhiring felt the weight of the life attached to him. His limbs operated on their own.

Chuck. His axe sunk into the ice.

Shink. Shink. His crampons pierced the slope.

He descended five feet and then braced himself, poised against the wall like a gecko.

Pasang, to his right, mimicked Chhiring's movements as best he could. He clenched his fist and punched it into rotten ice, but his hands didn't sink in like the pick of an axe. So he grasped Chhiring's outstretched arm and leaned against him. Intent on maintaining balance, Pasang stepped down, kicking in with his front points: *shink.*

They relied on instinct to read each other as the dance repeated—one man still as the other stepped, partners communicating with nods and grunts. The tether connecting them provided enough slack to maneuver, but they were all too aware that one false move could plunge both of them into the abyss.

Their headlamps formed a cocoon of light, and a hail of icy golf balls pierced through it, bouncing off their helmets. As the night wore on, the hailstones became bowling balls too heavy to ignore. Pelted by ice, Chhiring dodged the larger pieces, knowing he had to hurry. Soon the mountain might release something so big it would flatten them both.

Fortunately, "K2 sounds a warning before she tries to kill you," Chhiring later said. He listened for the telltale sound, and, midway down the Bottleneck, heard it: a prehistoric groan. Above, hurling at him, bashing and cartwheeling, was an ice boulder.

Chhiring tried to determine the mass's trajectory. "But I didn't know which way it was coming or the direction I should go," Chhiring recalled. "It was fifty-fifty," whether to duck left or duck right.

He guessed left. With barely time to shout, he plunged his ice axe to the side and lunged.

Simultaneously, Pasang let go, sliding on his stomach. He shuffled left, dangling off Chhiring's harness, which bore almost his entire weight.

Swooooof.

The block swished past and tumbled into black space. As it slammed into the slope, a gust of powder shot up from below.

The men drew deep breaths. "You OK?" Chhiring hollered.

Pasang, staring at the column of powder, didn't respond. "I thought I was already dead," he recalled.

After a pause, they resumed inching downward over alternating bands of hard blue ice and frost. To navigate these lips, holes, and bulges, they climbed side by side, holding hands. Sometimes Pasang clung to the tether between them as Chhiring supported the weight of his body.

Pasang wasn't sure what went wrong midway down the Bottleneck. Ice hit his helmet, and he could no longer hold on. All of a sudden he was falling—and so was Chhiring. Their bodies whisked down the Bottleneck. Their noses and chins raked the ice.

Chhiring hacked at the channel.

The blade sank in but did not catch.

Chhiring tried again, plunging in his axe. This time, granite repelled it, nearly flicking the tool from his hand.

Gaining speed, falling faster, they dropped another story. Another two. Another four.

Pasang clawed the mountain and banged it with his knee. Nothing slowed them.

"We were going too fast to survive," Chhiring recalled. "If I had seen someone survive this in a movie, I would have laughed."

But somehow their skulls missed the rocks that should have knocked them out. Their bodies missed the ice ramps that should have launched them into space. The tether between them held.

They'd fallen at least nine stories when Chhiring skimmed over the perfect patch of ice. The pick of his axe dug in, and, despite their speed, Chhiring held on. He gripped the shaft of the axe with his right hand, clamping it diagonally across his chest. At the same time, he angled the adze of his axe with his other hand, grinding the pick into the ice, squeezing in his elbows, and splaying out his knees. The axe dragged down the slope and his body slowed. Choking on ice chips, Chhiring flutter-kicked with both crampons. He stopped.

Chhiring was leaning hard against the ice axe, unable to see below. Shaking, he took a moment to listen to his heart beating. His calves and forearms burned, but he liked this pain. It reminded him that he was still alive.

Below, Pasang was panting and hacking. So we're both still here, Chhiring realized. They hadn't even dislocated their shoulders or broken their wrists.

"Keep going," came Pasang's rasp. The seracs were growling again, and fragments rained down. They needed to move. Fast.

Chhiring followed Pasang's bidding. It was miraculous that they'd survived the fall, and it saved them a tremendous amount of effort by depositing them near the Shoulder. With a *chuck,* a *shink,* and a *shink,* Chhiring stabbed his axe and his crampons into the slope and turned, grateful to see that the gradient had become less sheer. Pasang could move largely on his own now. Still, their progress seemed too slow. "I didn't know how long our luck would hold," Pasang recalled. As he continued downward, he counted the seconds like a mantra.

When they neared the end of the Bottleneck, climbing with barely any slack in the tether between them, Chhiring sensed something drop from above. It flew softly, without a rumble, an errant slab of granite aiming for their skulls. Chhiring and Pasang were exposed, in a channel with no room to maneuver.

Chhiring could do nothing. He exhaled, flattening his torso into a depression in the ice.

Pasang hunched, expecting his helmet to crumple like a can of Coke.

The block hit.

Chhiring tensed.

Pasang shrieked.

The blow never came.

The slab touched Chhiring's helmet and pulverized into crystalline dust. In the darkness, the layer had looked like rock, but it was only a sheet of sticky powder. Chhiring's *bhuti* was working.

He and Pasang continued downward until the slope merged into the Shoulder. Mist was thickening the air, and, in the distance, around a bend, a strobe light flashed.

▲ ▲ ▲

When Pasang staggered into Camp 4 at midnight, mist clung to the tents like cobwebs, too dense for him to see his boots. All around him, nervous climbers clutched radios and shone headlamps into the murk. Pasang avoided them. He couldn't bear to hear the death toll and hadn't the will to announce, "I'm alive."

His crampons crunched on the ice as he reached the ledge where he'd pitched his tent. Crouching down, he doubled over and vomited. Then he rose slowly to steady himself and wandered a few steps, bumping into a fabric dome. Groping for the tent's flap, he tore open the zipper, unstrapped his crampons, and flopped inside. Wrapping himself in a sleeping bag, he tried to switch off his mind and go to sleep, but his eyelids wouldn't stay closed. His thoughts raced, replaying the descent. Questions flooded in. Where was Jumik? Why was he late? Who would be dead in the morning?

Cold air suddenly gripped him, squeezing his chest. Pasang had visions of a tidal wave of snow sweeping over him and interring his body. His head pounded and his lungs constricted. He was suffocating.

Frantic and gasping for air, he thrashed, kicking off his sleeping bag. The tent spun. He rolled over and patted the ground, feeling for Jumik. Stop, he told himself. You're hyperventilating. Get back in the bag and calm down.

He sucked in a lungful of air and reassured himself. Jumik was a strong climber, and he'd be back before dawn. Now Pasang needed to stay warm and recover. He closed his eyes.

Whumpt.

A gloved fist slammed into the top of the tent. Pasang bolted upright as the fist continued to hammer. His hypoxic brain told him that less than a minute had passed since he'd entered the tent, but the light filtering through the fabric meant he'd been there for hours. The *whumpt*s came faster.

Woozy, Pasang turned on his side and let darkness envelop him. He felt Jumik roll in the sleeping bag beside him and heard his cousin's steady breathing. Pasang paced his breathing to match.

Deep sleep at this altitude was impossible, but this time, when Pasang closed his eyes, they stayed shut. Shrouded in a sleeping bag, he felt better—not safe, but contained.

▲ ▲ ▲

Some mountaineers consider a stove a crucial piece of safety equipment. A burner and a canister of propane can weigh less than a beer bottle, but if you find yourself without shelter in the Death Zone, that weight can save your life. A stove melts snow, and the drinking water prevents dehydration, which aggravates hypothermia and frostbite.

Those trapped above the Bottleneck on August 1, 2008, took a different approach. Although they had space in their packs for banners, cameras, camcorders, and flags, not one of them had carried a stove. They didn't even have emergency bivy sacks—wind-breaking, heat-reflecting shells that weigh less than a pound.

"No alpinist goes for the summit of an 8,000-meter peak with useless weight like a stove," explained Marco Confortola. "You don't go for the summit thinking you're going to bivouac." He had planned to make it to the top and back all in one day and wasn't going to be weighed down by safety equipment he'd never use.

But in the early hours of August 2, the Italian was wishing he had carried one. After posing for pictures and calling his sponsor from the summit, Marco had spent half the night pacing the slope above the Snow Dome—searching for the fixed line, the route to the Traverse, or anything at all that looked familiar. He backtracked, gesticulated, reviewed where he had gone, scouted, and returned to where he'd started. The icescape had changed, and Marco was lost.

As the temperature hovered at minus four degrees Fahrenheit, the Italian dug out a perch to rest on, planning to get up at dawn. Ger McDonnell, his messianic beard dripping icicles, joined him. Shivering, they slumped down within shouting distance of Wilco, who was pacing in the darkness.

Marco had enough juice in his sat phone to make a call, and he knew whom he wanted to reach: Agostino da Polenza. His mentor, who affectionately calls Marco "Stupido" behind his back, had also spent a night near K2's summit without a stove. Agostino had made it down despite losing the insoles of his boots, which blew away while he was rubbing his feet. Marco wanted to know how Agostino had survived.

After a few rings, Agostino picked up. He got right to the point: "Fall asleep and you'll die," Marco heard him say matter-of-factly. And when you get up in the morning, rub and extend your legs before you stand. "If you don't warm up your muscles, you'll fall."

Saving battery life, Marco ended the call. Without betraying emotion, he stood up again and paced alongside Wilco, searching futilely for the fixed lines. Ger rose and stared into the dome of the sky. "The stars were so dense," Marco recalled. "They pressed down on us like a blanket, trying to keep us warm." Nonetheless, he was shaking like a windup toy.

Around 1:30 a.m., they finally quit the search for a route and returned to their perches. Ger and Marco stayed together, and Wilco sat 15 yards away. To keep each other awake, Marco and Ger got creative. They clapped. They rubbed each other's legs. They beat their arms. They forced themselves to shiver even harder for heat. They sang a folk song that Marco's *papà*, Fonzi, had taught him for passing the time while herding goats. "La Montanara," a hymn of the Alps, describes the mountains as "sweet little dwelling-place of Soreghina, daughter of the sun." Ger must have appreciated the irony, Marco recalls, because the Irishman substituted Gaelic lyrics from the Irish band Kila: "Don't fail, don't fall, don't slip, don't wreck . . . do what you want, but be sure that's what you want to do."

This was not what they wanted to be doing. Marco fixated on a better place. He concentrated on the spores of light below—Camp 4 at 25,800 feet—a Shangri-la of stoves, tents, and the promise of survival.

▲ ▲ ▲

On the crown of the seracs, another man was crouched in the snow, trying to survive. It's hard to know how cold Karim Meherban became after taking a wrong turn, but he certainly suffered.

Hypothermia was unavoidable. As he shivered, Karim's blood would have shunted away from his fingers, toes, and skin, gathering around his vital organs. If his body temperature fell to 96 degrees Fahrenheit, amnesia and disorientation would have dulled his pain and fear. At 86 degrees, he would have passed out. At 79 degrees, Karim's heart and lungs would have stopped, but this is a reversible death. If rewarmed slowly at a hospital, a hypothermia victim can be resurrected hours after breathing stops, because the heart and brain require less oxygen when chilled. They don't usually degrade much, despite the loss of circulation, and they can start up again once body temperature rises.

Along with hypothermia, Karim surely suffered from frostbite, which tends to strike the fingers, toes, ears, nose, and other extremities farthest from the heart. Ice crystals crowd around the cells, causing them to burst from the pressure. This makes the extremities itch. The itch progressively evolves into a deep, dull pain, similar to that of pressure on a bruise. As his nerves, muscles, blood vessels, and tendons froze, the pain would have subsided as Karim's skin blanched to a waxy-white and then darkened to blue-gray.

But the cold didn't kill him. With the heat at sunrise, his veins would have dilated slightly, sending blood coursing through some of his thawing tissues and causing a throbbing pain far worse than what he would have felt before. His digits probably stayed frozen and wooden, making it difficult to clench an ice axe tightly. Nevertheless, a photo taken at 9:58 a.m. on August 2 shows a climber—almost certainly Karim—standing on top of the seracs, to the east of the summit.

A photo of the same spot taken nine hours later shows a skid mark. Karim, perhaps unable to warm his muscles properly before he stood, must have slipped, his body carving through soft snow or powder. Just before the lip of the overhanging glacier, the track stops. Next to it is a horizontal trail of boot tracks. The bootprints lead toward the junction above the Snow Dome.

▲ ▲ ▲

Battered and weary, Chhiring had thought of nothing but sleep as he trailed Pasang into Camp 4. When he found his tent, the flap opened and the arms of his friend yanked him inside. Eric Meyer locked him in a bear hug.

"Is it bad?" Chhiring asked.

Eric nodded. Eight sleeping bags were empty. He held out a Nalgene bottle of scalding Powerade, and Chhiring, his throat too tight to gulp, took small sips. He crawled into a sleeping bag but felt little warmth. Drifting in and out of sleep, he listened to the commotion outside the tent.

Sometime after daybreak, Chhiring overheard two raised voices. Eric, now outside the tent, and Pemba Gyalje, the Sherpa on the Dutch team, were debating what to do.

"The visibility is terrible right now," Eric said. The American team must descend, he continued, and so should you.

Pemba was crying, barely able to respond. "He was determined to recover what was left of his team," Eric recalled. Pemba's teammates, Wilco and Ger, were still lost somewhere on the mountain. "So I gave Pemba something that might help."

Chhiring rolled over in his sleeping bag and listened to the pills being administered. Pemba swallowed 30 milligrams of dextroamphetamine, a psychostimulant to keep him awake; 10 milligrams of Modafinil, another drug for workers on a graveyard shift; and 10 milligrams of Dexamethasone, to stall the onset of cerebral edema. No stigma attaches to mountaineers who take drugs in exigent circumstances, and Eric gave Pemba the medicine bottles in case he needed more.

When Eric ducked into the tent, Chhiring immediately pulled on his boots. Eric shot him a look that said, You want to die, too?

12

Survival

As night fell on summit day, Pasang's cousins, Tsering and Big Pasang Bhote, were deciphering fragments of radio chatter. Conflicting reports in a babel of languages told of confusion and death. Ten o'clock passed. "Our team should have been back by then," Tsering recalled. Another hour passed. And another. None of the seven summiters from the Flying Jump had returned.

Tsering and Big Pasang had moved up to Camp 4 to guide a second wave of Korean clients to the summit. "But no one was thinking of summits anymore," Tsering recalled. Worried, he and Big Pasang filled their bottles with juice and left to find their missing teammates.

Along the Shoulder, they spotted Mr. Kim. Skin chapped from exposure, eyes bleary with exhaustion, he looked tired but defiant, strong enough to make it back to camp on his own. He spoke to the Bhote cousins in a stammer, explaining that his climbing partner Ms. Go had lagged behind. "Serve her tea and help her down." Tsering pressed his boss to drink some juice himself. After reassuring Kim that he'd find Ms. Go and bring her back safely, he and Big Pasang continued up the Shoulder.

As they climbed, mist coalesced around them, obscuring the slope. Without fixed lines to guide them, the Bhote cousins often squatted and scrutinized the contours of the snow, searching for boot tracks. They took turns calling for Ms. Go, shouting the honorific "Didi" (Elder Sister), and listening for a response. After about two hours, their voices were spent and they still hadn't found her.

In the distance, Tsering saw something that made him think that Ms. Go was gone. High on a ridge, a dot of light plunged downward. A moment later, a second light mimicked the first. Although it was too dark to tell, Tsering feared that one of those climbers was Ms. Go. "It was a terrible thing to see," he recalled. He and Big Pasang climbed in the direction of the falling light. They kept calling, but their voices had lowered to croaks.

Finally, on a slope east of the Shoulder, the cousins heard a wail. The men hollered again. A woman's voice responded. Ms. Go hadn't fallen after all. As in a game of Marco Polo, the Bhote cousins exchanged shouts with her, blindly guessing where she stood in the mist. Sometimes it seemed as though she were only a few steps away; at other times, she sounded much farther off. Climbing toward the sound, Big Pasang spotted a flash. Ms. Go was clinging to an exposed band of granite on the unstable slope, blinking her LED headlamp off and on, off and on. One of her boots was jammed in a crack in the rocks, trapping her, but she smiled through gritted teeth.

Big Pasang climbed down and jimmied out her leg. Leashing her to his harness, he helped her plod toward Tsering. "We didn't talk with Ms. Go," Tsering recalled. "She was not in a state where she was able to communicate." Sandwiching Ms. Go between them and carrying her pack, they marched her back to Camp 4, arriving around 4:30 a.m.

Sobbing men mobbed Ms. Go as she arrived, smothering her in

hugs. An American with swollen eyes brought her a steaming mug of Powerade and announced into a radio: "She's alive and kicking." Tsering escorted her to her tent and filled up a water bottle, tucking it in her sleeping bag so it wouldn't freeze. He unstrapped her crampons, pulled off her boots. She was as comfortable as one can be at 25,800 feet. As Ms. Go shivered in her sleeping bag, Tsering crouched nearby, melting snow on the burner and worrying about Jumik.

About ten minutes later, Kim opened the tent flap and waved, signaling for Tsering to speak with him out of earshot of Go. "We were all so relieved to have found Ms. Go, and I thought Mr. Kim wanted to tell me how much he appreciated the rescue," Tsering recalled. "I was hoping he had good news about the others."

But Mr. Kim wasn't ready to give thanks yet. He gave his high-altitude porter the update. Pasang Lama, he said, was passed out in his tent. Jumik and three other members of the Flying Jump—Hwang Dong-jin, Kim Hyo-gyeong, and Park Kyeong-hyo—were still missing, probably somewhere above the Bottleneck. The radios weren't getting through to them. The weather, Mr. Kim feared, was deteriorating. You and Big Pasang, he told Tsering, need to head up immediately and bring the four missing climbers down to camp.

Tsering nodded but decided to consult with Pemba Gyalje of the Dutch team. Pemba had overheard the discussion. "It's too dangerous," he said. Pemba, like Chhiring and Eric, had assessed the lack of visibility, the potential avalanche conditions, and his own level of exhaustion. He'd determined that a rescue attempt at this time would cause more deaths, not fewer. Pemba was waiting to launch a search-and-rescue after the sun rose and visibility improved. "Don't go yet," he advised.

Tsering doubted he had a choice. Mr. Kim had hired him to help the Flying Jump immediately, not to wait. He found Mr. Kim again. As they were talking, Big Pasang joined them and listened, his face hardening. "Maybe he was thinking of Jumik's baby," Tsering recalled. "Jumik was my brother and his cousin, after all." Whatever the reason, Big Pasang was ready to go. He had already grabbed two oxygen cylinders, snapped fresh batteries into the radio, and filled several bottles with boiling water. Neither Big Pasang nor Tsering challenged Mr. Kim. "He had paid us some money," Tsering recalled, "so we acted as though he owned our lives."

▲ ▲ ▲

At 5 o'clock the morning after summit day, Wilco took an inventory. Frostbite had consumed his toes, but his friends were still there: Marco and Ger were dozing on a perch, three yards above him. The Dutchman approached their predicament as a mathematical equation, considering the variables: "I kept telling myself there has got to be a solution." He remembered the night well enough. He'd made it to the summit. The fixed lines had vanished. He had searched for two hours. Then the night had never seemed to pass. From 1:30 to 5 a.m., Wilco had sat apart from his friends. "I don't know why I didn't go over and sit next to them," he recalled. Too numb to feel lonely, "I just sat there by myself and waited for the sun to rise."

Now, with the sun blazing in front of him, he roused Ger and Marco with a loud croak. Marco barely looked up. He began rubbing Ger's thighs and forearms. Wilco, meanwhile, fantasized about water. It had been twenty-two hours since he'd drained his bottle below the summit, and the snow around him looked tantalizing. He wanted to scoop up a handful and melt it in his mouth. But he fought the urge. The slush would lower his body temperature and sap more energy than the hydration was worth. Trying to distract himself from the thirst, Wilco scanned the slope and wondered where the fixed lines were hidden. When he stood up, the crust beneath his boots squeaked, splintering under his weight. "It's unbelievable there wasn't an avalanche right then," he recalled. "The snow was so tense."

Once they had warmed their muscles, Ger and Marco rose, too, and the men fanned out, hunting for the fixed lines.

As Wilco searched, he removed his glacier glasses and rubbed his eyes. A breeze wafted across his face, and, gradually, his corneas began to freeze. It took him some time to notice it. At first, the faces of his friends became milky, and, blinking hard, Wilco strained to focus. An hour later, he was peering through a fogged-up windshield. "And I was thinking, 'I am so fucking fucked I don't know how to unfuck myself.' I couldn't see anymore and had to take action."

He turned to the others and told them he was going blind. "I said to Ger, 'Listen, I'm not going to discuss this. I'm going down. Directly down. It doesn't matter if I'm going in the right direction or not.'"

Wilco gripped his axe, plunged the heel of his boot into the snow, and headed straight down, dropping into a soup of white. "It was pure focus," Wilco recalled. Although he suspected that the path he was on led toward China, not Pakistan, Wilco was actually descending below the Snow Dome.

After about 200 feet, he heard a whimper. Confounded by the noise, he moved toward it and, a moment later, nearly bumped into something that made him gasp. As his mind processed the sounds and shapes, Wilco realized he was staring at a writhing knot of climbers. They were suspended upside down, hanging from the missing fixed lines, bound together in a snarl of secondary rope. The climbers were members of the Flying Jump—Pasang's cousin Jumik and two of his Korean clients.

The man at the top was hanging headfirst, his harness at his shins. About 10 yards below him, another Korean was curled on the ice, his face swollen, slashed, and bruised. He didn't respond to Wilco's voice. Below him hung Jumik. His eyes were glazed and his cheeks were covered in a gray crust, but he was alert enough to ask for gloves.

Wilco pulled out his spare pair, tugged them over Jumik's bare hands, and tried to understand why the men were tangled in so much rope. When the serac fall had cut the fixed line, the men had been attached to it by a safety leash and roped up to each other with a separate line. Falling, they must have somersaulted over each other. The two lines would have wound around them, twisting and cinching.

Wilco didn't want to imagine the horror of hanging upside down all night in the freezing cold. He moved Jumik into a more upright position and offered help, although he had no idea what he could do.

Jumik told him that help was on the way, and, after ten minutes, Wilco decided to leave. He descended toward a band of rocks. He tried to put the hanging men out of his mind. "They were trying to survive," he recalled, "but I had to survive, too."

Beyond the band of rocks was a sheer drop. Wilco turned back, "hanging over my ice axe, almost dead," he recalled, "and progressing centimeter by centimeter." He saw that Ger and Marco were far above him, kneeling beside Jumik.

"Where do I go?" Wilco shouted. He got no response. Too exhausted to climb up, he trudged forward, beneath the overhanging serac and saw a fragment of rope, his team's own five-millimeter Endura. It lay in the snow like a gift.

▲ ▲ ▲

By noon, Wilco was lost, wandering south of the Cesen route. He had made it through the Bottleneck with help from the rope but veered right, dropping off the Shoulder. "I really had no clue where I was," the Dutchman recalled. He hadn't recovered his sight, but even with perfect corneas, he wouldn't have seen much. A cloud bank obscured the slopes. Wilco went in the one direction he was certain of: down.

Pursing his lips to preserve moisture, he counted his steps. "I was busy with only one thing," he recalled. "Survival." Aiming to keep three limbs touching the mountain at all times, he backtracked when crevasses blocked his way. At one point, he saw more survivors, waved, and climbed toward them. The survivors ignored him, and, when Wilco finally reached them, they all turned out to be rocks. Defeated, he squatted in the snow. "I couldn't move any farther," he recalled. "I couldn't go to the left, I couldn't go to the right. I couldn't go down, I couldn't go up. I had no more strength. I was really trapped. That's when I was thinking I should make a phone call."

He pulled out his Thuraya sat phone. The keypad looked like pudding, and his mind was washed of all numbers except one. He felt out a familiar combination, and, at 9:30 a.m. Pakistan time, he heard the phone ring as it tried to connect to Utrecht.

A soft hello—the voice of his wife, Heleen—jolted Wilco. "I'm alive," he told her. Wilco tried to sound confident and paused, squinting. "I think I see people ahead."

Heleen sounded simultaneously shaken and relieved. "Are they moving?"

Wilco thought so. Switching off the Thuraya, he sculled forward, anxious to greet his rescuers. Again disappointed, he encountered more freestanding rocks.

The hours compounded. "I didn't have the guts to look at my watch," Wilco recalled. "I got frustrated at how slowly time was passing." He couldn't remember whether he slept. Sometimes his legs wobbled and tried to collapse. His eyes stung. He willed himself to keep going and to think of home. He began to regret the brusque call to Heleen. "Did I tell her I loved her?" Wilco couldn't remember. Squatting in the snow, he once again fished for the Thuraya in his pack and dialed.

This time, Heleen tried to orient him. "Do you see Broad Peak?" she asked.

"Of course I see Broad Peak," Wilco fumed. Why was she asking about the view? He was too unhinged to realize the significance of the question. Only climbers on the Pakistan side of K2 can see Broad Peak.

A few minutes later, Wilco hung up. The call reminded him of another he'd made four years earlier, and the memory buoyed him. From the summit of Everest in 2004, he had dialed Heleen and, shouting above the wind, asked her to marry him. Even then, Heleen had tried to orient him. "Just forget about this," she had said. "Get down safely. Then we can talk about it." That's probably how she felt now, Wilco realized. She wanted him to focus on climbing and survive so their toddler might have a father.

Each step was punishing on his frostbitten feet. The thirst was just as severe. As the day wore on, he wondered whether a swan dive was the solution. Everything looked milky, and he had no idea where he'd land, but a leap of faith seemed simple, even sensible—he'd certainly get down at breakneck speed. What remained of his reason fought against this idea. "If I landed in a crevasse," he considered, "nobody would ever find me."

Lights floated around him, burst apart, and dissolved. Deep in his pack, the Thuraya remained on, losing its charge. The sky darkened, and he readied himself for a second night in the Death Zone.

As he traversed toward a rock outcropping, Wilco spotted something yellow—another mountaineer—and climbed toward him. This man, Wilco was sure, had to be real. He was huddled in a sunbleached parka, and a rope led from his harness to another man, who seemed asleep on his belly.

Wilco introduced himself, but the strangers, long frozen, had nothing to say. Wilco wondered how long they'd been waiting for him. Lonely and lost, he stomped out a pit in the snow and sat out the night in the company of the dead.

13

Buried in the Sky

Snow Dome to Bottleneck

Once they had warmed their muscles, Marco and Ger rose from their perches and started down the mountain after Wilco. Around 8 a.m., they too encountered the three desperate men tangled in ropes. Marco couldn't tell whether they were alive until he noticed their shallow breathing. The sight was surreal, he recalled. "Maybe it was useless. Maybe they would die anyway, but we couldn't abandon them."

The slope was slick, and he and Ger moved like crabs. First, they tried to revive the men. Marco noticed that Jumik had lost a boot, so he took off his glove and pulled it over Jumik's exposed foot. Rooting through Jumik's pack, he found an oxygen cylinder, but the regulator was missing, making it useless. In the snow, Marco discovered a radio with live batteries. He called several frequencies for help. Someone answered. Marco asked for backup, and, in response, he heard a few words punctuated by static.

Ger, meanwhile, approached Jumik and raised his head to help him breathe. Then he tried to rotate the hanging man above him.

"They were like puppets on a string," Marco recalled. One would straighten and another would bend back. To help get the man upright, Marco wedged a ski pole under his armpit.

Sometime after 9:58 a.m., Ger turned and, without a word, climbed up the slope. Marco shouted after him, using his messianic nickname: " 'Jesus,' I cried. 'What the hell are you doing?' No answer. He didn't even turn around. . . . Nothing. He continued toward the top of the serac."

Marco continued with the rescue effort. He hammered his axe into the snow and attached the fixed line, creating a backup anchor so the chain of climbers wouldn't slide. He spent more time trying to free them—maybe an hour, but the passage of time was hard to calculate—and eventually he could do no more. He left. With only a ski pole for balance, he climbed along the Traverse and descended into the Bottleneck without an axe. "I clawed down by my fingernails," he recalled.

By the time he made it through the Bottleneck, Marco could barely walk. After that, he crawled, "moving with his hands and legs like a horse," recalled Tsering Bhote, who encountered Marco below the Bottleneck. "He had his buttocks up in the air. Sometimes, he slipped and crawled with the help of his hands."

Tsering and Big Pasang offered Marco oxygen. Gesturing, Marco indicated that he would never touch the stuff. Before he continued down, the Italian took a chocolate bar from his jacket and handed it to Big Pasang. "It was nice of him, but weird," Tsering recalled.

As Marco crawled toward the Shoulder, his mind, like his body, began to fail. The Death Zone does that to everyone. Scientists suspect it's the lower pressure that makes blood vessels leak, causing the brain to swell. Brain cells receive less oxygen and short-circuit. Neurons misfire. Climbers see and hear things. Marco heard an avalanche roar. A man wearing yellow La Sportiva boots surfed past him. Before he lost consciousness, Marco saw the man's blue eye pop from its socket. It rolled into his palm like a gumball, and Marco was certain it belonged to Ger.

▲ ▲ ▲

Ger kept his eyes and his wits. At Camp 4, two digital cameras were zoomed in on the upper slopes. Although observers couldn't see his rescue effort by naked eye, their memory cards capture some of what happened.

Evidence suggests that Jumik was freed. A photo taken at 9:58 a.m. shows a figure in a lime downsuit—Marco—and another in a red downsuit—Ger—working on the ropes binding Jumik. Another photo taken later shows the ropes, but Jumik is gone. Two eyewitnesses, Tsering and Big Pasang, spotted him near the Bottleneck around 3 p.m., and a photo from 3:10 p.m. shows Jumik, dead, below the Bottleneck.

Jumik couldn't have slid out of the rope tangle and down to the location where his body was found; he would have had to traverse 300 yards to get even near that trajectory. And Jumik was too entangled to have rescued himself. Clearly, Ger, the only able-bodied person in the vicinity after Marco left, helped him. Here's how it could have been done.

Sometime after about 9:58 a.m., Ger lumbered up the 50-degree slope, leaving Marco and the three tangled men below. Ger probably couldn't hear Marco shouting at him. Snow muffles sound; down hoods block it. Ger, according to Marco, continued up without turning around, climbing in the direction of the anchor point of the fixed line.

The upward slog would have been long, perhaps a hundred yards, and, given Ger's condition, might have taken him an hour. At least one ice screw had been gouged out by the falling serac, and Ger went up high enough to disappear from Marco's view. Trudging up the mountain, Ger would have paused to pressure-breathe, resting every few steps.

Many rescue techniques require a climber to reach the anchor point of the rope, and Ger had practiced rescues of this kind in the mountains of Alaska. Once at the anchor point, he would have studied the ice screw to assess how well it was holding. Depending on what he saw, he might have jammed it deeper into the ice, the goal being to establish a stable rope system that releases tension on the main line.

Unlike rescues dramatized by Hollywood, actual mountain rescues are slow-paced, technical affairs that prioritize risk management over speed. They commonly involve tying a complex series of knots. Ger's hands would have been clumsy from the cold as he tied and retied knots he knew by rote.

Matt Szundy, founder of the Ascending Path guide service in Alaska, taught and tested Ger on rescue techniques. He speculated that Ger "rigged a secondary anchor near the first, using an ice screw in his pack." Then, using a Prusik hitch and a Munter hitch, Ger would have created a series of pulleylike knots and loops that, thanks to friction and leverage, provided some slack and a strong backup anchor so that when he freed the tangled men, their bodies wouldn't go sledding down the mountain.

After creating the rope system, Ger descended toward the men. Now that he had enough slack to work with, he would have begun untying the climbers and equipping the people he freed. Jumik was missing a boot. Ger might have yanked a boot off another man and given it to him. Photos suggest Jumik was eventually worked free and able to stand.

Ger could do nothing for the man at the top of the tangle. He couldn't be revived, according to Marco and Wilco, the last living witnesses to see him. A grainy photo taken at 7:16 p.m. shows his body splayed in the same orientation as it appears in the morning photos.

But Ger may have rescued the man in the middle of the knot. The evidence is inconclusive. In the three grainy photographs of the rescue site—taken at 8:06 a.m., 9:58 a.m., and 7:16 p.m.—the man's position appears unchanged. But two eyewitnesses believe they saw him that afternoon with Jumik and Ger on the Traverse. Perhaps the shape in some of the photos is something other than a body, such as a pile of discarded rope.

Although the Korean was injured and weak, it is possible that he revived enough to climb. Mountaineers have gone from comatose to ambulatory under similar circumstances, as Texas mountaineer Beck Weathers did in 1996. Beck was in the upper reaches of Everest when a blizzard engulfed him in 80-mile-an-hour winds. His friends had left him in a hypothermic coma, assuming he would never wake. But, sometime the next morning, Beck opened his eyes, struggled to his feet, and began climbing toward camp. "I am neither churchly nor a particularly spiritual person," he later wrote, "but I can tell you that some force within me rejected death at the last moment and then guided me, blind and stumbling—quite literally a dead man walking." The Korean was injured and Jumik's foot was severely frostbitten, frozen to the ankle, but the two men may have felt the same way that Weathers had as they climbed up to the Traverse with Ger.

Somewhere along the way, a fourth man joined them, according to Big Pasang's radio calls. Who was he? It's hard to rule out a third Korean who hadn't been seen since the night before, but it is also possible the man was Pakistani high-altitude porter Karim Meherban. Photos suggest that Karim, after spending the night alone in the cold, slid down the crown of the serac, self-arrested, and managed to retrace his steps to the junction at the Snow Dome. There he could have met Jumik, Ger, and the Korean climber before they reached the Bottleneck.

Whoever they were—Jumik and Ger were among them, but it's impossible to identify the others with any certainty—four men were hobbling along the Traverse, driven by a force that rejects death.

▲ ▲ ▲

After accepting Marco's chocolate bar, the Bhote cousins resumed climbing toward the Bottleneck in search of survivors. By 3 p.m., Big Pasang had pulled ahead of Tsering by 900 feet. He looked up ahead and jubilantly reported on the radio what he saw: "Jumik is alive," he exclaimed, "and behind him are three men in red downsuits." He couldn't tell who they were.

Stowing the radio, Big Pasang may have waved and shouted at the men coming toward him and must have been overcome with relief. As Big Pasang approached the climbers, he may have heard a crack as an ice block fell. It bludgeoned one man—probably Ger, based on Big Pasang's description on the radio—and knocked him off the Traverse. "One man in a red suit with black patches was hit by falling ice," Big Pasang shouted over the radio to Pemba Gyalje and Tsering. "Now there are only three men descending."

Big Pasang probably tried to pick up the pace, eager to lead the three survivors out of the fall zone. Jumik was in front, so Big Pasang would have reached him first. Maybe the cousins embraced. Perhaps Big Pasang offered him some of the contents of his pack: water, bottled oxygen, and juice. He definitely attached Jumik to a rope.

As the two other climbers in red suits approached him, Big Pasang might have yelled up, reassuring them. All his effort was in vain. A thunderous boom ricocheted off the mountain.

▲ ▲ ▲

Contrary to legend, you can't start an avalanche by yelling or yodeling, but almost anything that deforms the snow can set one off: falling rocks, melting ice, rain, hail, an earthquake, a footstep. In nine out of ten cases, victims trigger the avalanche that kills them.

Avalanches can take various forms—ice, loose powder, heavy wet snow, rock and glacial flows—but the terrain the climbers traversed on the morning of August 2 was ripe for a dry-slab avalanche. Climbers on the mountain reported that each time they stepped on the snow, they heard a distinctive creak, and cracks shot across the snow's surface. They were climbing down a slope of about 40 degrees, an angle well within the 25- to 45-degree range that's common with dry slabs. Snow had been piling up for weeks, and the temperature had spiked over the previous few days, helping loosen layers of snow.

Skilled climbers will notice these danger signs, but predicting avalanches is imprecise even with the most sophisticated equipment. The chances of a flow depend on the snow's stickiness, the size and density of the ice crystals, how well those crystals are bonded, the steepness of the slope, the shape of the terrain, the temperature, the humidity, the location and force of the trigger. In broad terms, a slab avalanche occurs when a top layer of snow slips over a lower layer. Anything that makes the space between the two layers more slick (such as watery or ball-bearing ice crystals), or anything that adds pressure on the top layer (such as more snow) increases the likelihood of an avalanche.

Many people imagine an avalanche as being a lot of loose snow and ice tumbling down the mountain like a bunch of BBs rolling down a slide. When an avalanche starts, it's more like a plate sliding off a table. At first, a slab of snow breaks free from the mountain and moves down the slope. As it picks up speed, the slab shatters, breaking into increasingly smaller pieces that eventually become so tiny they flow like water. The material at the bottom of an avalanche is as fine as powdered sugar. Most avalanches flow at around 70 miles per hour; the big ones can reach 200 miles per hour and flow on for miles, washing up and down hills and valleys and striking with enough power to take out trees, houses, and entire towns.

The last, deadly avalanche of the day began all at once, with an enormous, thundering crack. Karim would have known what the sound meant. The men had about a second and a half to get off the snow slab. That wasn't enough time.

A moment after the crack, the slab slid out from under them. Within a second, the snow would have been moving at about 10 miles per hour, breaking into giant pieces. Two seconds later, the avalanche would have been sliding between 10 and 30 miles per hour, with chunks further fragmenting. Faster-moving snow at the surface of an avalanche carries more force than the slower-moving snow below it, causing a tumbling motion. For the next five seconds, the slide accelerated, the snow churning like the surf after a wave breaks. At this point, the men would no longer have known which way was up. When this happens in water, surfers sometimes call the condition "being washing-machined."

The snow, mixing with air, packed into the climbers' lungs and plugged their mouths, ears, and noses. Their goggles, hats, and mittens were ripped off. Big Pasang and Jumik were short-roped together. They spooled and threaded around each other, becoming tangled ever more tightly. This apparently broke their necks. Around 3 p.m., Pemba saw Big Pasang and Jumik tumble past him. They were dead at 3:10 p.m. when he photographed their bodies, tightly wound together in ropes. The snow around them was streaked with blood and tissue.

The flow would have reached its maximum speed, somewhere between 40 and 80 miles per hour, after roughly eight seconds. And then it would have begun to slow. Once it did, it probably took less than a few seconds to stop. The other two climbers were never found, suggesting that the avalanche sucked them down and buried them.

The snow probably would have cushioned them so that they remained conscious.

A trained climber would have tried to clear a space around his face, creating an air pocket before the slide halted completely. Then he'd have flailed out his arms and legs so his body would be easier to find.

Once the flow stopped, the snow would have compacted so tightly around him that he couldn't move even his fingers. Spitting to see which direction was up wouldn't have helped. The snow feels like concrete, too hard to dig without a shovel. In that situation, all a climber can do is wait, hope, and cough out the snow in the lungs, trying to relax and consume less oxygen.

More than enough air can diffuse through densely packed snow to keep a human alive, but warm breath causes the snow around the face to melt. Inevitably, that melting snow refreezes. This forms a capsule of ice around the climber's head, preventing fresh air from cycling through. As a result, he is forced to inhale and exhale the same air, with increasingly lower concentrations of oxygen. The climber, buried alive, slowly asphyxiates.

During asphyxiation, the heart initially beats faster. Breathing speeds up. People revived from this state commonly recall seeing a ray or tunnel of light. Many consider it a religious experience. Scientists have an explanation as well, but it hasn't been tested in a laboratory: Oxygen deprivation causes peripheral vision to decline, narrowing the field of view and giving the illusion of an ever-contracting tunnel of light. Survivors have described it as heavenly.

After about four minutes of asphyxiation, the brain goes into a manic version of REM sleep. Some researchers believe that this brainwave pattern delays damage to neurons. Victims revived from these moments often remember seeing their entire lives flash before their eyes. They report feeling relaxed, falling into a Zen-like trance that has been known to turn atheists into believers.

After that, the heart, starved of oxygen, slows; the pulse drops to roughly thirty beats a minute. Then the heart beats erratically and soon stops completely, quivering in place, jellylike. Breathing slows, then ceases. The body cools. Electrical activity in the brain diminishes and the central nervous system gradually shuts down.

If the climbers buried by the avalanche didn't form an air pocket in front of their mouths, they died within thirty-five minutes. With an air pocket, death could have taken about ninety-five minutes. If their bodies cooled quickly, they might have survived for hours in a state of suspension between life and death; hearts stopped, brains partially on, they could be summoned back. Doctors at a state-of-the-art hospital might have been able to revive them.

But the men buried by the avalanche on August 2 were never found. Their bodies stayed interred, cooling beneath the snow.

▲ ▲ ▲

When Tsering Bhote, climbing 900 feet below Big Pasang, saw the avalanche sliding toward him, he darted to the nearest rock, wrapped his arms around it, closed his eyes, ducked his head, and prayed. The snow hit the rock and parted, roaring past him on both sides, shooting over him. The noise resembled a jet engine at takeoff. Grains of ice sprayed him, blasting him with powder. He screamed but couldn't hear his own voice. Snow particles gusted into his mouth and nose.

As the roar continued downslope, gradually subsiding, Tsering opened his eyes and wiped them with his glove. All he saw was snow emulsified in air. Again he yelled, but the whiteness swallowed the sound, creating a hollow silence. He sucked in to breathe and felt the suspended ice crystals cake his throat. He coughed and snorted, panting. Still hugging the rock, he braced for more.

The powder around him drifted down and the sun tunneled through the dense white. As his ears stopped ringing, Tsering shook his head to dislodge the ice coating his hair. He relaxed his grip on the boulder and looked around, seeing only raked snow, bleak and featureless. Far below, a field of debris fanned into an embankment. Tsering recognized the contours of a mass grave. He hunted for a red splotch, something to signify a downsuit. He saw only chunks of ice and snow, no hint of where the men were buried. He yelled out for the other climbers, calling Jumik and Big Pasang by name, but "the goddess had hidden them well." So he moved downward, mindlessly placing one boot in front of the other, not caring what came next. He barely noticed Pasang Lama climbing toward him. When the two men met, Pasang was breathless. He explained that he and Pemba had ascended from Camp 4 as swiftly as they could to help the survivors. "What survivors?" Tsering replied. Unwilling to describe what he'd seen, Tsering turned away and traversed the slope to a rock outcropping and slumped down, shaking.

Pasang followed, crouched next to him, and held out a water bottle. Tsering refused the liquid and stared into the reef of clouds, contemplating the sky above and the sky below. "I didn't think I would lose my family," he said. "Somewhere in my heart I felt I would meet them below."

14

The Fearless Five

Soon after giving the Bhote cousins chocolate, Marco collapsed. Exhaustion had beaten him, and now, splayed out below the Bottleneck, he rested his head in the snow. An avalanche could have barreled down the slope at any moment and swallowed him alive, but he slept on, wavering in and out of consciousness.

Around 3 p.m., a hiss jolted him awake. Something dark glommed onto his nose and mouth like a slug. He knew instinctively to yank it off. Coughing, he tossed and turned his head and tore at the slug's rubbery hide. Unable to pull it from his face, he pried his fingers beneath its lip. The thing came loose, finally, releasing the suction around his cheeks, but then an oblong shape—a wrist—pressed it back into place. Marco tried slapping and pinching, but now the thing wouldn't budge. The hiss amplified to a wheeze, and dry air blew into Marco's throat and down his windpipe, inflating his lungs.

He reluctantly inhaled lungful after lungful of the gas. As he breathed, his vision sharpened and his mind rebelled. He realized that an oxygen mask was on his face. The wrist pressing it on him belonged to the Sherpa on the Dutch team, Pemba Gyalje. The hiss came from the regulator attached to the bottle. "Marco," said Pemba's soothing voice. "Marco. Marco. Marco. I'm trying to help you."

But Marco didn't want this kind of help. He had suffered plenty to avoid the bottle. Now, with each breath, he was ruining his record of climbing without supplemental oxygen. Why now, so close to high camp, should he surrender? To satisfy the recordkeepers, he'd have to climb the Savage Mountain all over again. Meanwhile, the Italian media might dig up an old taunt from 2004 when he had climbed Everest on the bottle: They'd call him *il bombolaro*, the bottle guy. Marco tore off the gas mask. Using it was exactly what he hadn't wanted. Pemba extended an arm and Marco, infuriated, grabbed it, pulling himself to his feet.

They had barely begun descending when something—Marco thought it was an oxygen cylinder, Pemba thought it was a rock— bounced down the incline and bludgeoned Marco in the nape, knocking him to his knees. Blood trickled from the puncture on his neck, and a dying avalanche, which had propelled the missile, flowed hard against him, threatening to whisk him away. Within seconds, Marco felt as though he were levitating.

Pemba grabbed him by the scruff, "like a lioness protecting her cub," and towed him to the side, out of the slow-moving flow. The avalanche slid past, blasting powder into the air and carrying the entangled bodies of Big Pasang and Jumik. Sickened, Marco shut his eyes, and Pemba, with the equanimity of a coroner, snapped photos.

To their far left, the man who had eaten Marco's chocolate bar came to rest. Ropes bound Big Pasang's corpse to Jumik; the Bhote cousins were aligned head-to-toe. Marco sucked in and looked away, contemplating something far worse than his tarnished record as Pemba photographed the streaks of gore in the snow.

Clouds moved in, "as if trying to hide the disaster," Marco recalled. He got moving, climbing side by side with Pemba, heading down the 50-degree slope toward the Shoulder. The nightmare was too real to talk about, so they made their way back to Camp 4 in silence.

▲ ▲ ▲

Locating Wilco the next day became a collaboration that stretched around the globe and into space.

As he wandered down the mountain, lost, GPS satellites installed by the U.S. military were orbiting 12,000 miles overhead, spitting signals to Earth. Wilco's phone grabbed several GPS signals. Using an algorithm based on the time the signals were sent and the satellites' positions, his phone calculated its latitude and longitude.

Every time Wilco called his wife, his 7.5-ounce phone quietly tossed its GPS coordinates to a Thuraya communications satellite floating 22,000 miles above equatorial Africa. This satellite then volleyed the data to Thuraya's computer server in Dubai.

The data sat there for a day, idling on the server. Thuraya's United Arab Emirates office refused to release any information about Wilco's location. Company policy promises its customers uncompromising confidentiality. The U.S. military uses Thuraya phones; so do spies, pimps, and politicians. Thuraya's policy protects its clientele from assassins who could use GPS coordinates to hone in on targets. Disclosing Wilco's location, the company feared, could put him in danger. Thuraya needed permission from the man himself.

Unfortunately, the subscriber was rather hard to reach. Tom Sjogren, Wilco's expedition tech provider, tried to reason with Thuraya and assure the company that he was telling the truth. "We had to convince them that a customer lost at 26,000 feet on K2 had other concerns than being ransomed by terrorists." It took several hours of verification, but Sjogren eventually prevailed. On the afternoon of August 2, he secured the data from Thuraya and plotted Wilco's rough location on a three-dimensional map of K2, e-mailing the information to Maarten van Eck, Wilco's expedition manager.

Aboard the *Archimedes* canal boat in Utrecht, Maarten further manipulated the data, factoring in his knowledge of Wilco's last-known location, photos of the mountain, and details about the routes. What he found surprised him. Everyone had thought Wilco would be somewhere above Camp 4, and climbers had spent hours scanning those slopes with binoculars. Maarten discovered that they were looking in the wrong place. Wilco was below Camp 4, at about 24,000 feet, south of the Cesen route. Maarten relayed this information to K2 Base Camp.

In Base Camp, a crowd of mourners lifted their binoculars and scoured the area Maarten had described. Even Hoselito Bite, the Serb whom Wilco had evicted during a windstorm, pitched in to help. "I'd have even climbed up to help that asshole," Hoselito recalled. "This was no time to nurse resentment." But no one spotted Wilco, even with clues to his location. Fog obscured Camps 3 and 4, and the prevailing opinion was that Wilco was tough but K2 was tougher.

Nadir, the cook for the Serbs, disagreed. "Wilco wasn't the type of man to give up," he said. After rescuing Shaheen from Camp 2, Nadir was back in the kitchen, wishing he could do more than prepare lunch. He didn't really expect to find Wilco, but he figured that if nobody had spotted him yet, he should leave the grill. "Everyone had lost their appetite anyway," he recalled. Long after others had quit, Nadir continued to scan the slope in a grid pattern, even when all he could see were clouds.

Around 3 p.m., the fog lifted, and Nadir spotted a dot south of the Cesen, above Camp 3, just where the GPS geometry had predicted. At first, the dot appeared to be a rock, but, after studying it, Nadir decided that the object was unquestionably orange—and moving. "This had to be Wilco," who had been wearing a mango-colored North Face downsuit. But a moment later, fog rolled in and others couldn't see the spot.

Three and a half hours later, the fog burned off, and Chris Klinke, an American, sighted the orange dot. It was definitely a survivor. Chris became ecstatic and alerted others. Base Camp radioed Wilco's teammate, Cas van de Gevel, near Camp 4.

Guided by bearings radioed from Base Camp, Cas descended toward the dot. As the sky darkened, he switched on his headlamp, but soon it went out. Cas crouched, trying to swap dead batteries with live ones. His fingers were stiff with cold, and all the batteries dropped from his grasp and slid down the slope. Forced to stop, Cas pulled a sleeping bag from his pack, wrapped it over his head like a shroud, and waited. He spent the night less than 700 yards from Wilco. At first light on August 3, he intercepted the last survivor near Camp 3.

Wilco could march, but his gait was robotic. His face resembled a barbecued bell pepper, and his lower lip was swollen, ready to pop. His eyes were poached. Cas had known him for twenty-five years, and when he grabbed his friend in a bear hug, both men began to cry. "I thought I'd never see you again," Cas said. Unable to speak at first, Wilco accepted a liter of water and downed it. His throat now wet, Wilco rasped something to his friend, but it took a few tries before he could be understood. Cas was anxious to hear what he had to say.

"I'm fine," said Wilco. "I'm feeling good."

▲ ▲ ▲

At Base Camp, the vacant tents unsettled everyone, but the dome of the first victim was the strangest. As the glacier melted around its perimeter, Dren Mandić's red-and-blue tent appeared to rise. On a four-foot pedestal, too prominent to avoid, it resembled a *stupa*. "I tried not to look at it," Pasang recalled.

Entering his own tent was intolerable enough. Inside, his cousins' sleeping bags were rolled in the corner. Jumik's socks were paired on top of each other. Big Pasang's wallet was wedged inside a shoe. The neatness of the space repulsed Pasang and made him imagine his cousins, entombed in the glacier, being ground into scrap.

He was unsure what to do with their gear. The various equipment—down gloves, glacier glasses, parkas, sleeping bags—were valuable. The Flying Jump had provided it all, but Pasang doubted that his family would accept anything with Kolon Sport's twin-tree logo. He left the tent and asked another cousin, the team cook, what to do.

Take whatever you want, Ngawang Bhote replied. "You're a stranger to them. A few weeks from now, Mr. Kim won't remember your name."

Pasang didn't care. He didn't want to remember his name either.

Pasang heaved, crying, and Ngawang gripped him by the shoulders. "I have good news," he said. On the day before the summit bid, Ngawang had received a call from Kathmandu. Jumik's wife, Dawa Sangmu, had given birth to a son on July 29. Ngawang had tried to radio high camp to surprise the new father, but terrain blocked reception. And then Jumik had died. Ever since, Ngawang had been burdened with good news. Now, he told Pasang everything he knew about the baby, a healthy boy named Jen Jen.

The birth of a baby buoyed some survivors, and Ms. Go went around to the occupied tents to announce it. In the Serbian tent, Nadir, the team's cook, listened to her and wondered what would happen to the fatherless child. He tapped a stubby metal pick with a mallet, incising letters on an aluminum dinner plate; then he took out a semipermanent Magic Marker. On the surface of the plate, he glossed over the name Karim Meherban and added *HAP PAK* to identify him as a high-altitude porter from Pakistan.

Carrying several of these memorial plates, Nadir and a kitchen hand named Nisar Ali hiked to the Gilkey Memorial, the putrid burial cairn beyond Base Camp. With fishing line, Nadir strung the shiny plates around the rocks, and Nisar Ali found and buffed an old, oxidized platter engraved with the name of his father, Lashkar Khan, a high-altitude porter who died on a 1979 French expedition. In all, eleven new names were added to the memorial in 2008.

Miraculously, neither a twelfth nor a thirteenth plate was added. Wilco and Marco limped into Base Camp, skeletal but alive. Eric Meyer turned the Dutch mess tent into a field hospital, propping the two men against the soap-suds pattern of Cecilie's inflatable IKEA sofa. Most of the survivors he had treated needed food, water, and sleep, or blisters disinfected and dressed. Wilco and Marco, however, were living cadavers. After enduring three days in the Death Zone, Wilco had lost twenty-two pounds. Frostbite had tinted his feet violet, and much of his skin had the consistency of cheese. Marco had similarly severe frostbite, plus a concussion.

It was hard to tell how deep the frostbite had penetrated. To treat the patients, Eric soaked their feet in warm water. He injected Wilco with the clot-busting drug alteplase and the anticoagulant heparin. As the pain intensified, he offered morphine and Valium. Chhiring worked as the physician's assistant. He fetched supplies for Eric, monitored the IVs, maintained the temperature of the tubs, and served tea, bread, and Powerade. On breaks, he walked over to his *chorten* in the center of camp and prayed, thanking the goddess for his deliverance.

Across camp, the Flying Jump survivors were arranging a deliverance of their own. Askari Aviation had quoted a price of $60,000 to dispatch the Fearless Five pilots. It was an expensive and unnecessary chopper ride, but Pasang and the Koreans were going to fly back to town. When Eric learned of this, he thought of the dead sherpas' children in Kathmandu and Shimshal. "If the Flying Jump saved the 60 grand and trekked out like the rest of us," he told Chhiring, "they could have set up those kids for life."

▲ ▲ ▲

The Fearless Five provide a peculiar taxi service. The elite Pakistani military unit is stationed in Skardu to defend a frozen wasteland called the Siachen. The glacier, fifty miles southeast of K2, has little strategic importance, but, at an altitude of 21,000 feet, it is the world's highest battleground, occupying disputed ice between India and Pakistan. The two countries disagree where their border should be drawn, and they've fought for control of the glacier since 1984. The war has cost more than four thousand lives, mostly due to cerebral and pulmonary edema. A ceasefire has held since 2002, but the Fearless Five are constantly training for a flare-up.

During the first days of August, K2 upstaged India. Foreign nationals needed help and Pakistan's oft-maligned military seized the opportunity to score a public relations coup. As the tragedy unfolded, the Fearless Five pilots were in the mess hall, standing around a flat-screen TV. Soft leather sofas faced the screen, but the men never considered sitting. "We were ready to move," said Major Aamir Masood, who had been trained to suit up and get airborne within two minutes. Conversing with his colleagues in clipped British English, he felt restless. "I dislike the wait before a rescue mission," he said, noting that the tenets of the Fearless Five—sacrifice, courage, devotion, pride, and honor—do not include patience.

At first, Masood could only watch the reports on the Geo Television Network. Wilco and the Flying Jump had been evacuated days before, but Marco still needed an airlift on August 6. Wind gusts were stalling takeoff.

At lower altitudes and better conditions, you have a margin of error," said Major Suleman Al Faisal, one of the pilots. "We don't have any margin in the Karakorum. Every mission is high risk." Altitude makes flying a helicopter formidably complicated. The downwash generated by the main rotor blades depends on air density, and the thinner the air, the harder the rotors have to work to produce the same amount of lift. Fuel also burns less efficiently in thin air, so pilots must keep flights short or they'll run out of gas. The Karakorum's unpredictable winds, inconsistent visibility, and uneven terrain magnify the danger. Fortunately for the men being rescued, the Fearless Five are among the best high-altitude aviators in the world. Selected from a pool of combat pilots, they undergo years of specialized training to fly rescue missions in the Karakorum.

Masood, whose jet-black beard matched the shade of his aviator sunglasses, waited, monitoring the weather, until finally, at 12:30 p.m., his team received clearance. Within 120 seconds, Masood's team conducted about two hundred mechanical checks—a list they'd committed to memory—and buckled themselves inside the chopper's slanted seats. Masood trusted his machine absolutely. The green Ecureuil B3 Mystery, with a single rotor, had a sister that touched the summit of Everest in 2005, and Masood loved its power at altitude. The rotors whirled, the skids lifted, and the Mystery was soon flying east, followed by a second, the backup helicopter that wouldn't land unless Masood's mission failed. The two choppers, noses angled downward, cruised over the Baltoro Glacier toward K2.

Fifty-five minutes later, the chopper was circling Base Camp. Winds were gusting at a relatively calm 20 miles per hour, and Masood could see that the climbers had tied socks to their ice axes to signal a wind change. As the Mystery sank toward the glacier, grit shot into the air. "It's like being in a blender," said Masood. "You can't see a thing."

As the helicopter touched the ice, Rinjing Sherpa, a mountaineer from the Makalu region, raced toward the fuselage with Marco riding piggyback. Rinjing dumped the Italian into the chopper's open door and jogged backward, his head held low to avoid flying debris.

The Mystery lifted off. Marco, cradling a liter of Coke, pointed to Masood's camcorder and signaled for him to pass it over. Marco trained the lens on a freewheeling blur of glaciers below. As the camera quivered, K2 receded from sight.

▲ ▲ ▲

When Shaheen heard the *whup-whup-whup* of rotor blades beating overhead, he was strapped to a mule, plodding slowly back to town, still recovering from the illness that had nearly killed him. For days, with each passing helicopter, his mind spun. At first, he told himself that the helicopters were a sign of homesickness encouraged by a liberal insurance policy, but as more choppers crossed the Baltoro, he knew something had gone wrong. He spurred the mule.

Reaching the village of Askole in the heat of the day, he didn't bother to have his lungs checked at the local clinic. He only wanted the names, and they were easy to come by. News had already filtered in from Skardu, and it was even worse than Shaheen had imagined. Eleven were dead on K2, among them two Shimshalis, Karim Meherban and Jehan Baig.

"I took it like a knife in the gut," Shaheen recalled. He tried to think straight, but his thoughts circled, emphasizing every mistake he might have prevented if he had led the climb as planned. He never would have sanctioned the recovery of Dren's body. He would have tried to dissuade anyone who wanted to climb past the 2 p.m. turnaround time. So many lives—including Jehan's and Karim's—might have been spared if only he hadn't fallen ill.

Shaheen prayed that word hadn't yet reached Shimshal. He felt that he needed to be the one to deliver it. "I loved Karim and Jehan like brothers," he explained. "I led them to K2. I was the only man who should face their families." So he calculated: How fast was this information moving? How fast could he move himself? If he were lucky, he could get to Shimshal within a day or two. If the village's one satellite phone, used for natural disasters, were switched off, he might arrive in time. He hitched a ride to Skardu, and, on the main drag at College Road, found a truck bound for Hunza.

But in Shimshal, the phone had already rung. Shaheen had been too late even before he'd heard the first rotor blades above the Baltoro. Jehan's death had been reported to his mother, Nazib, on August 3, and, later that evening, another call had come in. By daybreak, nearly everyone in the village knew that Karim had died—everyone, it seemed, except Karim's wife, Parveen. No one had had the stomach to tell her about the second call confirming her husband's death, so Parveen assumed that Karim had survived. "After hearing what had happened to Jehan, I felt I had to see Karim right away," she recalled. So Parveen had decided to leave Shimshal and meet Karim along the Karakorum Highway. "That way, I could see my husband a day sooner."

At 7 a.m. on August 4, she waited on the mud stoop next to her general store, desperate to catch a lift. The bus, a battered military jeep, came on time, but the driver, Merza Aman, told Parveen he wasn't driving through the gorge until 11 a.m. "It was the lie of a good man," Parveen recalled. "Merza wanted to save me the trip." At 10:45 a.m., Parveen returned to the bus stop, unaware that Merza had left at 8 a.m. with his passengers.

Another hour passed. Those who saw her waiting wouldn't make eye contact, and Parveen began to understand. Finally, Didar Ali, a farmer, came to the stoop and told her the truth: Karim had never returned to high camp.

Parveen's first instinct was to reach her children, Umbreen, Abrar, and Rahmin. She ran to their elementary school. When she walked into the classroom, Parveen didn't have to ask whether her children had been told the news by classmates. Their faces said it all.

▲ ▲ ▲

At the Fearless Five base, Marco was lifted from Masood's chopper into the backseat of a military van. The Italian nodded off, unsure of his surroundings, until he woke in front of a dusty playground with swings and a canary-yellow seesaw. Squat buildings on the periphery resembled concession stands at a fairground. Painted in candy-apple red, the sign on one building read MORTUARY. Another cautioned: OPERATING THEATRE. NO ENTRY. VISITORS NOT ALLOWED. This was the Combined Military Hospital in Skardu.

Nurses helped Marco out, lowered him into a wheelchair, and pushed him into the operating theatre. The bright room smelled rancid, a mixture of renal failure and nail-polish remover. Following faded instructions taped to the wall, the nurses lowered Marco's feet into tubs of lukewarm salt water and told him the pain would get worse.

Within an hour, reporters from the local stations, now working as correspondents for international media, had pushed past the NO VISITORS sign on the swinging door. They fended off doctors ordering them to leave and mobbed Marco's cot, shoving microphones under his chin. The reporters tossed Marco questions, snapped photos of his feet, and videotaped his grimaces. Marco, communicating in rudimentary English, was so exhausted he could barely make sense. But he was photogenic enough for the Associated Press, and his sentence fragments, strung together by reporters, managed to offend and enthrall. "I was surprised by his interview," South Korean climber Go Mi-sun later wrote in an e-mail to Ger's family. "Marco had a mental breakdown."

Media outlets around the world picked up the story. Many romanticized the horror and misrepresented important details. It was widely reported, for instance, that Pasang's cousin Jumik had learned of his son's birth during a satellite phone call from the summit. That is fiction, according to Jumik's wife. In the *New York Times*, a front-page article about the disaster displayed a photo of Gasherbrum IV—the wrong mountain. *ExplorersWeb*, the insiders' website for mountaineering news, ran a column titled "K2's Double Tragedy," castigating Base Camp bloggers for releasing premature casualty lists that traumatized some victims' families.

The disaster captured the attention of viewers around the world. In London, Jerry del Missier, the president of Barclays Capital, was engineering the "Deal of the Century," the acquisition of Lehman Brothers, involving $47.4 billion in securities and $45.5 billion in trading liabilities. He took a break to send worried e-mails to Kathmandu. Jumik Bhote was his friend and had climbed with him. In Dublin, President Mary McAleese, a fan of Ger's, released a statement consoling his family: "Following so closely on their righteous pride, and that of the country, at Gerard becoming the first Irish person to scale K2, it is truly heartbreaking that they must now contemplate the loss of a beloved son and brother." She dispatched a diplomat from Tehran to meet Ger's family in Pakistan. In Islamabad, Vincenzo Prati, Italy's ambassador to Pakistan, prepared a note for Marco: "Hoping you've unwound from your tremendous efforts on K2." The note included an invoice for $10,614, the cost of Marco's airlift.

The press, meanwhile, vied for the chance to interview Wilco. Inside the lobby of Islamabad's Regency Hotel, the Dutchman hunkered below a crystal chandelier and rested his bandaged feet on a Louis Quatorze chair. He tried to be polite as reporters swarmed over him, but his mind was still on the mountain. What do these people know about fighting for your life? he thought, while the cameras flashed. He held up his bandaged hands, as requested. "I guess it's showtime," he said.

15

The Next Life

As the survivors returned to Islamabad, Pakistan's Ministry of Tourism invited them to the Committee Room of the Green Trust Tower. A press release stated that government officials were hosting a "tea party" on August 8 to "pay tribute to the heroes who took part in this noble rescue that saved human lives."

At 4 p.m., sixteen guests crammed around a rectangular conference table on the twelfth floor. Fans sliced the air as condensation pooled in the window frames. A bureaucrat passed around crackers and bottled water, and, despite the swelter, poured steaming tea. He gave the climbers gifts: lapel pins enameled with Pakistan's flag and picture books of alpine flora.

The room hushed as Dr. Shahzad Qaiser, secretary of the Ministry of Tourism, slid behind a makeshift podium. Sweating in a suit and tie, Qaiser read from prepared remarks. He commended the rescuers for their courage, thanked the people of Pakistan for their hospitality, and apologized as though K2's seracs had fallen in violation of ministry protocol. He and everyone else around the table had a patchy understanding of the events and limited insight from the Pakistani mountaineers, who were not present to explain what they had done. Of the lead team, only Pasang Lama and Pemba Gyalje attended the tea party.

As Qaiser spoke, Nazir Sabir—the Hunza mountaineer and president of the Alpine Club of Pakistan—sat at the opposite end of the room, wishing the tourism secretary would make it fast. Nazir had a headache from arguing with Alpha Insurance agents about Jehan Baig's policy. His printer had run out of ink, so he couldn't produce the summit certificates that the climbers wanted to frame. Everyone knew our party was a farce, he recalled. The ministry couldn't smooth over the loss of eleven lives by serving tea and cookies. When Dr. Qaiser finished speaking and sat down, nobody clapped.

When it was Wilco's turn to speak, he didn't try to stand on his frostbitten feet. His cheeks, crusted over from exposure, had sunk inward, and his fingertips were starting to swell into purple grapes. He waved a bandaged hand at Nazir. "You need to train your high-altitude porters," he snapped.

Wilco was among several survivors who felt that the Pakistanis had failed him. Some blamed Shaheen Baig, accusing him of feigning his illness. As more facts surfaced, Wilco came to a better understanding, but his perspective at that moment reflected a widespread stereotype. "Pakistani high-altitude porters are not the right kind of climbers for K2," he said. "They are just too lazy to do the work."

Nazir tried to keep the tone civil: "Some of our high-altitude porters aren't as trained as Sherpas, but we are not ashamed of them," he said. "They are not expected to do everything, and you cannot blame them for every problem." No one had debriefed the Pakistanis yet, he reminded his guests, and speculation was fueling a blame game.

Sitting to the right of Nazir, Brigadier M. Bashir Baz, the head of Askari Aviation, chimed in. "Pakistan treated you well," he shouted at the Europeans. "Some of you did not pay for evacuations, but we picked you all up. Your mistakes cost Pakistan a great deal of money."

Disgusted, Nazir forgot Wilco and turned on Baz. How could Askari Aviation lecture his distraught guests about the bill? Nazir got in his face, and the two men shouted at each other in Urdu. Someone restrained Nazir, yanking him away from the brigadier. Sixty-five-year-old Ashraf Aman, the first Pakistani to summit K2, then sprang out of his seat like a jack-in-the-box. He shouldered his way toward the brigadier. "This is a tea party," he pleaded.

Someone threw a punch, and Ashraf tackled the brigadier. Ministry bureaucrats dove between the two and pried them apart. Unexpectedly, Mr. Kim kicked back his chair and lunged at Wilco. You maligned me to the Korean media, he charged. Wilco had done no such thing. Ministry bureaucrats pulled Kim off the bewildered Dutchman.

By then, Nazir had seen enough. He stormed into the hallway. Mr. Kim followed and jumped in front of him, blocking his way and stuttering something in Korean. You don't understand what we're going through, Kim's expression seemed to say.

Nazir said nothing. His brother had been buried by an avalanche on Mount Diran, a peak he could see every morning from his driveway. I've lost fifty-eight close friends and a brother to the mountains, Nazir thought to himself. He shoved past Kim and stomped down twelve flights of stairs. The tea party was over.

▲ ▲ ▲

Chhiring avoided the receptions. After trekking back from K2, he picked up his summit certificate and boarded an empty flight to Kathmandu. Loneliness pressed in on him. To distract himself, he stared out the window of the plane. In the valley below, the smoke from the brick factories undulated in the air currents like strands of seaweed. When the plane jolted to a stop on the runway, Chhiring grabbed his pack and stepped out into a sheet of rain.

He had not spoken with his wife since leaving for K2, and he prayed Dawa would be waiting inside the terminal. He scanned the corridors of Tribhuvan International, trying to spot her—or anyone he knew. Stray cats swatted dung beetles across the pink marble floors. Bug-eyed TV monitors flickered with snow and cryptic numerals, informing travelers that they had missed the last flight.

Chhiring switched on his cell phone, but the network was overloaded as usual. Taking a bus to Boudhanath, he trudged home through leech-infested mud, rehearsing what he'd tell his wife. K2 had never been worth it, he planned to tell Dawa. I've always loved you more than any mountain.

When he unlocked the front gate of his house, his white spaniel, Dolkar, whipped his tail so fast it nearly tipped him off-balance. Chhiring gave the dog a pat and, climbing up the stairwell, found his brother, Ngawang, in the rooftop prayer room. But his little brother and the dog were not the ones Chhiring wanted to see most. He wandered down the hallway, through the kitchen, and into the bedroom. His wife was gone.

▲ ▲ ▲

As August wore on and the monsoon moved northward, Big Pasang's widow felt as though she were sinking. On September 6, when a doorman led her into the Hotel de l'Annapurna, Lahmu considered turning around. Inside the hotel's opulent lobby, she felt tense, perched on the edge of a leather couch in front of a man who was blaming himself for the death of her husband.

Mr. Kim was in Kathmandu, preparing to leave for Manaslu,

another 8,000-meter peak. He looked weary. His eyes teared as he provided life-insurance paperwork and helped Lahmu fill it out. Kim, speaking through the interpreter, told Lahmu about the perils of climbing. He told her that he was the president of a mattress company and could not offer much money or ask his sponsor, Kolon Sport, for further support. He handed her a thick envelope with Big Pasang's earnings and a donation from the survivors of the Flying Jump, a sum of about $5,000.

After Lahmu accepted the envelope, Kim appeared to relax. He ordered tea. The interpreter ordered a soda. Kim offered to take Lahmu to a restaurant where the entrées cost more than her month's rent. But Lahmu doubted that her young daughter would accept the breast of the woman caring for her while she was away. Kim shook her hand and left. Lahmu didn't expect to hear from him again.

She didn't hear much from Pasang Lama, either. He had become a pariah in the Bhote family. When Pasang returned from K2, Jumik's older brother, Pemba Jeba, was unsparing. You abandoned my brother to save yourself, he told Pasang. Jumik and Big Pasang are dead, and you're alive. How could you have let this happen?

Pasang avoided his relatives, but he asked himself Pemba Jeba's question, again and again. How could I have let this happen?

"I hate climbing," he told anyone who would listen. He found himself in a bar drinking *chang* so cheap it didn't have a name. It tasted like lye, and he liked it that way; that's what he thought he deserved. A greasy wad of rupees was all he had left over from the climb, and he spent the money as fast as he could, draining jug after jug until he passed out. He woke up in a gutter one morning, filthy and lost, not knowing where he was or where to go. Pasang was convinced he never wanted to see another mountain again.

Two weeks later, he took a job with the Flying Jump and left for Manaslu, the world's eighth-highest peak.

▲ ▲ ▲

Pushing a cart of duffels through Los Angeles International Airport, Nick Rice was just bones wrapped in cellophane. One blogger dubbed him "Freddy Krueger's cousin." Nick's life had been saved by a soggy pair of socks. Now he wanted to gulp down a life-affirming Starbucks Frappuccino, lock his bedroom door, and hide. Hobbling on a bandaged right foot, he plowed through a wall of video cameras and microphones. "Twenty-seven interviews so far," he said in response to a question from TMZ, adding that he intended to return to K2 whenever he could find a sponsor.

Many climbers faced a similar spectacle—so much so that, in Holland, Cas van de Gevel had to plan an escape. "Wilco, good luck with all this media shit," he told his friend before flying south to meet his girlfriend in Málaga. "I hope they never find me."

Cecilie, devastated by the death of her husband, had difficulty getting out of bed. When she could, she paced the beach near Stavanger, Norway, and watched waves beat the shore. "The pain was physical, too," she explained. "Every part of me hurt, every muscle." Gradually, she started to run on the sand, "so I didn't have to think." Each day, she ran farther and faster. Eighteen months later, she had completed the first unsupported, unassisted crossing of Antarctica.

Marco adapted to fame better than the others. As Italian journalists reported his amputations—"my little pedicure," as he put it—his cell phone twitched with texts and his inbox filled with fan mail. He moved out of his mother's place and purchased a hot tub with rotating jets and a bed with a mirror on the canopy. The media attention turned him into a toeless sex symbol. His story was covered in newspaper articles, television specials, talk-show appearances, two book deals, and a five-page spread in *Vanity Fair*, which featured Marco performing planche push-ups over a lead pipe. The Italian Olympic athletes association awarded him a medal for heroism. Dolce & Gabbana inquired whether he would model underwear; Italian housewives nearly swooned in anticipation.

But Marco had alienated Pemba Gyalje, the Sherpa who had saved his life. In Marco's memoir, he characterized Pemba as a porter, not an equal, and misidentified him as "Pemba Girgi." Scrutiny intensified when Pemba complained to Shaheen Baig's climbing partner, Simone Moro, in a searing four-hour interview. Moro, in turn, dissected Marco's errors on K2 for the newspaper *Corriere della Sera*.

Pemba's interview with Simone "made my mama cry," Marco recalled. He considered himself "persecuted like Bonatti," the Italian martyr of K2—until he flew to Kathmandu to visit Jumik Bhote's mother. Gamu Bhoteni met him beside a frog pond at the Hotel Mala. With her was Jen Jen, her grandson. Marco was moved. "Holding Jumik's baby was one of the great privileges of my life," he said. "I told Jen Jen, 'I wish I'd been strong enough to bring your papa home.'"

Gamu asked to see Marco's stubs, and he unlaced his sneakers. She examined the amputations briefly, then waited for him to pull on his socks. "You are fortunate, sir," she said. "You can conceal your sorrow inside your shoes."

Marco nodded and pressed her hand. "K2 was good to me."

Across town, Pemba Gyalje must have felt the same. His double rescue had attracted fame, and visitors to his home in Kathmandu could squish down on the living room sofa and stare up at an effigy of their host: a five-foot-by-three-foot poster of Pemba Gyalje's face on the cover of *National Geographic Adventure*. The magazine had christened him "The Savior."

▲ ▲ ▲

By helping Pasang down the Bottleneck, Chhiring had pulled off one of the most heroic rescues in K2 history; by sacrificing his ice axe and anchoring it to a rope system, Pasang had anonymously prevented many climbers from wandering off-route to their deaths. Both men had played crucial roles in leading the climb and keeping others alive, but hardly anyone knew it.

"The mainstream media focused on the rescues of August second and third," Pemba noted. Those rescues involved Western lives. But the cameras eventually reached the Bhotes in Kathmandu. In January 2009, Pemba Gyalje's agent, Pat Falvey, arrived at the Hotel Marshyangdi with a film crew and an $800,000 budget. Pat was producing a documentary about the tragedy, and Pemba had agreed to conduct the interviews in Nepali. Pat met with the Bhotes, introducing himself as a ragpicker-turned-millionaire.

"I owe Ger this film," Pat told Pasang Lama. Four years earlier, Ger had found Pat dying on Everest and short-roped him down the mountain, saving his life. Now Pat wanted to ensure that Ger received credit for his heroism on K2.

Pat offered to fly the Bhotes to Switzerland to shoot a reenactment on the Eiger. They would wear the same Kolon Sport suits used on K2. Pasang decided the idea was cool and offered to show Pat his summit footage, but his cousin Pemba Jeba objected. Pemba Jeba distrusted foreigners who'd pay $2,270 per minute for his brother's last memories, and he had seen enough Hollywood films to fear that Jumik would be depicted by a test dummy leaking red dye and corn syrup. "What do you know about survival?" Pemba Jeba implored Pasang. Gamu, Jumik's mother, had burned her forearms and chest in grief. His widow, Dawa Sangmu, had spent her nights inside the same Kolon Sport sleeping bag that Jumik had taken to K2. Their infant, Jen Jen, would never know his father.

Pemba Jeba snatched the summit footage. "I am saving this video for Jen Jen," he said.

Pasang didn't try to justify himself. "My life didn't make sense anymore," he recalled. He had survived K2 but wasn't sure he could survive now. The crime of survival weighed upon him. It was the guilt of breathing when other men—better ones, he felt—no longer could.

During the filming, Pasang met Chhiring for the first time since August. He thanked him, but the pain was transparent. Pasang's spirit seemed to be cannibalizing his body. He smelled sour, of beer and sweat, and spoke in monosyllables. Chhiring, unsure what to say, invited him to go climbing.

▲ ▲ ▲

Under the skylight of the great hall, Parveen, Karim's widow, served Nazir Sabir tea and *chilpindok,* a flatbread soaked in melted goat cheese. As they waited for Jehan's mother to join them, Nazir thanked her. "I wanted to come to Shimshal to pay my respects to you," said the Alpine Club president. The house filled with mourners; soon it was standing room only. Finally, Nazir broke the silence. He asked how the families were doing.

For a time, no one spoke. Then Karim's father, Shadi, broke down. "I've been cut in half," he said. "I hide my grief in front of my grandchildren, but they see it. They feel it."

Karim's four-year-old, Rahmin Ullah, skimmed the air with a toy Pan Am jet, as his grandfather spoke. "He still believes his father will return from K2," Shadi explained.

Children are the most affected when their fathers leave for the mountains, Muhammad Raza, the local schoolteacher, told Nazir. The students become distracted in class and silent during recess. They spend too much time alone. As climbing season ends, they start to laugh again, and they listen for the rumble of jeeps along the riverbed. Once their fathers are safely home, he said, "The children become themselves again."

For the children whose fathers would not return, it was different. Jehan's son, Asam, had borrowed a cassette player. The boy spent hours alone, listening to a tape he had made. "Long live my father," the tape repeated. "Long live brave Jehan." The ten-year-old had become withdrawn, said Nazib, his grandmother.

Jehan's youngest son, eight-year-old Zehan, had grown to resent Western expeditions that employ Shimshalis. When his grandmother was discussing the downturn in tourism, the boy had blurted out: "I hate foreigners. Why do they come to climb mountains and kill our fathers?"

The elders worried for the children but had no solution except the passage of time. No one had dealt with deaths like these. Karim and Jehan were the first Shimshalis to die in modern mountaineering. The community had banded together to help the widows, but for some, it was hard even to look at the White Horn, where Karim and Jehan had learned to climb. Shaheen Baig found the memories so unbearable that he had quit mountaineering for a time and left Shimshal to work as an oil prospector in the Taliban-occupied North-West Frontier Province.

Nazir nodded, knowing he could do little else but listen. And even that felt inadequate, for soon the families had nothing more to say. The great hall became quiet. Nazir cupped his hands, lifting them toward the skylight. He tried to compose himself, but soon he wept openly with Shadi. Struggling to keep his voice steady, he twice recited the Surah Ikhlas, a Quranic verse, for the lost men:

> *Say: He is Allah, the One and Only.*
> *God, the Eternal, Absolute.*
> *He begets not, nor is He begotten.*
> *And there is none like Him.*

After the prayer, almost all the men were sobbing. Grief made it hard for Shadi to stand. Nazir supported him, helping him rise. Outside, the sun tinted White Horn's glacier a brassy gold. Nazir realized he'd have to leave soon or navigate the Shimshal gorge in the dark. Shadi led him down the irrigation channel, along the jeep track, to the place he'd last seen his son.

▲ ▲ ▲

As the disaster on K2 was unfolding, Dawa tried to follow the online reports. Sometimes Chhiring's wife asked tourists at Internet cafés to decipher the news. Otherwise, she had to guess what *ExplorersWeb* was reporting in a foreign language she couldn't read. Kathmandu's electrical grid fizzled daily, for eight hours at a time, so Dawa often went without any news at all. She had to go on instinct and tended to imagine the worst.

The stress of the expedition had been too much. She'd needed to get her mind off K2, so she had stayed with German friends while her daughters attended summer school. But in the first days of August, even fast Wi-Fi couldn't confirm whether Chhiring was among the living. Newspapers listed sherpa fatalities but typically failed to provide names.

"The only time I didn't suffer was when I was asleep," she said. She tried calling Chhiring's brother Ngawang, to see whether he'd heard anything, but the circuits were overloaded. In early August, still unsure what had happened and unable to reach anyone who could tell her, Dawa summoned her courage and headed home.

As she opened the gate, Dolkar the spaniel yelped and spun in circles, charging ahead to alert his master. Moments later, Dawa was reunited with her husband. She wanted to reproach Chhiring for going to K2 against her wishes, but she couldn't do it. She was too grateful to see him alive. As Chhiring told her a sanitized version of the climb, Ngawang gathered up relatives and neighbors, and soon a dozen people had arrived. Instead of debating love and death, Dawa found herself snatching fermenting socks off the rug, chopping vegetables, and scrambling to host a party. Things were back to normal.

But not everything was the same. Chhiring now considered mortality when he deliberated about future expeditions. As anticipated, his ascent of K2 netted a sponsorship offer to climb another deadly peak, Nanga Parbat. Chhiring declined it. Instead, he decided to spend the summer with his family and climb Makalu, a statistically safer mountain, with two Swedes. Dawa appreciated the compromise and set forth her terms: "Stay away from Annapurna, K2, and Nanga Parbat"—the most dangerous mountains—"and you may climb Everest and the others."

Chhiring agreed. Survival had given him strong resolve to hold onto Dawa and the rest of his family and friends. Perhaps this was why, for a second time, Chhiring couldn't leave Pasang Lama behind. He was taking him along to Makalu. Dawa considered it a good partnership, and when Chhiring and Pasang left for the mountain, she gave them a tepid blessing.

▲ ▲ ▲

At Makalu Base Camp, everything reminded Pasang of his cousins. The village where they were born was nearby, two days on foot. While dicing potatoes for dinner, Pasang had a dim memory of Jumik hiding boiled potatoes from his mother; while exploring the foothills, Pasang thought of a hot spring where the cousins used to bathe; while preparing gear for the summit assault, he remembered how Big Pasang first showed him an artificial claw he dubbed "the crampon."

One afternoon before the Makalu summit bid, Pasang and Chhiring huddled around a stove, heating beer in a pot. Pasang spoke of his most recent climb with the Flying Jump on Manaslu. His family had called him a collaborator. "They tried to stop me from working for the Flying Jump again, but I didn't listen," he told Chhiring. The money was good, and there was a fair chance of getting killed, which seemed attractive at the time. Chhiring asked him if he still felt that way. Pasang put down the mug and, unwilling to say more, studied a rising cloud bank.

The despair that haunted Pasang also unsettled Chhiring. He usually slept soundly at altitude, but that night Pasang heard him tossing. They didn't speak much while climbing to the summit on May 2, and they could barely grin for their clients' victory photos. Pasang turned to Chhiring and tried to point out his village, but Hungung remained smothered in low-lying clouds.

The sky above was a bright celestial blue. As Pasang stalked the summit plateau, he lost a crampon and slipped. Chhiring shot out a hand to grab him, but Pasang slid from his grasp.

Plunging down on his back, Pasang felt more freedom than fear. He gripped his axe and, for a split second, still had a choice. What he chose surprised him. "I decided I didn't want to miss this life," he recalled. "Would the next be any better?" He wasn't ready to find out, so, twisting onto his stomach, he hacked his axe into the slope. His body fishtailed and skidded to a halt. Choked on adrenaline, Pasang stood up and smiled. The rush had cleared his head, and, on his way down from the summit, he had an idea. "I need to climb every 8,000-meter peak," Pasang confided to Chhiring.

"Don't get married," his friend advised, "until you've bagged all fourteen."

On the descent, their Swedish clients had a crazy inspiration, too: take a hot shower in town, then go for a second 8000er. Soon, Chhiring, Pasang, and the Swedes were making a beeline for Lhotse, Everest's conjoined twin. Eighteen days later, all four were on the top, completing the fastest doubleheader of the season.

From the summit of Lhotse, Chhiring pointed southwest to Rol-waling, the place where his mother had died and his father had gone mad, the valley he'd left to become a porter. He told Pasang what the elders used to say: The world began in Rolwaling, and it would end there. Then it would begin again.

Acknowledgments

This tragic climb impacted many lives, and we owe a special debt to the survivors who shared their experiences, as well as those family members who spoke about the loved ones claimed by K2. Patient with our questions and generous with their time, they helped us understand a more complete story. Heartfelt thanks to:

Qudrat Ali, Guldana Baig, Khanda Baig, Nazib Baig, Shaheen Baig, Ngawang Bhote, Pemba Jeba Bhote, Phurbu Bhote, Dawa Sangmu Bhoteni, Gamu Bhoteni, Lahmu Bhoteni, Phurbu Chejik Bhoteni, Hoselito Bite, Marco Confortola, Muhammad Hussein, Chris Klinke, Pasang Lama, Tsering Lama (Chhiring Bhote), Nela Mandić, Gisela Mandić, Roberto Manni, J. J. McDonnell, Margaret McDonnell, Parveen Meherban, Shadi Meherban, Eric Meyer, Lars Nessa, Damien O'Brien, Denise O'Brien, Iso Planić, Nick Rice, Nadir Ali Shah, Chhiring Dorje Sherpa, Ngawang Sherpa, Ngawang Thundu Sherpa, Pemba Gyalje Sherpa, Dawa Sherpani, Cecilie Skog, Annie Starkey, Fredrik Sträng, Cas van de Gevel, Wilco van Rooijen, Pedja Zagorac, and Alberto Zerain.

Mountaineering historians Jim Curran, Ed Douglas, Jennifer Jordan, and Ed Webster offered insightful comments and corrections to the manuscript. It was a privilege to get to know some of the primary sources and their family members from historic K2 climbs, including Erich Abram, Liaquat Ali, Sultan Ali, Zulfiqar Ali, Ashraf Aman,

Haji Baig, Lino Lacedelli, Jamling Tenzing Norgay, Leonardo Pagani, Tony Streather, and Bruno Zanettin.

We couldn't have understood many important sources without a team of excellent translators. Thank you to Rehmat Ali, Ragnhild Amble, Aleksandra Basa, Hussn Bibi, Erik Brakstad, Snighda Dhungel, Oddvar and Anne Hoidal, Paola Meggiolaro, Paolo Padoan, Aava Shrestha, Gava Shrestha, and Ester Speggiorin.

For providing us with important information and helping us out, we'd especially like to thank: Suleman Al Faisal, Ahmad Ali, Qudrat Ali, Zaman Ali, Ashraf Aman, Dee Armstrong, Judy Aull, Raj Bajgain, Banjo Bannon, M. Bashir Baz, Seanan Brennan, Joëlle Brupbacher, Eddie Burgess, Dana Comella, Marty Davis, Jerry del Missier, Karen Dierks, George Dijmarescu, Fred Espenak, Pat Falvey, Yan Giezendanner, Asif Hayat, Soukat Hayat, Brian Hogan, Lance Hogan, Shah Jehan, Katie Keifer, David Kelly, Sher Khan, Sultan Khan, Gourish Kharel, Richard Klein, Sonia Knapp, Dorie Krahulik, Joe Krahulik, Ab Maas, Caroline Martin, Major Aamir Masood, Dan Mazur, Dean Miller, Simone Moro, Colm Ó Snodaigh, Rónán Ó Snodaigh, Rossa Ó Snodaigh, Mario and Rosina Padoan, Dan Possumato, Nathaniel Praska, Jake Preston, Ronnie Raymar, Muhammad Raza, Syed Amir Raza, Joe Reichert, Rebecca Rice, David Roberts, Alexander Rokoff, John Roskelley, Richard Salisbury, Araceli Segarra, Janmu Sherpa, Jigmeet Diki Sherpa, Ngawang Oser Sherpa, Pasang Sherpa, Tshering Mingma Sherpa, Shujaat Shigri, Tina Sjogren, Tom Sjogren, Ryan Smith, Sam Speedie, Jelle Staleman, Matt Szundy, Hirotaka Takeuchi, Dana Tredway, Mueen Uddin, Maarten van Eck, Jaffer Wazir, Freddie Wilkinson, Yaqub, Ellen Zuckerman, and Katie Zuckerman.

Special thanks to: University of Maryland professor of anthropology Janice Sacherer, an authority on Rolwaling, for reviewing the book for accuracy and sharing with us her original research, which will be published as an academic ethnography; Cambridge University professor Hildegard Diemberger, for discussions about Buddhist religion and mythology and the Bhote culture; Professor Cynthia Beall of Case Western Reserve University, for discussions of her genetics studies; the late Dr. Klaus Dierks, for his photographs of Rolwaling; Jean-Michel Asselin, for his photographs of Chhiring during his first Everest expedition; Kunda Dixit, editor of the *Nepali Times*, for sharing his knowledge of Nepal's political history; Dr. Michael Su, for answering our medical questions; mountaineer Jamie McGuinness, for reviewing the manuscript many times and improving accuracy throughout; Nazir Sabir, for insightful analysis and for facilitating our interviews in Pakistan; documentary filmmaker Nick Ryan, for his tireless collaboration; Wilco van Rooijen and Lars Nessa, for reading the manuscript in advance of publication; Kelly McBride, a journalism ethics expert at the Poynter Institute, for providing advice on how to make the best writing and reporting decisions; the Multnomah County Library and the American Alpine Club reference librarians, for helping track down obscure books and articles; Brian Wannamaker and the Falcon Art Community, for providing Peter with a work space and a fun, supportive environment in which to write; the Corporation of Yaddo, for granting Amanda a residency and providing her with a sanctuary to write; Adrian Kitzinger, for creating our maps; and Kathleen Brandes, for fearlessly copyediting our manuscript.

Our agents, Stephen Barr and Dan Conaway, picked forty pages out of the slush pile at Writers House and brought this book to life. Their guidance has been invaluable. Our editor, Tom Mayer, steered us with insight and good sense. His dedication to our book brings to mind Saint Jerome.

Our writing process involves a degree of self-mortification as we rewrite each other. This would not have been possible without the majesty of Google Docs, which allowed us to collaborate closely even when we were thousands of miles apart.

Peter's partner, Sam Adams; Amanda's husband, Paolo; and Amanda's sons, Eli and Matteo, all deserve special recognition. Their love and patience were unwavering.

Background Notes

The notes below provide additional background information about this book and our research. When multiple versions of a story existed—as they frequently did—we chose the interpretations that best fit the verifiable facts. For the folklore based on historical events, we checked known facts but related the storytellers' perspective as well. We hope that we have made clear, within the text itself, when we are speculating and what supports that speculation. We maintained editorial control, but K2 survivors Wilco van Rooijen and Lars Nessa reviewed the manuscript for accuracy. Others—such as anthropologists Cynthia Beall and Janice Sacherer; alpine historians Ed Douglas, Jennifer Jordan, and Jamling Tenzing Norgay; *Nepali Times* editor Kunda Dixit; and mountaineer Jamie McGuinness—scrutinized specific sections pertaining to their areas of expertise and, in some instances, reviewed the book in its entirety. After the manuscript was completed, we returned to Nepal with interpreters and reviewed it with Chhiring and Pasang for accuracy.

Just as climbers have conflicts of interest, writers do, too. Before the disaster, Amanda knew several characters, including Marco and Karim, who was her high-altitude porter on Broad Peak in 2004.

Peter quickly found out that being an effective journalist in Nepal and Pakistan is far more complicated than practicing traditional newspaper journalism in the United States. Although reporters are generally expected to avoid getting involved with a story, Peter lived with Chhiring and Pasang and spent about two months trekking with them to their villages, interviewing their friends and families, and gathering information while hiking, hanging out, and learning the art of mountaineering.

Some of the characters went out of their way to help us gather information. Nazir Sabir arranged interviews, and we hired his trekking company to help us get around Pakistan. Damien O'Brien, Gerard McDonnell's brother-in-law, became our friend, and he shared photographs and recordings from the expedition and his original research. Chhiring and Pasang put their lives on hold so Peter could go with them to their villages. Shaheen Baig did the same for Amanda in Shimshal. We agreed to reimburse them for their time and expenses, based on the equivalent rates set by trekking companies, so we could spend as much time with them as necessary during the three years it has taken to complete this book. We did not ask for exclusivity to their story. After completing most major interviews, we wanted to help the families and communities of those who were lost on the mountain. We discussed how to do so with Chhiring and Pasang and decided to donate a part of the proceeds of this book to the Gerard McDonnell Memorial Fund, a trust directed by the McDonnell family for the education of the Bhote, Meherban, and Baig children, and, through other charities, help the communities of Chhiring and Pasang.

We relied on photos, videos, and site visits for location descriptions. When we couldn't reach a certain place, such as the Bottleneck of K2, we had the characters take us to locations with a similar look and feel. In some instances, we asked interviewees to reenact what happened. We also observed several reenactments on the Eiger by Chhiring, Pasang, Tsering Bhote, and Pemba Gyalje while Nick Ryan's documentary was being filmed. For the descriptions of the trek to K2, Amanda had trekked this route in 2004. We relied on her recollections, in addition to interviews and photos. Sound descriptions are based on what characters remembered hearing or recordings from the actual events.

We adapted some words to English phonetics. For consistency and readability, we refer to the same person by the same name throughout the book, even when that name sometimes changed because of the cultural context. In a few instances, we use sources' nicknames or alternative spellings because their first and last names were identical to those of other characters. Many places above 8,000 feet in Nepal have both Tibetan and Nepali names. When there were multiple names for a place, we applied the name used locally.

For biographical research, we received help from photojournalists who captured images of Chhiring's childhood and teen years. These images from Jean-Michel Asselin and the late Dr. Klaus Dierks complemented the anthropological research of University of Maryland professor Janice Sacherer, who studied Rolwaling during the period of Chhiring's childhood, and the mythology studies of University of Cambridge professor Hildegard Diemberger, who studied the cultures of the Upper Arun Valley during the period of Pasang's childhood.

For the action sequences and dialogue exchanges, we relied on interviews conducted with witnesses separately and, when possible, together, asking them what they said and did. When film footage of the incidents was available, we used their recorded words. The majority of the interviews were conducted in the sources' native languages. We relied on interpreters and, for ease of reading, all the quotes were translated into English.

PROLOGUE: THE DEATH ZONE

The descriptions of the climb down the Bottleneck in this chapter (and in chapters 11 and 12) come from the recollections of Chhiring, Pasang, and Pemba. We also viewed photographs and videos of this location.

5 "at the beach" Mine Dumas, quoted in Hugues's memorial blog.

1: SUMMIT FEVER

The descriptions of Beding and Chhiring's childhood are from interviews with him and his family during Zuckerman's three-week trek to Rolwaling in 2009 and subsequent interviews with the authors in Kathmandu in 2009 and 2010. The standard version of Beding's history, and much of the Rolwaling history, comes from correspondence with Professor Janice Sacherer and her writings.

12 "like a yam between two boulders" According to King Prithvi Narayan Shah, founder of the Shah dynasty in Nepal.

13 job description According to the common usage, *sherpa* means a high-altitude mountain worker of any ethnicity, and the word is spelled with a lowercase *S* to distinguish it from the ethnicity, which is spelled with an uppercase *S*.

13 150,000 Sherpas Government of Nepal Central Bureau of Statistics, *2001 Nepal Census, Population by Caste/Ethnic Groups.* The most recent ethnic-group–specific census was conducted in 2001, when the Sherpa population was 125,738 and .64 percent of the total population; 150,000 is an estimate for 2008.

13 Rolwaling Sherpi tamgney See Janice Sacherer, "Sherpa Kinship and Its Wider Implications," in *Han Language Research—34th Session of the International Han Ji-no-kura Language and Linguistics Conference Proceedings* (Beijing: Zhaojia Wen Feng Shi National Press, 2006), pp. 450–57.

14 astonishing amounts of potatoes In 1977, Sacherer did a study in which she calculated that an average Rolwaling family who ate nothing but potatoes most days of the year would consume approximately twelve pounds a day, for a diet of 6,000 calories. The potato represented a revolution in food security with three times the calorific value of barley, the Sherpas' alternative crop.

14 giant horse and plow This is according to Rolwaling's oral tradition, dating back to 1870. See Janice Sacherer, "Rolwaling: A Sacred Buddhist Valley in Nepal," in Rana P. B. Singh, ed., *Sacredscapes and Pilgrimage Systems* (New Delhi: Shubhi Publications, 2010), pp. 153–74. The written tradition differs. Tibetan texts of the thirteenth century describe *beyuls* as always present on earth but rendered invisible by Guru Rinpoche's powers of meditation to preserve them until sanctuary was needed.

14 center of the universe This is based on the version told by Ngawang Thundu Sherpa, Chhiring's father. As he recounted the legend, relatives and friends interjected with elaborations. Some parts of this story are based on these elaborations.

16 120 years old The actual mortality rate in Rolwaling was much starker during Chhiring's childhood. According to a 1973 survey of Beding, preadolescent mortality was 28 percent, and hardly anyone lived past seventy. Death in childbirth, disease, hunger, and nutritional deficiency were commonplace. See Ove Skjerven, "A Demographic and Nutritional Survey of Two Villages in the Upper Rolwaling Valley," *Kailash: Journal of Himalayan Studies* (Kathmandu) 3, no. 3 (1975).

16 land of three borders The Buddhist text, *Tseringmi Kangsu*, makes reference to Takar Dolsangma's flight to a mountain in a northern region that straddles three borders. Rolwaling *lama* Ngawang Oser Sherpa believes this mountain to be K2. The Tibetan translation of Chogori (possibly *Chomo go ri*), as well as the nearby Chogo Lungma (*Chomogori lungma*) Glacier, invokes five mountain deities, likely the Tseringma sisters.

17 Hrita Sherpa This is based on Sacherer's research.

17 "most isolated, traditional and economically backward" Janice Sacherer, "The Recent Social and Economic Impact of Tourism in a Remote Sherpa Community," in Christoph von Fürer-Haimendorf, ed., *Asian Highland Societies: An Anthropological Perspective* (New Delhi: Sterling, 1981), pp. 157–67. Sacherer gives a comprehensive description of the local economic forces.

19 Pem Phutar See photo included in this book. Chhiring's paternal grandfather had been a porter for the Merseyside Himalayan Expedition in 1955. After this service, Pem received a commendation letter, which he kept inside a box at his home in Rolwaling. This family history came as a surprise to Chhiring, who discovered the letter in 2011. Pem had never told his son—Chhiring's father—about his experience as a porter. Of Pem, expedition leader C. P. Booth wrote: "He has carried heavy loads over difficult country and has proved to be a safe and steady porter under the most adverse conditions."

19 two members of the 1934 expedition The men who abandoned the Sherpas on Nanga Parbat were actually Austrian but their German-run expedition was blamed. The tales of unlucky Germans appear to have surfaced in modern Sherpa folklore during the late 1930s.

20 "remain a virgin" John Roskelley, *Last Days* (Mechanicsburg, PA: Stackpole Books, 1991). Roskelley actually had more than one goddess to contend with. The mountain is shared by up to five Buddhist goddesses, one on each of the five summits seen from Beding, as well as two Hindu gods, as evidenced by the two summits seen from Kathmandu. Shiva, also known as Shankar, resides on the highest summit, sharing it with Tseringma. Parvati (Gauri), Shiva's consort, occupies the second highest summit with one of Tseringma's sisters. Roskelley trampled on the highest summit, presumably offending the two most powerful deities—Shiva and Tseringma.

20 ill effects from the climb John Roskelley was unaware that his climbing partner, Dorje, had objected for religious reasons. He believes his conquest of Gauri Shankar and the subsequent flash flood were unrelated.

20 **The third died** Personal correspondence, Professor Janice Sacherer, October 2011. See also "Tsho Rolpa, GLOFS, and the Sherpas of Rolwaling Valley: A Brief Anthropological Perspective," Mountain Hazards, Mountain Tourism e-conference, 2006.

21 **If driving rules exist** See "Traffic Fatalities in Nepal," *Journal of the American Medical Association* 291, no. 21 (June 2, 2004).

21 **World Health Organization standards** See Sumit Pokhrel, "Climatology of Air Pollution in Kathmandu Valley, Nepal" (master's thesis, Southern Illinois University Edwardsville, May 2002).

24 **up this high** This encounter is based on Chhiring's recollection.

26 **twenty-three permanent residents** This was the population of Beding when Zuckerman visited in spring 2009 during the trekking season. The population is higher at other times of the year.

26 ***Playboy* centerfold** In 2006, Playmate Martyna Wojciechowska summited Everest.

2: DOORWAY TO HEAVEN

This version of the 1939 Fritz Wiessner expedition was interpreted by elders in Rolwaling, but we supplemented the story with details from Wiessner's writings and accounts of alpine historians, including Maurice Isserman, Jennifer Jordan, Andrew Kauffman, William Putnam, and David Roberts. The actions of the climbers are consistent in both accounts. Although Pasang told Wiessner that he saw a supernatural being, historians rarely attribute the problems of the climb to Takar Dolsangma, as Buddhists in Rolwaling do. For information on the 1954 Italian expedition, we interviewed Lino Lacedelli, Erich Abram, and Bruno Zanettin of the 1954 expedition on K2; Leonardo Pagani (son of Guido Pagani of the 1954 expedition); Sultan Ali, Liaquat Ali, and Zulfiqar Ali (son and grandsons of Amir Mehdi of the 1954 expedition); and Haji Baig (friend of Amir Mehdi during their 1953 Nanga Parbat expedition). The description of Chhiring and Dawa's argument comes from several interviews with them in Kathmandu during 2009. The sequence of quotes is from Dawa's recollection, and each quote is what the speaker remembers saying. We also visited the house in Colorado where the argument took place.

28 **highest pass** The Karakorum Pass is 18,290 feet, or 5,575 meters.

28 **affirmed the title** Charles Close et al., "Nomenclature in the Karakoram," *The Geographical Journal* 76, no. 2 (August 1930), pp. 148–58.

29 ***Chogori*** Correspondence with Sacherer. In Tibetan, *Cho* means "god," *Go* means "door," and *Ri* means "mountain." Balti is a form of archaic Tibetan once written in Tibetan script. Persian script was imposed during the Islamic conversion of Baltistan in the sixteenth century.

31 **averaged 0.7 for the previous decade** The Himalayan Database calculates

the rate based on all those who attempt the peak, not just those who succeed. Although it is common practice, calculating the death rate based on the number of summiters is misleading: "This is sort of like calculating auto death rates by using only the number of drivers and ignoring all the passengers," explains Richard Salisbury of the Himalayan Database. "Death Analysis" in *The Himalaya by the Numbers*.

33 **"most bizarre tragedy"** See Galen Rowell, *In the Throne Room of the Mountain Gods* (San Francisco: Sierra Club Books, 1977). See also Jennifer Jordan, *The Last Man on the Mountain* (New York: W. W. Norton, 2011).

33 **heard a rustle** According to *lamas* who interpret this incident from a Buddhist perspective. Wiessner did not report seeing or hearing a goddess.

33 **"No, sahib"** This is what Wiessner heard Pasang say. Correspondence with David Roberts, who got the quote from his interview with Fritz Wiessner in 1984. The quote also appears in Roberts's *Moments of Doubt and Other Mountaineering Writings* (Seattle: The Mountaineers Books, 1986).

34 **sunbathed nude** Wiessner was sunbathing in the threshold of his tent. It's likely he became sunburned, which would have severely sapped his strength, making the climb the next day all the more grueling. See Jordan, *The Last Man on the Mountain*, pp. 190–91.

34 **"fear of the evil spirits"** Fritz Wiessner, "The K2 Expedition of 1939," *Appalachia* (June 1956).

34 **They turned around** Wiessner left his sleeping bag in camp, intending to use one he thought had been left for him lower down the mountain.

34 **"a funny little noise"** Fritz Wiessner, interview with David Roberts, 1984.

34 **"dug in"** Wiessner interview with Roberts, 1984.

34 **"how stupid"** Wiessner interview with Roberts, 1984.

35 **"sabotaged"** Ed Webster, "A Man for All Mountains: The Life and Climbs of Fritz Wiessner," *Climbing* (December 1988), quoting Wiessner interview.

35 **three rescuers** The fourth member of the rescue team, Tensing Norbu, stayed behind in a lower camp. When the rest of the team never returned, he went down to Base Camp and told others what had happened.

35 **nearly full moon** Wiessner interview with Roberts, 1984.

35 **lunar charts** "Planet Notes for July and August, 1939," *Popular Astronomy* 47 (July 1939), pp. 314–15. (Data courtesy of Maria Mitchell Observatory, Harvard; provided online by NASA Astrophysics Data System.)

35 **bigger problem than a turquoise dragon** Headlamps were invented in 1972 by Petzl. The handheld bulbs that Wiessner and Pasang would have used to light their high camps were too dim for effective night climbing.

37 **"This is it!"** See Maurice Isserman and Stewart Weaver, *Fallen Giants* (New Haven, CT: Yale University Press, 2010), p. 313.

38 **"wiggled himself loose"** Charles Houston interview with Bill Moyers, 2004.

39 fifty years of polemic See Lino Lacedelli and Giovanni Cenacchi. *K2: Il prezzo della conquista* (Milan: Mondadori, 2004).

39 Amir Mehdi He is also sometimes referred to as Amir Mahdi or Mehdi Khan.

39 join their summit bid This is the account Amir Mehdi gave his family when he returned to Hassanabad, Hunza. Interview by the authors, 2009, in Hassanabad, Hunza, with Mehdi's son, Sultan Ali, and grandsons Liaquat Ali and Zulfiqar Ali, and the recollections of Mehdi's friend and fellow porter on Nanga Parbat in 1953, Haji Baig, in Gilgit (interview with Zuckerman, 2009). Bonatti acknowledged that he offered Mehdi a shot at the summit but says this was a trick to motivate him to carry the oxygen bottles.

39 "yelling crazily" Bonatti interview with David Roberts, 2003. Bonatti declined the authors' request for an interview. "I'm 80 years old," he replied, "and tired of talking about the bivouac!" He died in 2011.

39 two sizes too small The Italians had provided army boots for their high-altitude porters, but Mehdi's feet were too big for any of them. The Italians wanted to stretch and cut the boots to fit, but Mehdi objected, fearing this would slash their resale value.

39 sipping chamomile Compagnoni said that he wanted to pitch the tent out of the fall-line of the seracs. Although this sounds plausible, he chose an inconvenient location that was exposed to rockfall.

40 oxygen allegedly ran out See Robert Marshall, *K2: Lies and Treachery* (Herefordshire, UK: Carreg Ltd., 2009). The summit photo shows that the oxygen systems had been carried to the summit. If the bottles had been empty, they would have been discarded as unnecessary weight. The frost on Lacedelli's beard corrresponds to the shape of an oxygen mask.

40 "Like an elephant" Erich Abram interview with Paolo Padoan, November 2009.

41 a single summer See Jim Curran, *K2: Triumph and Tragedy* (Boston: Houghton Mifflin Harcourt, 1989). For a survivor's account, see Kurt Diemberger, *The Endless Knot: K2, Mountain of Dreams and Destiny* (Seattle: The Mountaineers Books, 1991).

41 "Conquistadors of the Useless" Lionel Terray used this term for his autobiography, *Conquistadors of the Useless: From the Alps to Annapurna* (Seattle: The Mountaineers Books, 2008, reprint).

42 "more resort than wilderness" See Ed Douglas, "Mount Everest: a not so novel feat," *The Guardian*, May 19, 2010.

43 forty summit-hungry climbers Estimates of the number of summiters who passed Sharp vary.

45 "treat me like a sherpa" Chhiring is using the term *sherpa* (with a lowercase S) to mean any high-altitude mountain worker.

3: THE PRINCE AND THE PORTER

The description of the massacre is from the official reports issued by the government of Nepal during the summer of 2001. The initial June 14 report, by a two-member panel of Supreme Court Chief Justice Keshav Prasad Upadhyaya and House Speaker Taranth Ranabha, compiles the testimony of crime-scene investigators and all surviving witnesses. We supplemented our account with a visit to the palace and the massacre memorial site, photos of the crime scene, discussions with Kunda Dixit of the *Nepali Times*, and interviews with Dr. Raghunath Aryal, the royal astrologer who knew many of the victims and was familiar with the locations. We also corroborated these accounts with the BBC Panorama documentary about the massacre, *Murder Most Royal*, and Jonathan Gregson's book, *Massacre at the Palace: The Doomed Royal Dynasty of Nepal* (Talk Miramax, 2002). The quotes are what witnesses heard, and Ketaki Chester's interviews with Kunda Dixit and the BBC were a major source for these quotes. The descriptions of Pasang's childhood are based on interviews with him during Zuckerman's trek to Hungung and the Upper Arun Valley in 2009, and from interviews with his friends, family, and neighbors. The interactions with Ms. Go are based on Pasang's recollections. The description of the Hotel de l'Annapurna is from the authors' observations of the hotel and Pasang's recollection. The authors interviewed Pasang, Ngawang Bhote, and Tsering Bhote about this meeting at the hotel.

48 bloodbath See Jonathan Gregson, *Massacre at the Palace: The Doomed Royal Dynasty of Nepal* (Talk Miramax, 2002). See also *Murder Most Royal*, a BBC Panorama documentary (2002).

49 probably opium According to official investigation reports, Dippy was smoking "a special kind of cigarette prepared with a mixture of hashish and another unnamed black substance." The description and effects match those for "black hash," an opium-and-hashish mixture that the prince liked to smoke. No one tested the exact composition of the joint.

49 lower social standing Not by much. Devyani's mother is a member of the royal family of Gwalior state in India. Queen Aishwarya nevertheless considered the maharajahs of Gwalior to be beneath the royalty of Nepal.

49 stripped of royal status Despite the laws of succession set forth in the constitution, Queen Aishwarya could have "excommunicated" Crown Prince Dipendra just as his uncle, Prince Dhirendra, once had been.

49 high cholesterol King Birendra's last conversation with his wife, Queen Aishwarya, concerned his family's predisposition to high cholesterol.

50 an aunt Princess Ketaki Chester interview with the BBC in 2002. Information from the official report is supplemented by Ketaki Chester's June 2011 interview with Kunda Dixit of the *Nepali Times*.

50 last words "*Ke gareko?*" in Nepali. This is according to official reports and subsequent interviews with witnesses, including Ketaki Chester's 2011 interview with Kunda Dixit.

50 Two relatives Gorakh Rana, the husband of Dipendra's sister, Princess Shruti, and Dr. Rajiv Raj Shahi, the king's nephew, sprang forward to help.

50 "That's enough" "*Pugyo Babu*" in Nepali. *Babu* is a term of endearment for younger brothers, sons, and grandsons in Nepal.

50 from the landing This comes from Ketaki Chester's interview with Kunda Dixit, 2011. It is also possible that Dipendra shot his brother from a position in the garden beside the stairs, according to the official investigation report.

51 surrendered From Ketaki Chester's 2011 interview with Kunda Dixit.

51 shot her in the face Queen Aishwarya's face was so mutilated that a porcelain mask, painted to resemble her, was used during her funeral.

51 released a statement The statement may have been mistranslated or misreported at the time. See Gregson, *Massacre at the Palace*, p. 214.

51 clumsy cover-up See Ketaki Chester's interview with Kunda Dixit. Prime Minister Girija Prasad Koirala consulted with Queen Mother Ratna, who asked that he provide full disclosure to the public. Her instructions were not followed, and the ensuing media blackout allowed conspiracy theories to flourish.

52 "how do you tell your boss" Dr. Raghunath Aryal interview with Padoan in Kathmandu, 2009.

53 "grave human rights crisis" See *Report of the U.N. High Commissioner for Human Rights,* U.N. GAOR, 60th Sess., UN Doc. A/60/359 (2005), available at www.nepal.ohchr.org. See also *Nepal: Heads of Three Human Rights Organizations Call for Targeted Sanctions*, The International Commission of Jurists (April 18, 2006).

53 forced to flee The estimated number of refugees varies from 100,000 to 150,000, according to UNHCR, Human Rights Watch, and Amnesty International.

55 sneak in Interviews in Hungung were conducted by Zuckerman in 2009. As a journalist, he was not permitted in the region, so he snuck in.

56 250 people This estimate is based on Zuckerman's observation during the height of the tourist season in 2009. Others have given different estimates, ranging from fifty to several hundred. The discrepancies may be a result of migration during the tourist season as well as the various meanings of *Hungung*, which, depending on context, can refer to an individual village, a collection of villages, or a region of the Upper Arun Valley.

58 "wasn't safe to stay" This is based on interviews with Pasang's parents in Kathmandu and his relatives and friends in Hungung. The village is now peaceful.

61 publicity stunt Most pundits were other climbers, interviewed by the authors in Kathmandu. Ms. Go was not overtly criticized in mainstream climbing blogs, such as *ExplorersWeb* and *Everest News*. Pasang had a vague understanding of the controversy surrounding Go, based on his online research and conversations with others, but it's unlikely he knew the level of detail as described here.

62 kept rain out Lahmu Bhoteni, 2009 interview with Padoan at the home Lahmu shared with Big Pasang in Kathmandu.

4: THE CELEBRITY ETHNICITY

For the details on Sherpa genetics, we examined more than twenty studies. Cynthia Beall, professor of anthropology at Case Western Reserve University and an authority on Tibetan genetics, compiled much of the data. Although Beall's research focuses on Tibetan highlanders, she said her research is generalizable to Sherpas. Evolutionarily speaking, Sherpas split from Tibetan highlanders very recently. To make this section easier to understand, we use the term *Sherpa* when, in many instances, the researchers studied Tibetan highlanders. We also interviewed Beall, and this section includes information from ongoing research. For the ethnicity details, we drew extensively from interviews and correspondence with Professor Sacherer and Professor Diemberger. The biography of Tenzing is based on an interview with his son, Jamling Tenzing Norgay, visiting Tenzing's private museum at his home (Ghang La in Darjeeling), viewing his mountaineering gear at the Himalayan Mountaineering Institute Museum in Darjeeling, and library research, with *Tiger of the Snows* by Tenzing Norgay (with James Ramsey Ullman) serving as a primary source and Ed Douglas's *Tenzing: Hero of Everest* serving as our main secondary source.

64 Sherpa® diaperbag These are all real products, and the Sherpa trademark signs are part of the product names as advertised.

65 red-blood-cell count One of the best overviews of the research on this topic is C. M. Beall, "Adaptations to Altitude: A Current Assessment," *Annual Review of Anthropology* 30 (2001), pp. 423–46.

65 populations well adapted to altitude In extreme altitudes, Sherpas' bodies will ramp up red-blood-cell production, but not nearly as much as the bodies of other populations do.

65 dominant genetic trait Researchers have yet to identify the location of this gene, and the Sherpa red blood cells affected by this gene have yet to be compared with red blood cells in other populations.

66 oldest Sherpa clans See Michael Oppitz, "Myths and Facts: Reconsidering Some Data Concerning the Clan History of the Sherpa," *Kailash* 2 (1974), pp. 121–31. When Oppitz wrote the clan history, he used the term *Khamba* throughout. At the time of his paper's publication, he was unaware of the linguistic distinction between *Khampa*, meaning someone from Kham in eastern Tibet, and *Khamba*, meaning a poor, landless wanderer. The latter can be a derogatory term.

66 as much as 30 percent Interview and correspondence with Sacherer, October 2010.

66 **naming system** The naming system varies among villages and families. The version here is based on the system in Rolwaling.

67 **roughly twenty clans** The number of clans that are Sherpa is disputed. This number reflects an inclusive definition of the ethnicity. By the narrowest definition, there are only four clans plus a handful of subclans.

68 **one of four types of Bhotias** See Ed Douglas, *Tenzing: Hero of Everest* (Washington, DC: National Geographic, 2003), p. 6. The four Bhotia ethnic groups are Sikkimese, Sherpas, Drukpas, and Tibetans.

68 **the *Mayflower*** Sacherer provided this analogy.

68 **Good faith** Communication with Sacherer based on an unpublished manuscript, "The Sherpas of Nepal: Using Anthropology to Reconstruct History."

69 **bloodthirsty barbarians** Zuckerman interview with Professor Hildegard Diemberger, University of Cambridge, 2010. Buddhists are not vegetarian, per se. No sin attaches to consuming the flesh of an animal that has died of natural causes. Slaughter, however, is a sin. And, as sin goes, there are varying degrees. Diemberger emphasizes the distinction between slaughter for consumption and sacrificial slaughter. Tibetan Buddhists, including Sherpas, do eat meat of slaughtered animals for essential nutrition, although they feel guilty about it and try to avoid direct responsibility by nudging the animal off a cliff or buying their steak from a Muslim butcher. Slaughter for consumption can be justified from the Buddhist perspective because it provides nourishment for the body, fueling it to perform good deeds. But Sherpas draw the line at sacrificial slaughter, which they regard as a gratuitous waste of life.

69 **"stab you in the back"** See Douglas, *Tenzing: Hero of Everest*, p. 11.

70 **Tsechu, a pilgrimage site** The name of the birthplace of Tenzing Norgay has been subject to half a century of translation error. *Tshe-chu*, which means "long-life water" in Tibetan, is a well-known pilgrimage site in the Kharta region. In some biographies of Tenzing Norgay, Tshe-chu was replaced by the word *Cha-chu*, which means "hot mineral springs" in Tibetan. See Ed Webster, *Snow in the Kingdom* (Eldorado Springs, CO: Mountain Imagery, 2000).

71 **recruitment hub** In the 1930s, Everest was attempted from the north side in Tibet, and the expeditions were exclusively British. Britain had a choke hold on Everest permits thanks to its influence with the Tibetan government.

71 **"never get a job"** Tenzing Norgay (with James Ramsey Ullman), *Tiger of the Snows* (New York: Putnam, 1955), p. 30.

72 **compensate Sherpas preferentially** See Douglas, *Tenzing: Hero of Everest*, p. 12.

72 **"his attractive grin"** See Eric Shipton, *That Untravelled World* (London: Hodder & Stoughton, 1969), p. 97.

73 **any mortal** Tenzing had also come very close to the summit in 1952 with Swiss partner Raymond Lambert. The duo had reached 28,215 feet, just 813 feet shy of the summit.

73 "single cramponed foot" Jamling Tenzing Norgay and Broughton Coburn, *Touching My Father's Soul* (Harper San Francisco, 2001), p. 93. Other books give slightly different versions of this incident.

74 "like a giant fish" John Hunt, *The Ascent of Everest* (London: Hodder & Stoughton, 1953), p. 209.

74 "A few more whacks" Edmund Hillary, *High Adventure: The True Story of the First Ascent of Everest* (Oxford: Oxford University Press, 2003, anniversary edition), p. 226.

74 "under her wings" We used the version that appeared in the *New York Times*. Tenzing's choice of metaphor also belies his origins. His biographer, Ed Douglas, learned that "hen" is the local name for Everest in the Kharta region.

74 Union Jack Tenzing held up four flags strung in the following order: the United Nations, the United Kingdom, Nepal, and India. The Union Jack is the most visible in the photograph. Tenzing's face was obscured by the oxygen mask. Ed Douglas wrote that this anonymity allowed every nation to project its dreams onto this iconic image.

74 "on television" See Tenzing Norgay, *Tiger of the Snows*, p. 272.

75 press conference. This version of the press conference is from Jamling Tenzing Norgay's recollection of how his father, Tenzing, described it. Contemporary British sources describe Hunt's press conference less critically. Hunt's comments were based, in part, on Hillary's account of having to drag Tenzing up the Hillary Step. No known transcripts exist.

75 "it doesn't matter" Hillary did eventually say that he was first on the summit, but he waited to do so until after Tenzing's death.

76 "draw their knives" See Douglas, *Tenzing: Hero of Everest*, p. 11. James Ramsey Ullman's notes for *Tiger of the Snows* are in the Princeton University Library. Although anthropologists sometimes use the term *Bhotia* to mean a larger grouping of which Sherpas and Tibetans are part, Tenzing is using the term *Bhotia* interchangeably with Tibetan.

5: INSHA'ALLAH

Both authors visited Shimshal in April 2009, and Padoan traveled with Shaheen Baig through northern Pakistan in June 2009. The authors interviewed Shaheen's wife, Khanda, his children, his parents, his close friend Qudrat Ali, his climbing partner Simone Moro, and his employer, Nazir Sabir, as well as the families of Karim and Jehan. The folklore of the region is from stories locals told Zuckerman and Padoan, supplemented with academic studies and Pam Henson's *Shimshal* (Obisan Press, 2006) and *The Women of Shimshal* (Shimshal Publishing, 2010). Many of the details relating to the Baltit Fort are based on the authors' visit to it and interviews with Soukat Hayat of the Baltit Heritage Trust. For descriptions of Younghusband's exploits, we relied on his own accounts in *Wonders of the Hima-*

laya (John Murray, 1924) and *The Heart of a Continent* (John Murray, 1896), as well as Peter Hopkirk's *The Great Game* (John Murray, 1990). We supplemented the research with Patrick French's biography *Younghusband: The Last Imperial Adventurer* (HarperCollins UK, 2004), and *Where Three Empires Meet* (Longmans, Green, 1918) by contemporary historian E. F. Knight. Knight was present during the siege of Hunza as a reporter for British newspapers. Some of the details about the Mir are also from R. C. F. Schomberg, who wrote *Between the Oxus and the Indus* (Lahore: al-Biruni, 1935) and befriended Safdar Ali in exile. For the campaign to defeat the Mir, we also drew from Algernon Durand's *The Making of the Frontier* (London: Thomas Nelson & Sons, 1899). The quotes and details, such as the Mir's conversations with Younghusband, appear in several of these accounts and are based largely on Younghusband's own writings. The physical descriptions are from photographs and the contemporary accounts. For the details of the porter selection process, we interviewed Haji Baig, the only living high-altitude porter of the 1953 Nanga Parbat expedition, and we visited the Durbar below the Baltit Fort where the selection took place. The Mir's ceremonial coat is on display at the Darbar Hunza Hotel. As mentioned above, Padoan climbed with Karim on Broad Peak in 2004, so some of the observations about him are from their interactions. The descriptions of Karim's interactions with his family and his departure for K2 are based on interviews with his wife, Parveen, and his father, Shadi.

79 **a strange creature** For further reading, see Michel Peissel, *The Ants' Gold* (New York: HarperCollins, 1984), in which the author sets out to solve this mystery posed by Herodotus. The legend of the gold-digging ants was popular with Alexander and his troops.

79 **"bigger than foxes"** Herodotus, *The Histories*, 3.102–5.

79 **marmots** Marlise Simons, "Himalayas Offer Clue to Legend of Gold-Digging 'Ants,'" *New York Times*, November 25, 1996.

79 **"the Bride"** Iftikhar Haider Malik, *The History of Pakistan* (Westport, CT: Greenwood Press, 2008).

81 **had to be secured** For further reading, see Peter Hopkirk, *The Great Game* (London: John Murray, 1990).

81 **considered marriage "coercive"** For more details, see Patrick French, *Younghusband: The Last Great Imperial Adventurer* (HarperCollins UK, 2004), p. 283.

82 **"bullets and stones whizzing"** Francis Younghusband, *The Heart of a Continent* (London: John Murray, 1896), p. 228.

83 **vodka and brandy** See Francis Younghusband, *Wonders of the Himalaya* (London: John Murray, 1924), p. 183.

83 **"hereditary failings"** E. F. Knight, *Where Three Empires Meet* (London: Longmans, Green, 1918), p. 350. Knight portrayed Safdar Ali in harsh terms, but the Mir eventually found his apologist. Colonel R. C. F. Schomberg, who befriended Safdar Ali during his exile in Yarkand, claims that at least one instance of fratri-

cide (the killing of a fourth brother in Shimshal) was "self-defense." Schomberg could find no excuse, however, for the other killings. See R. C. F. Schomberg, *Between the Oxus and the Indus* (Lahore: al-Biruni, 1935), p. 153.

83 **"redeeming feature"** Algernon Durand, *The Making of a Frontier* (London: Thomas Nelson & Sons, 1899), p. 230.

83 **"paying blackmail"** Younghusband, *Wonders of the Himalaya*, p. 199.

84 **"soap for his wives"** Younghusband, *Wonders of the Himalaya*, p. 201.

84 **"poor creature"** Younghusband, *Wonders of the Himalaya*, p. 202.

84 **on a platter** Knight, *Where Three Empires Meet*, p. 361.

84 **"pomade and cosmetics"** Knight, *Where Three Empires Meet*, p. 487.

84 **pseudoscientists** See, for example, Ralph Bircher, *The Hunzas: A People without Illness* (Bern: Huber, 1936).

85 **20 rupees** In 1953, the exchange rate for one U.S. dollar was 3.3 Pakistani rupees.

86 **hereditary Mir** Crown Prince Ghazanfar Ali Khan would have ascended the throne in 1976 if Pakistan had not disbanded the kingdom two years earlier and stripped his father of royal status. The Mir's family continues to wield significant political power in the elected government. As a show of respect, the crown prince is called "Mir" by foreign dignitaries.

87 **Wakhi** Wakhi-speaking people of Shimshal are considered a distinct ethnic group from the Hunzas. During the Great Game era, many Hunza raiders employed by the Mir assimilated into Wakhi villages.

87 **taste the summit** Simone Moro was even closer to the summit when he turned around at 2 p.m. In 2011, Moro would pioneer the first winter ascent in the Karakorum on Gasherbrum II.

89 **crystal palace** The mythical palace is translucent with gaudy pearl and coral decor. Gottlieb W. Leitner, *The Hunza and Nagyr Handbook* (Calcutta: Superintendent of Government Printing, 1889), p. 6.

91 **"What about carpentry?"** This conversation is based on Shadi's recollection.

6: THE APPROACH

We rode a jeep along the same route that Karim took. We based these descriptions of the ride to Askole on that road trip. Further descriptions of Askole are from Padoan's trek to K2 as well as from videos and conversations with climbers about what they were doing during their trek to Base Camp in 2008. Because of political instability, many of the LAPs interviewed for this section were interviewed not in their villages but rather in Skardu or Machulu. (They were compensated for their three days of travel expenses.) The description of K2 Base Camp is from photos, videos, and interviews, as well as from Padoan's visit to the Gilkey Memorial in 2004. The descriptions of what the porters carried are from interviews with the climbers. Chhiring described sky burials, but his description was supplemented with the writings of anthropologist Sherry Ortner. The incident involving Mr. Kim and the quartz rock was described by several sherpas as well as by Jamie McGuinness.

95 "rolling down avalanches" See E. F. Knight, *Where Three Empires Meet* (London: Longmans, Green, 1918), p. 359.

96 *LAPs* In Balti, low-altitude porters are called *khurpas*. For clarity and consistency, we use the term *low-altitude porters*, even in translations where the speaker used the word *khurpas*.

99 Yaqub As a LAP, Yaqub was responsible for bringing his own food. The expedition kitchen crew is responsible only for feeding the HAPs and the clients. (As with many other porters, Yaqub doesn't use a last name.)

101 the uninsured Although expeditions could buy more extended coverage for their porters, Raza said he'd never heard of that happening in his thirty-four years with the company.

101 uninsurable Of course, you can insure anything if you're willing to pay a high enough premium. Celebrities often insure such body parts as legs, faces, buttocks, and breasts, for exorbitant premiums, but this hasn't caught on with the 8000er set.

103 sky burial The practice differs throughout Tibet and Nepal, depending on the materials available.

7: WEATHER GODS

The discussion of the attack on the Danish Embassy is based on news reports from Al Jazeera and videos. Pakistan's Ministry of Tourism and Alpine Club president Nazir Sabir provided details of the climbing rates and the reasons behind the changes. Shaheen described his encounter with Hugues, and photos on Hugues's blog corroborated many of the details. The description of Ger's injury is from interviews with friends and family, including Annie Starkey, Banjo Bannon, and Joëlle Brupbacher. The description of Roeland van Oss's near-death experience is based on interviews with Jelle Staleman and Wilco. The description of Yan Giezendanner's workstation is from Padoan's visit to his home in Chamonix. The description of the final team meeting is from interviews with several of the men who were present, as well as from video footage.

108 seven times more A permit to climb Everest from the south side in Nepal was $70,000. As with K2, up to seven mountaineers are included in the price of the permit.

110 "would be obscene" This is what Shaheen heard Hugues say. The photographs of the corpse appeared on Hugues's blog on July 9, 2008.

111 "completely bitchy" This dialogue did not occur between Nick and Wilco.

They were interviewed separately about their feelings toward each other and their quotes were spliced.

112 customary toll The Dutch team brought 4,000 meters of new lightweight Endura rope, which cost $5,500, and they fixed the route along the Cesen to Camp 4. A donation to the team that brings the rope and fixes it is customary on 8,000-meter peaks. Wilco was asking for $450, a reasonable sum under the circumstances.

116 ideally, below 18,000 feet This is equivalent to 5,484 meters; the benchmark many climbers use is 5,600 meters.

118 "'Only use this outside'" Mountaineers have to settle for an open tent flap.

118 "eating priests" Correspondence with Yan Giezendanner, December 2009.

119 Dutch weather god Ab Maas of the Royal Netherlands Meteorological Institute was the first to report the weather window to the mountaineers at Base Camp. His prediction was ten days in advance of the window.

121 four camps Camp 1 is usually at 6,200 meters; Camp 2 is at 6,700 meters; Camp 3 is at 7,300 meters; Camp 4 (the Shoulder) is a large site where tents can be pitched at heights between 7,700 and 7,900 meters.

121 about 19,000 feet Wilco's Camp 1 on the Cesen route was at 5,800 meters.

121 20,300 feet Wilco's Camp 2 on the Cesen was at 6,200 meters.

121 about 23,500 feet Wilco's Camp 3 on the Cesen was at 7,150 meters.

122 Muhammad Hussein He was also known as "Little Hussein."

122 Muhammad Khan He is also listed as Muhammad Sanap Akam on summit records.

122 rope, ice screws, and pickets The rope supply consisted of 400 meters from the Dutch team and 200 meters from the Italian team.

8: GHOST WINDS

The rescue of Shaheen is based on interviews with Shaheen and Nadir. Yan's discussions with Hugues are from Yan's recollection, and all of Hugues's quotes are also from Yan's recollection. Wilco's discussions with Maarten are from both men's recollections. Hoselito's discussion with Wilco about the tent is based on interviews with both men and corroborated by Pemba. All quotes in the conversation between Hoselito and Wilco are from our interviews with the men who said them and as reviewed by Wilco and Hoselito.

127 "K2: A Little Shorter/A Lot Harder" Mike Farris of the American K2 International Expedition created this motto.

9: THROUGH THE BOTTLENECK

The scenic descriptions of the mountain are based on interviews with the climbers, their photographs, and video footage. The descriptions of the conflicts in the lead team are from interviews with all surviving members. The descriptions of the traffic jam in the Bottleneck come from about a dozen of the mountaineers who were there, plus several photos. We based the description of Cecilie's encounter with Dren Mandić on her memoir and interviews with her. Cecilie's account was corroborated by Chhiring, Pasang, and Lars. The descriptions of the attempted recovery of Dren's body come from interviews with Fredrik, Muhammad Hussein, Iso, and Pedja, plus footage from Fredrik's documentary *K2: A Cry from the Top of the World*. The description of Jehan's slide down the mountain is based primarily on the versions told by Muhammad Hussein and Iso, who had unobstructed views. Dr. Fred Espenak of NASA's Goddard Space Flight Center provided information about the eclipse above K2. Pasang's encounter with Alberto comes from interviews with both men. The scene on the summit is from interviews with the people described and from photographs. The detail about Kim and Jumik playfully smoking a cigarette is from Pasang.

143 **"the essentials"** The Italians still had a second coil of 100 meters, and the Dutch team had brought 400 meters of rope. This would have been enough if the fixed lines had been set in the appropriate locations.

143 **$385** This is based on 2008 prices. Zuckerman examined and tried on some of the oxygen cylinders that Pasang used, and Pasang demonstrated how he prepared them.

143 **turn up the flow** The maximum is four liters a minute.

144 **Sure, Eric replied** This conversation is based on Chhiring's recollection. (Eric had only a vague recollection of their exchange, which is why his words aren't in quotation marks here.)

144 **"He won't be coming"** Paolo Padoan interviewed Alberto in Vitoria-Gasteiz, Spain, in 2009.

145 **Muhammad Hussein** Zuckerman interviewed Muhammad in his village of Machulu in 2009.

145 **procedure on Everest** On Everest, an army of sherpas fixes lines systematically, and every team contributes with supplies, porters, or payment. The Bhotes tried to deliver extensive fixed lines on K2, but, given the time frame of the project—a few hours' lead time before the main group—this was unrealistic.

149 **"being a gentleman"** Hoselito, who didn't see the fall, bases this theory on Dren's personality.

154 **a perfect corona** A total eclipse of the sun was visible in areas of China, far to the north of Shimshal.

155 **years preparing** Wilco also remembered the summit time of the 1995 K2 expedition in which he took part. The team reached the summit at 6 p.m. and descended safely to Camp 4 by midnight.

159 **"at the beach!"** This was the August 4 entry on Hugues d'Aubarède's memorial blog by his girlfriend, Mine Dumas.

10: ESCAPE FROM THE SUMMIT

The encounter with Mr. Kim is from Pasang's recollection, as are most of Pasang's encounters with Kim, who declined to be interviewed. To understand Kim's perspective, the authors reviewed transcripts of Kim's interviews with Fredrik Sträng, who filmed him throughout the climb for the documentary *K2: A Cry from the Top of the World*. We also reviewed transcripts from Kim's interviews with Ryu Dong-il on behalf of author Freddie Wilkinson for his book *One Mountain Thousand Summits*. Several climbers described the rope system, including Chhiring and Pasang. Cas van de Gevel described the death of Hugues. The sounds are based on climbers' descriptions. For Jumik's fall, we do not know the precise time this serac calved, but it was a separate serac fall from the one that killed Rolf at 9 p.m. The descriptions of Rolf's death come from interviews with Cecilie and Lars, as well as from Cecilie's memoir, translated from Norwegian by Erik Brakstad, and their video footage, translated by Ragnhild Amble and Oddvar and Anne Hoidal.

164 **stumbling and falling** Between 1953 and 2008, twenty-four of the sixty-six deaths on K2 occurred during descent from the summit.

166 **"You go first"** This quote is according to Cas's recollection.

167 **two Koreans with Jumik** Neither Marco nor Wilco could positively identify the two Korean climbers tied to Jumik.

169 **"Where's Rolf?"** This quote is what Cecilie remembers saying; the quote after it is how Lars remembers responding.

169 **"stars and loneliness"** See Cecilie Skog, *Til Rolf: Tusen fine turer og en trist* (Oslo: Gyldendal Norsk Forlag AS, 2009). Excerpts translated by Erik Brakstad.

170 **streaked down** The next morning, Jumik was found hanging about 70 vertical meters (230 feet) below the Snow Dome.

172 **all available rope** Lars carried 50 meters of rope for emergencies. After the serac fall, this coil would be the key to survival for those trapped above the Bottleneck.

172 **The visitation** This is based on interviews with Chhiring.

173 **"No axe"** The quotes from exchanges with Pasang and Chhiring are from interviews with both men.

11: SONAM

Pasang's encounter with the specter of Mr. Kim is based on interviews with Pasang. The description of the bivouac is from interviews with Marco and Wilco; from Marco's memoir, *Giorni di Ghiaccio* (*Days of Ice*, 2009); and from Wilco's memoir, *Surviving K2* (2010). The specific lyrics that Ger substituted during the singing served as his climbing mantra. They were written by the Irish band Kila. Dr. Michael Su provided details about what would have happened when Karim became hypothermic. Eric provided information about what drugs were given to Pemba. Go Mi-sun died on Nanga Parbat in July 2009, three weeks before our scheduled interview with her. We did, however, obtain copies of e-mails she sent about the K2 climb, and we talked to other climbers about what she told them had happened.

180 **when Pasang closed his eyes** Pasang originally arrived at Camp 4 around noon on July 31, and it was now roughly 6 a.m. on August 2.

180 **"useless weight"** There are some celebrated exceptions. Dan Mazur and Jonathan Pratt survived a bivouac on K2 at 28,000 feet and kept their fingers and toes, thanks in part to a lightweight stove.

180 **minus four degrees Fahrenheit** This figure (equivalent to -20°C) is Marco's estimate.

183 **skid mark** This photo was taken from Camp 4 by Pemba at 7:16 p.m.

183 **"Is it bad?"** This exchange (and the one between Pemba and Eric) is from Chhiring's recollection but corroborated by Pemba and Eric.

12: SURVIVAL

The accounts involving Tsering, Big Pasang, and Go are from interviews with Tsering. Padoan and Zuckerman both interviewed Tsering on separate occasions in Kathmandu in 2009. Zuckerman did a followup interview with him in Grindelwald, Switzerland, in 2010. Tsering's conversation with Kim is told from Tsering's perspective but corroborated by Pemba, Eric, and Chhiring. Wilco's assertion that Jumik said help was coming is corroborated by the conversation between Lars and Go in Base Camp. The details of Wilco's descent are from interviews with him and from his memoir.

185 **Tsering** Tsering Lama was more commonly known as Chhiring Lama, reflecting the Nepali pronunciation of his Tibetan name. We refer to him by his Tibetan name to avoid confusion. He also sometimes goes by Chhiring Bhote in other books and articles.

189 **corneas began to freeze** Even a slight breeze at this altitude can begin to freeze the corneas when a wind shield (such as goggles) is removed. Vision gradually becomes cloudy, and it takes at least six hours to recover sight. To avoid this,

high-altitude mountaineers keep their eyes closed for five to ten seconds at a time and roll their eyeballs around on every third or fourth breath.

189 **After about 200 feet** Wilco estimates that Jumik and his two Korean clients were hanging 50 to 70 vertical meters (164 to 230 feet) below his bivouac site.

190 **twisting and cinching** This is what Wilco and others later figured must have happened.

190 **help was on the way** When Ms. Go left Jumik the night before, she promised to send help, according to Lars, who spoke with Go at Base Camp on August 4 or 5.

190 **"I had to survive, too"** This quote is from a 2009 interview with Wilco at his home in Voorst, Holland.

190 **Wilco was lost** See Wilco van Rooijen, *Surviving K2* (2010), p. 127.

190 **three limbs** Or two limbs and an ice axe, maintaining three points of contact.

191 **familiar combination** The number was also on speed dial, but the phone's memory failed. Wilco had to dial by "feel."

191 **"I'm alive"** Wilco's conversations with Heleen are from his recollection.

13: BURIED IN THE SKY

The descriptions of the entangled men are from interviews with Marco and Wilco and from photographs taken by Pemba and Lars. The description of Big Pasang's radio calls comes from interviews with Pemba. The description of the avalanche assumes a dry-slab avalanche because that is consistent with the conditions described by Tsering and what photos suggest. Several books provided details of what happens and what to do during an avalanche. *The Avalanche Handbook*, by David McClung and Peter Schaerer (Seattle: The Mountaineers Books, 2006), was an especially good source. Dr. Michael Su provided many of the details about asphyxiation and dying. The interaction between Tsering and Pasang is based primarily on interviews with Tsering but supplemented by interviews with Pasang and with Jumik's mother, Gamu.

193 **Around 8 a.m.** A photo by Lars, taken from Camp 4 at 8:06 a.m., shows Marco and Ger first encountering the tangle of men and Wilco descending below them.

194 **after 9:58 a.m.** Pemba's 9:58 a.m. photo taken from Camp 4 shows Marco leaning over Jumik's head as Ger kneels beside him.

194 **"nice of him, but weird"** Marco doesn't recall giving any chocolate to Tsering and Big Pasang.

194 **an avalanche roar** Marco does not believe what he experienced was a hallucination. During a 2010 interview with documentary filmmaker Nick Ryan, Marco acknowledged that the body could have been anyone wearing yellow La Sportiva Olympus Mons Evo boots and a red downsuit. Ger and Karim both wore that gear.

195 **taken at 9:58 a.m.** This photo was taken by Pemba from Camp 4.

195 **Jumik is gone** Pemba took this photo at 7:16 p.m. from Camp 4.

195 **photo from 3:10 p.m.** Pemba photographed the corpses of Jumik and Big Pasang at 3:10 p.m. from a few feet away.

195 **rescued himself** This is the assessment of Wilco and Marco, the last surviving witnesses to see Jumik alive.

196 **sledding down** Or Ger may have used a simpler system. He might have rigged up a second rope that he had attached to the two living climbers and then cut the first rope.

197 **two eyewitnesses** They were Big Pasang and Tsering, as described later in this chapter.

197 **"dead man walking"** See Beck Weathers with Stephen G. Michaud, *Left for Dead: My Journey Home from Everest* (New York: Villard Books, 2000), p. 7.

198 **four men** Big Pasang and Tsering counted four men, and Big Pasang reported this over the radio.

198 **reported on the radio** Pemba received this radio call while he was trying to revive Marco.

198 **thunderous boom** Tsering heard it.

202 **death** What's considered the moment of "death" varies among doctors, cultures, and jurisdictions. We define it here as the moment when breathing and circulation stopped.

203 **"lose my family"** This quote is from an interview with Tsering and corroborated by Pasang.

14: THE FEARLESS FIVE

The description of Marco's rescue is from interviews with Pemba and Marco, supplemented by Marco's memoir. The descriptions of Wilco's descent are based on interviews with Wilco, Cas, Pemba, Nadir, Tom, Maarten, Hoselito, Chhiring, and Chris. The description of Pasang's return to Base Camp is from interviews with Pasang and Ngawang Bhote. The field hospital description is based on photographs and on interviews with Eric and Chhiring. We also discussed the treatment with Wilco and Marco. The scene at the Gilkey Memorial is from interviews with Nadir, supplemented by photos of the memorial and interviews with Hoselito, who was nearby. The authors visited the Fearless Five at the military base in April 2009, including the mess hall and barracks. The landing at Base Camp and Marco's airlift were videotaped by the military. We reviewed this footage and interviewed the pilots involved in the rescues. Shaheen's return comes from interviews with him. Zuckerman and Padoan visited the hospital rooms used by Marco and Wilco and interviewed the medical personnel who treated them. We also relied on information broadcast by media outlets. Details about personal responses to the disaster stem primarily from news reports but also from interviews with Dawa Sherpa and Jumik's friends with Internet access, Judy Aull and Jerry del Missier.

205 **might dig up** And they did. See Cristina Marrone, "Confortola scalerà da solo «È un campione ma antipatico»," *Corriere della Sera*, February 7, 2010.

205 **"like a lioness"** See Marco Confortola, *Giorni di Ghiaccio* (Milan: Baldini Castoldi Dalai Editore, 2009), p. 128.

206 **afternoon of August 2** All times refer to the local time on K2. Utrecht, Holland, was four hours behind K2. Denver, Colorado, was eleven hours behind K2.

207 **Maarten** Padoan interviewed Maarten van Eck in Utrecht, Holland, in October 2009.

208 **the orange dot** Zuckerman interviewed Chris by telephone. Chris was credited in the media as the first person to spot Wilco, but he does not dispute Nadir's earlier sighting.

208 **near Camp 3** Strictly speaking, Wilco was not rescued. He had located Camp 3 on the Cesen route and was approaching it on his own. Cas climbed toward Wilco, meeting him about 100 meters from camp, while Pemba remained in Camp 3, standing in front of his tent.

209 **"a stranger to them"** Ngawang Bhote interview in Kathmandu (2010) with Snighda Dhungel, Padoan's translator.

210 **$60,000** This is based on Eric Meyer's recollection of his discussion with English-speaking members of the Flying Jump as they arranged their evacuation from Base Camp. The average cost for an airlift is $6,000 per person, and approximately ten members flew out, so this estimate is reasonable. Askari Aviation told the authors that the Flying Jump's airlift cost a total of $13,000, but mountaineers said these figures were inaccurate.

211 **Siachen** The name of this wasteland means "place of many roses" in Balti.

212 **Ecureuil B3 Mystery** Didier Delsalle landed an Ecureuil/AStar AS 350 B3 on the summit of Everest on May 14, 2005, for two minutes.

212 **Rinjing Sherpa** In addition to carrying Marco to the chopper, Rinjing, along with his brother-in-law, George Dijmarescu, and Mingma Sherpa, intercepted Marco above Camp 2 and helped him descend to Base Camp.

15: THE NEXT LIFE

For the description of the tea party, Zuckerman visited the room where the meeting took place and spoke to members of the Ministry of Tourism about it. The quotes are from interviews with Nazir and Wilco. The meeting between Lahmu and Mr. Kim is from interviews with Lahmu and a visit to the hotel where the discussion took place. The description of Nick Rice's return is from interviews with him and his sister, Rebecca Rice, and video footage. For the scenes with Nazir

Sabir, we joined him on his drive to Shimshal and attended the meeting with the families of Karim and Jehan. The quotes come from followup interviews with those who spoke; it would have been insensitive to have our interpreter translating during a memorial service. The quotes of Jehan's children were reported by their grandmother, Nazib. Chhiring's return home is based on interviews with him, Dawa, and Ngawang. Pasang's return is based on interviews with Pasang, Pemba Jeba, Tsering, Dawa Sangmu, Lahmu, and Gamu. The descriptions of the doubleheader climbs are from interviews with Chhiring and Pasang.

218 **Jehan Baig's policy** Alpha Insurance eventually compensated Jehan's family.

218 **"the right kind of climbers"** This quote is from interviews after the tea party when Wilco, Nazir, and others recalled what they were saying and thinking at the time. Unfortunately, the party was not taped by the ministry, and Geo TV and Dawn TV had lost their tapes of the meeting.

222 **unsupported, unassisted** Cecilie, with American Ryan Waters, crossed Antarctica using strictly their own muscle power. For previous crossings of Antarctica, skiers had used wind for propulsion.

223 **"Pemba Girgi"** Marco Confortola, *Giorni di Ghiaccio* (Milan: Baldini Castoldi Dalai Editore, 2009), p. 102.

223 **Jumik Bhote's mother** This visit was in April 2010. Padoan and Joëlle Brupbacher were present with translator Snighda Dhungel.

223 *National Geographic Adventure* See "The Savior and the Storm on K2," *National Geographic Adventure* (December 2008/January 2009).

224 **"focused on the rescues"** Pemba Gyalje interview with Padoan, Nick Ryan, and Pat Falvey at Pemba's home in Kathmandu, January 2009.

224 **rescues involved Western lives** Freddie Wilkinson was a notable exception to the media focus on Westerners. By November 2008, Wilkinson had broken the story, investigating and writing the first article about Chhiring's rescue of Pasang. See "Heroes in Fine Print," *The Huffington Post*, November 12, 2008. Wilkinson followed the article with a longer piece: "Perfect Chaos," *Rock and Ice*, December 2008. He also wrote the first book about the tragedy from the Sherpa perspective: *One Mountain Thousand Summits* (New York: New American Library, 2010).

224 **$2,270 per minute** This figure is based on the amount paid to Wilco for his video footage.

226 **little else but listen** That is only true of this particular meeting. Nazir continued to do a great deal for the families. He coordinated a fundraising effort for the support of the families, contributing his own money, and ensured that they were treated fairly by insurance companies.

Selected Bibliography

BOOKS

Biddulph, John. *Tribes of the Hindoo Koosh*. Calcutta: Superintendent of Government Printing, 1880.

Bonatti, Walter. *The Mountains of My Life*. New York: Modern Library, 2001.

Bowley, Graham. *No Way Down: Life and Death on K2*. New York: HarperCollins, 2010.

Clark, John. *Hunza: Lost Kingdom of the Himalayas*. New York: Funk & Wagnalls, 1956.

Confortola, Marco. *Giorni di Ghiaccio*. Milan: Baldini Castoldi Dalai Editore, 2009.

Curran, Jim. *K2: The Story of the Savage Mountain*. London: Hodder & Stoughton, 1995.

Douglas, Ed. *Tenzing: Hero of Everest*. Washington, DC: National Geographic, 2003.

French, Patrick. *Younghusband: The Last Great Imperial Adventurer*. Hammersmith: HarperCollins UK, 2004.

Gregson, Jonathan. *Massacre at the Palace: The Doomed Royal Dynasty of Nepal*. New York: Talk Miramax, 2002.

Hopkirk, Peter. *The Great Game: On Secret Service in High Asia*. London: John Murray, 1990.

Houston, Charles S., and Robert H. Bates. *K2, The Savage Mountain*. New York: McGraw-Hill, 1954.

Hunt, John. *The Ascent of Everest*. London: Hodder & Stoughton, 1953.

Isserman, Maurice, and Stewart Weaver. *Fallen Giants: A History of Himalayan Mountaineering from the Age of Empire to the Age of Extremes*. New Haven, CT: Yale University Press, 2010.

Jordan, Jennifer. *The Last Man on the Mountain: The Death of an American Adventurer on K2*. New York: W. W. Norton, 2010.

Kauffman, Andrew J., and William L. Putnam. *K2: The 1939 Tragedy*. Seattle: The Mountaineers Books, 1992.

Knight, E. F. *Where Three Empires Meet*. London: Longmans, Green, 1918.

Lacedelli, Lino, and Giovanni Cenacchi. *K2: Il prezzo della conquista*. Milan: Mondadori, 2004.

Leitner, Gottlieb. *The Hunza and Nagyr Handbook*. Calcutta: Superintendent of Government Printing, 1889.

Norgay, Jamling Tenzing (with Broughton Coburn). *Touching My Father's Soul: A Sherpa's Journey to the Top of Everest*. San Francisco: Harper San Francisco, 2001.

Norgay, Tenzing (with James Ramsey Ullman). *Tiger of the Snows: The Autobiography of Tenzing of Everest*. New York: Putnam, 1955.

Ortner, Sherry B. *Sherpas Through Their Rituals*. Cambridge, UK: Cambridge University Press, 1978.

———. *Life and Death on Mount Everest: Sherpas and Himalayan Mountaineering*. Princeton, NJ: Princeton University Press, 1999.

Peissel, Michel. *The Ants' Gold*. New York: HarperCollins, 1984.

Schomberg, R. C. F. *Between the Oxus and the Indus*. Lahore: al-Biruni, 1935.

Skog, Cecilie. *Og De Tre Polene*. Stavanger, Norway: Wigestrand, 2006.

Tenderini, Mirella, and Michael Shandrick. *The Duke of the Abruzzi: An Explorer's Life*. Seattle: The Mountaineers Books, 1997.

van Rooijen, Wilco. *Overleven op de K2*. National Geographic, 2009. (Published in English as *Surviving K2*. Diemen, Netherlands: G+J Publishing, 2010.)

Viesturs, Ed, and David Roberts. *K2: Life and Death on the World's Most Dangerous Mountain*. New York: Broadway Books, 2009.

Webster, Ed. *Snow in the Kingdom: My Storm Years on Everest*. Eldorado Springs, CO: Mountain Imagery, 2000.

Wilkinson, Freddie. *One Mountain Thousand Summits: The Untold Story of Tragedy and True Heroism on K2*. New York: New American Library, 2010.

Younghusband, Francis. *The Heart of a Continent*. London: John Murray, 1896.

———. *Wonders of the Himalaya*. London: John Murray, 1924.

PERIODICALS

DeBenedetti, Christian. "The Savior and the Storm on K2," *National Geographic Adventure* (December 2008/January 2009).

Kodas, Michael. "A Few False Moves," *Outside* (September 2008).

Power, Matthew. "K2: The Killing Peak," *Men's Journal* (November 2008).

Sabir, Nazir. "K2: A Letter from Nazir Sabir," *The Alpinist* (August 2008).

Wilkinson, Freddie. "Perfect Chaos," *Rock and Ice* (December 2008).

FILMS

Disaster on K2 (The Discovery Channel, March 2009).

Hillary and Tenzing: Climbing to the Roof of the World (PBS, 1996).

K2: A Cry from the Top of the World (Mastiff AB, Stockholm, Sweden, 2010).

Murder Most Royal (BBC Panorama, 2002).

Index

Page numbers in *italics* refer to maps.